AF064595

Singing the Coast

Place and identity in Australia

Margaret Somerville
and Tony Perkins

Aboriginal Studies Press

First published in 2010
by Aboriginal Studies Press

Reprinted 2011, 2019

© Margaret Somerville and Tony Perkins, 2010

All rights reserved. No part of this book may be reproduced or transmitted in any form or by any means, electronic or mechanical, including photocopying, recording or by any information storage and retrieval system, without prior permission in writing from the publisher. The Australian *Copyright Act 1968* (the Act) allows a maximum of one chapter or 10 per cent of this book, whichever is the greater, to be photocopied by any educational institution for its education purposes provided that the educational institution (or body that administers it) has given a remuneration notice to Copyright Agency Limited (CAL) under the Act.

Aboriginal Studies Press
is the publishing arm of the
Australian Institute of Aboriginal
and Torres Strait Islander Studies.
GPO Box 553, Canberra, ACT 2601
Phone: 61 2 6246 1183
Fax: 61 2 6261 4288
Email: asp@aiatsis.gov.au
Web: www.aiatsis.gov.au/asp/about.html

National Library of Australia
Cataloguing-In-Publication data:

National Library of Australia Cataloguing-in-Publication entry

　　Author: Somerville, Margaret.

　　　Title: Singing the coast / Margaret Somerville; Tony Perkins.

　　ISBN: 9780855757113 (pbk.)
　　ISBN: 9780855757229 (ebook PDF)

　　Notes: Includes index.
　　Includes bibliographical references.

　　Subjects: Aboriginal Australians — Folklore. Mythology, Aboriginal Australian. Aboriginal Australians — New South Wales — History.

　　Other Authors/Contributors: Perkins, Tony, 1947-

　　Dewey Number: 398.20899915

Printed in Australia by SOS Print + Media

Cover: Collecting pipis, Corindi Beach, photography by Margaret Somerville.

*For Gumbaynggirr people
past and present
who inhabit
No Mans Land
differently*

Garby Elders: Keith Lardner, Cecil (Bing) Laurie, Jerry Flanders, Bruce Laurie and Michael McDougall, 2000. Photograph by Jessica Somerville

Singing the Coast has opened up part of the NSW coastline through language and stories both traditional and contemporary, that are lived but have been, until now, largely unspoken.
Gary Foley

Singing the Coast is one of the most beautiful and important books to enter our world in recent time. It is a journey within meeting places: where sea and land meet, and where oral and written modes of storytelling weave together. It is drenched in love and knowledge, and blessed with the always astonishing generosity of Indigenous Australians. Read, enjoy, and find yourself ambushed by its subtly transformative power.
Deborah Bird Rose

An impressive work of stories intricately woven together like a mosaic which reveals the important message of living in harmony with the land and waterways. Particularly powerful is the varied life included: paperbarks, birds, animals, amphibians, reptiles, as well as the connection the book engages and demands of the reader.
Dr Greg Blyton

This book bears testimony to the art of listening in a context where the voices of such communities, and the injustices and the creative adaptations, have too often been rendered silent or ignored. It provides an intimate picture of the formation of the community and a compelling portrayal of the social world created and sustained by people in 'No Mans Land'.
Dr Barry Morris

Contents

Illustrations	vi
Acknowledgments	vii
Notes on language	ix
Map	xi
Prologue: In the beginning	xiii
Chapter 1: *Singing differently*	1
Chapter 2: *Crying-songs to remember*	24
Chapter 3: *Making home in No Mans Land*	54
Chapter 4: *Eating place*	87
Chapter 5: *Spirits in places*	121
Chapter 6: *A language of landscape*	153
Chapter 7: *Connecting the dots*	188
Epilogue: The place of creation	223
Notes	226
References and further reading	228
Index	230

Illustrations

(between pp. 82–83)

Moonee Moonee Beach. Photograph by Margaret Somerville
Shadow on sand. Photograph by Margaret Somerville
Bing Laurie, 2000. Photograph by Barry McDonald
Bushtucker walk. Photograph by Margaret Somerville
Red Rock band. Photograph courtesy Estelle and Doreen Richards collection
Red Rock picnic. Photograph courtesy Estelle and Doreen Richards collection
Red Rock Estuary. Photograph by Margaret Somerville
Sapling house with Teddy McCrystal, 'Armi' and Maggie Blakeney, 1920s. Photograph courtesy Yarrawarra Cultural Centre collection
The Old Camp, 1998. Photograph by Margaret Somerville
Lake entrance. Photograph by Margaret Somerville
Clarrie Skinner and jewfish, 1930s. Photograph courtesy Estelle and Doreen Richards collection
Milton fishing, Corindi Beach. Photograph by Jessica Somerville
Collecting pipis, Corindi Beach. Photograph by Margaret Somerville
Preparing curry pipi gravy with johnny cakes. Photograph by Margaret Somerville
Elders sitting on bank at Jewfish Point. Photograph by Margaret Somerville
Old mangrove tree at Jewfish Point. Photograph by Margaret Somerville
Val on the Island, 1930s. Photograph courtesy Val Cohen (Smith) collection
Val and family on the Island, 1940s. Photograph courtesy Val Cohen (Smith) collection
Val and Rosina on the Island. Photograph by Margaret Somerville
Islands in Nambucca estuary. Photograph by Margaret Somerville
Deep mapping: Tony, Ken, Gary with Meg Goudling. Photograph by Margaret Somerville
Mapping at Scott's Head. Photograph by Margaret Somerville
Nunguu Miirlarl. Photograph by Margaret Somerville
Split Solitary Island. Photograph by Margaret Somerville

Acknowledgments

Many people were involved in the research that led to the writing of this book. Some were interviewed, some were part of the organisational support, and others were members of the communities where this research took place. It is important to acknowledge all of the Gumbaynggirr people who have collectively worked against all odds over several generations to preserve the hidden stories of their coastal places since white settlement. They continue to look after these places, even when they no longer have access to them, through their storytelling. It is to them we owe our continuing gratitude and respect.

I want to acknowledge the teams of researchers from Yarrawarra Aboriginal Cultural Centre Corindi Beach, Muurrbay Aboriginal Language and Culture Centre Nambucca Heads, and the University of New England, Armidale, who carried out this research. Tony Perkins, Dee Murphy and Cheryl Brown were the Yarrawarra members of the team and Wendy Beck, Anita Smith and myself were the university researchers on the team in the first phase of the research. In the second phase of the project Ken Walker, Gary Williams, Pauline Hooler and Virginia Jarrett worked with Meg Goulding and myself under Tony Perkins' continuing leadership. Meg Goulding developed the processes of deep mapping with the project team in this phase of the research. A team of trainee researchers from Jalumbo, Yarrawarra's research and consultancy arm, including Dee Murphy, Sue Tompkins, Richard Preece and Ian Brown, interviewed Gumbaynggirr Elders for the final phase of the project about regional place knowledge.

Some of the stories that are quoted in the book have been previously printed in local materials, in particular, the Yarrawarra Place Stories Series Books 1–5 authored and produced by the team of researchers. An earlier version of part of Chapter 2, Crying-songs to remember, appeared in a special edition of the online journal *Altitude*, edited by Anne Brewster.[1]

A very special thanks to Dee Murphy who has unfailingly sustained the challenging role of broker between the Aboriginal community at Corindi Beach and the research project in all of its stages. She has undertaken a cultural edit of the book, working with Gumbaynggirr oral storytellers to ensure that their language, stories and cultural meanings are appropriately represented. A very special thanks also to Dr Kerith Power who was a sounding board during all stages of the research and writing and provided unfailing support in so many ways.

Both stages of the project were generously supported by the Australian Research Council, through a competitive scheme across all disciplines and all universities in Australia. This funding made it possible to produce an extensive research base for both of the Aboriginal organisations to make full use of in their ongoing cultural work. It enabled the training of Gumbaynggirr researchers to continue this work in their communities and in the broader arena of government departments. Monash University has supported the production of this book through a generous grant to support my new position as Professor of Education (Learning and Development). The Institute of Regional Studies, Monash University has also provided support for my position as Research Director of the Institute, enabling me to employ research assistants to help with the editing of the text. The ARC funding, and other grants from the Aboriginal and Torres Strait Islander Commission and the Australian Institute of Aboriginal and Torres Strait Islander Studies, assisted with the production of other important research outcomes, and has supported the work of research assistants including Helen Edwards, Alison McConnell-Imbriotis, John Duley, Kristal Yee and Phoenix de Carteret. Miriam Potts has made a significant contribution to the editing of the final text and Sue Collins has been a precise and exacting editor who has greatly assisted the final version of the text to come into being.

The various stages of the research and other projects it has generated have left a lasting legacy for Gumbaynggirr people, their communities and places. We hope that this book will extend this process to other coastal landscapes and communities around Australia.

Notes on language

This book is constructed from the space between oral stories and written text. The writing itself follows the process of creating knowledge from oral stories. It derives from research undertaken over a ten-year period where the stories of many Gumbaynggirr people were recorded. We hope to make evident the processes of cultural translation by including these stories as they were transcribed from their oral form.

What follows are some insights into the process and conventions we followed in creating this written text. Margaret Somerville collaborated with Tony Perkins to record his substantial body of cultural knowledge, which was documented in the form of oral stories. Thus, both Tony and Margaret are acknowledged as co-authors: the authorial voice is Margaret's, in conversation with Tony.

Tony and Margaret are acutely aware of the politics of representation; that writing from the space in-between Aboriginal and non-Aboriginal voices and identities is a risky business. Over her time in recording conversations with Tony and other Garby Elders, Margaret developed techniques for recording stories and simultaneously clarifying meanings. While Tony can read and write, he has never wanted to become a writer or a reader of written words, so in seeking feedback on what she'd heard in conversations, Margaret read his words back to him and recorded his responses. Still, the English language had to be bent to hold traces of Gumbaynggirr meanings. Reading these stories requires that readers enter the process of translation, and listen carefully to the traces of the voice that remain in the written text. It is slow learning that requires slow and careful reading.

The transcription and presentation of Tony's stories provided the template for the way the voices of others were generated as written text. Tony was keen that the written form of his voice should be as close as possible to the way he speaks so that that his words as they appear on the page reflect the meanings of the stories and places that he wanted to convey. There are variations between the way that some words are spelt within a single story, for example 'fella/fellows', depending on the emphases in the conversation. Apostrophes are used to represent letters not sounded out at the beginning of words, like *'cause* (because), *'em* (them) and at the end of words, like *thinkin'* or *runnin'*. On occasions, words are elided, like *m'Grandmother*. There are similar differences across other speakers. In some quotations, the voices represent more than one individual, in the hope that the reader gains a sense of the multiple individual voices telling their stories, as well as the collective story of a people.

The spelling of local place names, colloquial language and Gumbaynggirr language words also hover in that imprecise world where words are not fixed in written form. Local place names change over the years as the politics and practices of naming changes. Words and language have power. Northern Gumbaynggirr language speakers who can still speak language, for example, developed their own spelling, which is different from the conventional orthography developed within the language work in southern Gumbaynggirr country. Where Gumbaynggirr language words are used, we have followed the 2008 edition of the *Gumbaynggirr Dictionary & Learner's Grammar*. The dictionary enables us to create a written text that is readable and accessible, but this also, in some senses, elides the complexities of language and place. We hope the shifting and complex nuances of place and identity are available to readers throughout the book.

Margaret Somerville and Tony Perkins
March 2010

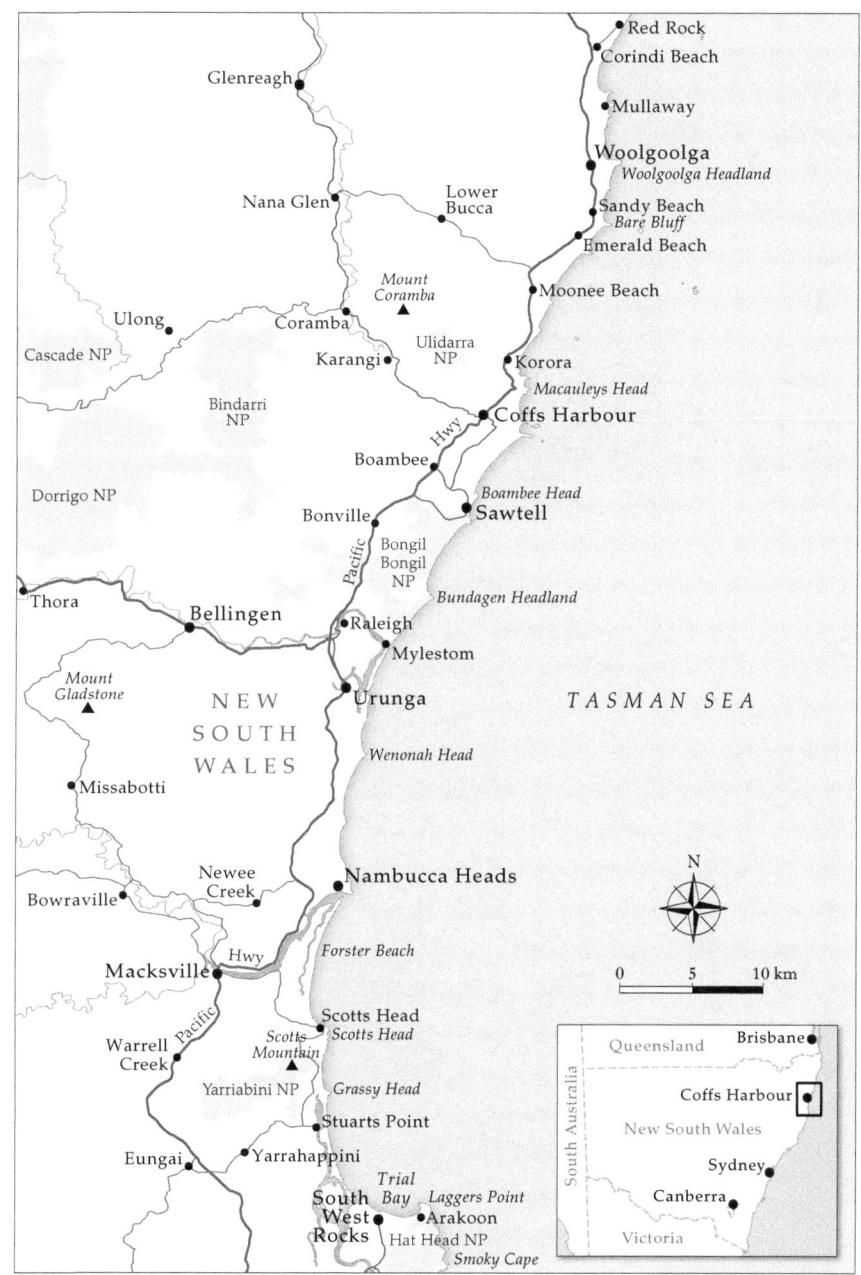

Northern New South Wales coast. Map by Damien Demaj, demap.

Aboriginal and Torres Strait Islander people are respectfully advised that this publication contains names and images of deceased persons, and culturally sensitive material. AIATSIS apologises for any distress this may cause.

Conversion table

Imperial to metric equivalents follow:
one inch = 25.4mm
one foot = 30.5cm
one yard = 91.5cm
one mile = 1.61km
one ounce = 29.3g
one gallon = 4.6ll
one acre = 0.405ha

Prologue: In the beginning

Moonee Beach, 2008

In the beginning was the mother place.

I am parked at the estuary at Moonee Beach looking through the curved branch of a eucalypt. It is a blue, sunny day, low tide, with strands of blue-green water winding across the wide stretch of sandy estuary. All is rounded here. The rounded knoll of a shady reserve with tents and cabins is bordered by a sweeping curve of golden sand and curved channels of water. Beyond is a small protected beach flanked by two close headlands. A sprawling grassy dome guards the southern end of the beach and, to the north, low dark bushes mark its reach. Past the curve of sand, hazy in the distant blue sea, are the two curves of an island split in two.

I am unusually anxious with the pressure of meaning. I do not know this place or where I have to go to understand. As I walk across the sand I can see by the ripples that at high tide the water covers the whole estuary and I wonder, if I go exploring, whether I will be able to get back. I have been here once before and remember the fast pull of water in the channels at mid tide. These winding channels get really deep and I don't yet know what the tide is doing. The only way to get to the beach and the northern headland is across the deepest channel. But as I watch a mother wades across with her three children and lies down on the sandy beach, face down in the sun, while her children play. I know it will be safe, for a while.

I go back to the car and put on swimmers and shirt, leaving camera, recorder, shoes and clothes behind, and head to the dark bushes at the northern end. I wade through the water, hat on my head, wondering if I'll have to swim back. I remember the funny story of Jimmy Runner swimming across the estuary at Red Rock, with his hat and watch on his head, to meet a woman. Once on the other side the beach opens out, a fresh breeze blows from the sea and blue-green waves break rhythmically on the sand. My bare feet are tender so I find a sandy pathway through dune grass and low prickly bushes to the deep shady forest of coastal banksias. A fine thick cover of low grass is soft underfoot so I walk along here to get the feel of the forest. I pass a small collection of objects gathered together at a fireplace where the Yarrawarra workers have been clearing weeds and rubbish. Dee says they refused to work at the mother place so it can't be here. I read these signs; there are no answers here, only questions.

I feel a sort of pressure to find a special meaning in this place, the place of creation. And yet I find most meaning in the everyday, in reading the intimate details of the marks on the vast sandy expanse of estuary. Everywhere are patterns of tiny balls of sand and thumb-sized crab holes, worm trails and three-pronged bird prints crowded around the channels. Last night's shower has left dimples of rain all over and the tide leaves its ripples as it washes over the sand. Along the edges, around the broad curve of the estuary, are patterns of driftwood and debris left from the tide's reach. This morning there have already been plenty of people making new marks after high tide's clean wash. There are patterns of human footprints, of bare feet, feet with shoes, children's and dogs' footprints, round and round, running, playing. I read it as a place of play, rich with life.

Walking back I see a young woman with a baby tucked close to her in a sling talking to another young mother with a baby in her belly. Their kids run round and play in the safety of the shallow waters. Aah, a deep breath of recognition. This is enough for today, I think, for the time being the place has given me all that I need. I leave for my meeting with Tony, who has sent me here to this place.

CHAPTER 1

Singing differently

Well, this is where the story began. It started here when the whole tribe decided to go out here huntin. There was no sea here then and they left two women behind to camp here. And they were la-de-da, out there hunting and all that. And unbeknowns to them there was a young man in a cave just off this point here. There was a cave out there he hid in because he was into these two women. He wanted to marry one of them, poor bastard. And when they got out of sight he come out of the cave and come up to these two women and asked them to marry him. And they both refused so he bashed them up and he left.

And in that time the women decided to get some honey and the sap from this special vine. And apparently this young fella come back and asked them two or three times, ya know, 'Ngiinda ngaanya baalgu?' 'Will ya marry me?' And they kept on refusing him. Anyway, to pacify him a bit they offered him this honey drink which had this herb in it which they got from the vine, this special thing, it turned him into a mopoke. So he flew away. That's how they got rid of him, but because they got cheesed off with everybody then for leaving them here at the mercy of that young fella, they decided to get even.

Apparently they went from here to Moonee Moonee Creek, that's up near Coffs Harbour, and that's where they got the ganay, the digging stick, from. And they decided that one would go north and one would go south and as they went they would stick their yam sticks into the ground and one would chant 'Giduurra! Become sand!' and other one would chant 'Ngaarruwa! Become water!' So they went from up there, one went this way and one went that way. They went right around Australia chanting this song. (Ken Walker)

This story begins in the time when the world was being made, before the sea and sand, before the beaches and headlands that shape our coastline. At Moonee Moonee Beach, north of Coffs Harbour on the mid north coast of New South Wales, the two sisters made their yam sticks, ganay, from the ganayga tree. From here they set off to make the sand and the water with their digging sticks. The older sister went to the south, in the direction of the strong southerly winds, and the younger sister to the north, where the weaker winds come from. They chanted their song all the way around Australia, making the sea and sand, and creating the coastline of our island continent. At Split Solitary Island, just off the coast from Moonee Moonee Beach, they met up again. Here you can see their digging sticks crossed over each other where they left them when they rose to the heavens to become part of the Seven Sisters, joining earth country to sky country.

Ken Walker tells this story of The Women Who Made the Sea for Gumbaynggirr people learning culture and language at Nambucca Heads. In the old days these stories were told as songs, sung in ceremonies to keep the country strong. Like all creation stories, connections to country are made again each time the story is told, and people and country are renewed. In this book we want to tell the stories of these places for you the reader so that we can all learn to 'sing' these coastal places again.

Australia is a nation of coast dwellers. Most of us live on the fringes of our island continent. Our coastal places are the fastest growing areas of Australia and as these places are developed their former landscapes and ancient stories are overwritten with grids of streets and buildings. These ancient stories tell us about the changing shapes of this island landscape from before the last ice age, from the time of Gondwana when Tasmania was joined to the mainland by a land bridge. Stories will continue to be told as coastlines change with the rising seas, and many islands in the Pacific Ocean come to exist only in the minds of their storytellers and the hearts of their people. Our creation stories and songlines are typically seen as belonging to the desert where Indigenous spirituality resides and tourists go in their thousands to the great rock Uluṟu. But our coasts shape our lives and our identities; it is where we live. In this book we ask: How can we learn to 'sing' our coastal landscapes differently? How can we bring traditional understandings of singing the country, singing for the renewal and wellbeing of people and places, into a contemporary present?

Today you can fly from Sydney to Brisbane and see the folds of tree-covered mountains and coastal plains rimmed with the thinnest strip of golden sand. There are shapes of estuaries, rivers, lakes and lagoons, islands, headlands and beaches. With familiarity you get to know the markers of these places. Just out of Sydney the hammerhead of Barrenjoey marks the end of Sydney's northern beaches. Then the blue water seeps into the land making the lace waterways of Pittwater and the Hawkesbury. Somewhere around the Central Coast a familiar sequence of headland, beach and estuary begins, repeated up the coast in an endless pattern of sand, water, rock and tree. At Red Rock, on the mid north coast of New South Wales, there is a distinctive wide-bellied estuary with curled sand islands in the middle. They called this place Ngaalgan, the ear, deep listening in Gumbaynggirr language. Headlands and beaches continue until, just before Brisbane, a different pattern of coastline begins.

Driving up the Pacific Highway through this country you pass through the landscapes of nine different Aboriginal language territories. On the outskirts of Sydney you enter Darkinyung territory at the Hawkesbury. Wonnarua and Awabakal areas are around the Central Coast and Newcastle. Travelling north from Newcastle you pass through Warorimayi land and at Forster–Tuncurry you move into Birrbay country. Just north of Port Macquarie you are in Dhanggati territory then, after you cross the Nambucca River, just before Nambucca Heads, you come into Gumbaynggirr country. At Yamba you cross the Clarence River, leaving Gumbaynggirr for Bundjalung territory that stretches as far as the Gold Coast. Then, just south of Brisbane, as the landscape changes again, you move into Yuggera country. Within each of these language groups or nations there are many smaller clan groups with distinct names and authority in local places.

If you walked along the beaches through these places it would take you weeks or even months. You would get to know these local places more intimately through your body's movements and senses. You would feel the sand under your feet, the puffing up-and-down rhythm of headlands, and always the smell of salt in the air. At estuaries and rivers you would have to find a way to cross the water. When the tide is high you would camp beside the estuary, waiting until you could wade ankle deep through the shallow water that spills into the sea. At Arrawarra, just north of Coffs Harbour, there is just such an estuary that marks a crossing-over place to enter into the northern Gumbaynggirr country of the Garby Elders.

> It was Yirrawarra, that's its original name, but over time it just got changed and changed. That's like a meeting ground, like a place where you come from over Nana Glen or over Glenreagh way, come across to there, and like a big gathering there. Or you comin' across, you're enterin' someone else's clan area, 'cause you come across from those fellows' area over there. See, up at Yulong, down to Nana Glen, Glenreagh, they all come over that way, 'cause they're all with the different clans of people, and they come over, then Yellow Rock fellas come up, from all over, and that's how they used to meet. There was a lot of camps goin' right back through there, right behind where that midden is there, you see. (Tony Perkins)

We want to invite you to cross over into this country of coastal landscapes differently. It is the work of translation, of moving across. For the Gumbaynggirr people who live at Corindi Beach this place is understood and experienced as the centre of a contemporary global world. When outsiders visit Yarrawarra Aboriginal Cultural Centre these language words welcome you to country.

Giinagay nginda?	How are you?
Yaam ngaya ngulungginyay	I am a Gumbaynggirr Elder
Yaam nganyundi wajaarr	This is my country
Darruyagay, biyambaygu yuraal	So be happy and eat food
Yarrawarra	at Yarrawarra
	(Bing Laurie, 2000)

These words invite you to sound the landscape, to feel it slowly with your tongue, to take it into your bodies. If it is a warm winter's day the air is filled with the sound of rosellas chattering as they eat sweet banksias. The smell of salt air wafts in with the hum of the sea nearby. You might go on a bush tucker walk, winding through swamp mahoganies and white-trunked paperbarks. There you can taste geebungs, sarsaparilla, lilly pillies and the pungent sweet-salt of the fruit of the pigface flower, bright pink beauty of the dunes. You'll see toe holes where Uncle Clarrie Skinner climbed the tree to collect bush honey, and scars on trees where bark was cut to make canoes. At the end of the walk the coastal swamp opens to a surprise of bright blue, with white egrets dipping into a mangrove-lined lagoon. There's a small trail of water where the lagoon opens to the sea, a deep blue-green sea just visible through the opening in the dunes.

~

Northern Gumbaynggirr people called this place No Mans Land. They settled in the swampy wetland around Corindi Lake when the first selections were taken up by white people and they found 'they was livin' on someone else's land'. The narrow coastal strip where they came to live was the only available place that remained when fences divided their land and robbed them of their freedom to move through their country.

The fence was a powerful symbol of colonisation for northern Gumbaynggirr people. While unseen maps enabled selections to be allocated by the colonisers from a distance, separating people from country in unimaginable ways, the fence represented the materiality of colonisation. Until the signs of the fences appeared on the landscape, the Gumbaynggirr had no idea of the methods of enclosure of land that represented an entirely different view of our relationship to country.

> They kept on being forced and forced out and the only way to work out where to go to live, where you should be, where no-one could touch you, was when you seen a fence like that, with a river or a creek when you were off on the other side of it and lived.
> Nobody owned it, nobody really owned that side of it, and in the finish that's the only way everybody's worked out where to go, was to get on the other side of the fence, and *anyone* owned it. *They* owned the other side of the fence, along the creek banks and that. That's why you find a lot of – goin' back now a lot of camps later on, might be in the sixties and that, or in the fifties, them times, you find a lot of camps along the back of the beaches or headland or along the edge of a creek or lake or something, 'cause they all jumped over the other side of the fences. No Mans Land, that's what they called it. (Tony Perkins)

No Mans Land was a hidden place. Hidden behind the dunes in the Corindi Lake area, the people were largely able to avoid the intervention of authorities such as the Aborigines Protection Board and the Church. It gave them a different sort of freedom. The place was known up and down the coast as a place where you could escape the watchful eye of government authorities. It was a place where you could speak language. People came there to protect their children from being taken away by the Welfare.

> Yeah, we believe that we were one pocket that never came under the Welfare Protection Board or the churches or anything like that. I think they honestly somehow completely missed this section. Because they obviously had went through everywhere else, up and down, but right here they seem to have missed this section. An' I suppose in one sense it's

unique that there's only a very small group that's left that's never been through, you know, that system. They've always retained that freedom, and it's probably very rare to see.
(Tony Perkins)

In the in-between space of No Mans Land the Old People continued to eat food from their local places, to build their own shelters and to incorporate chosen elements of white culture into their daily lives. The idea of No Mans Land was a powerful and ongoing story for the people who settled at Corindi Lake. Neither water nor land, the swamp was the quintessential in-between space where new stories could be born. They called the small estuary in No Mans Land 'the Lake'. As a typical coastal estuary, the Lake was fed by rain waters from the inland and sea waters from high tides and big seas. They lived by these rhythms of the Lake; it was the centre of their world.

The Lake was their survival. It was the most immediate and plentiful source of everyday food. 'That Lake was plentiful with crabs, prawns, fish, you didn't have to go over to the sea throwing out a line. It was all in the Lake.' In the brackish upper waters there were turtles, waterbirds, fish and eels. The children learned to fish and swim in the safe waters of the Lake. 'We used to walk up there when we were kids with a bit of wire and drive the fish backwards, catch them that way.' They learned how to look after the Lake from the Old People. 'We used to go and get food and do it in such a way that you wouldn't kill everything out.' The Old People camped around the edges of the Lake in bark shelters made from the trees that grew there. Tony remembers going with his grandfather, Clarrie Skinner, to collect the bark to make their huts.

> I still remember goin' with me grandfather, old Clarrie Skinner, just remember goin' with him, and I was probably about ten, eleven. And he used to take me, instead of goin' to school sometimes, he'd take me across the other side and I still remember him.
>
> He used to get bark off trees from over there, sheets of bark, and he'd tie it all in bundles and we'd bring it back and they used to use it for the walls and for the roof. They were

getting it off those – like a swamp mahogany type tree, or a stringybark an' that sort of stuff, they used to get it off them. The stringybark was the one they used to get most of all. They'd get it off that 'cause it used to come off like in sheets. (Tony Perkins)

Tony learned about country from his grandfather. First he learned the practical skills that sustained life in that place. When he was about ten or eleven, the time when a boy would begin the learning involved in making the transition into manhood, his grandfather began teaching him the rules of living in this country.

I remember him sitting me down, and I still know, I can still see the spot today, like, it's not very far from here where he took me one day and I was about, probably eleven, eleven or twelve, and he was tellin' me about different ways of when anybody disobeys people and don't respect and that type of thing and he was showin', he was explainin' to me about how punishment is served on them in the traditional way and what type of plants were used to do it. And I can still remember that as clear as clear today, how he told me it was done, and what they used. At the time I was only about twelve year old, when he told me. (Tony Perkins)

Tony remembers the exact spot where his grandfather began to teach him this deeper knowledge of country because this sort of knowledge is learned in country. When access to the special places where the higher levels of learning took place was no longer possible, the initiated men taught the young men through stories. The marks of initiation on their bodies established their authority to tell these stories.

But my grandfather he would – I remember him showin' me the initiation marks on him, on his chest, an' that sort of thing I seen. He explained, you know, what that was for, what it was about. And I saw Bing and Bruce's father, 'cause my grandfather and Bing and Bruce's father they were stepbrothers, sort of like brothers. They were brothers. I saw both of them. They both showed me and explained the marks and things on the body from initiation. (Tony Perkins)

The scars hold the knowledge of these men in bridging the time before and the time after white settlement. They are evidence of these mens' authority in country and the means through which Tony gains his authority to tell this story in place, and of places. They are also symbolic for Tony of the whole process of translation in telling this story. By the time of his generation the young men were no longer being fully initiated and the Old People had decided on a new mode of passing on their knowledge about country.

My grandfather was telling me that it's like a jigsaw puzzle. He said this is how it'd work. We will keep all, we've got the knowledge and the law inside of us, he said that. We will, over a long time, watch the young children growing up, which was us. And we will work out which ones to tell certain things to and what he told me was that you will all come home at some times and when you do you'll all talk about different things and he said you'll all be told different things, and you'll all put the jigsaw puzzle together on all the information that has been, that we will be giving to each person that we can trust. And what he was saying, I think, was that the information'll never be lost because each person'll be carrying a part and when it comes together you'll work out the Law and the culture and the whole lot for yourself. (Tony Perkins)

The people who were given the pieces of the jigsaw puzzle, the young people of the next generation, are now the Elders of today.[2] Each of them holds different aspects of traditional knowledge — of food, plants and animals, of land and special places, of medicine, healing and spirit knowledge, of language, music and song. It is this knowledge that we draw on in this book. Tony himself was partially initiated but, like many other young men in those times, was too busy being part of the new world to complete the full initiation cycle.

Having grown up by Corindi Lake with his grandfather and large extended family, as a young man Tony left the area to look for work. Between the late sixties, when he left, and the early eighties, when he returned, he saw remarkable changes.

> When I look back I saw the bark huts down there, then the tin huts, and I saw people come up to brick homes. I saw people change from living out of the Lake to going to the shop. Before that they were down there at the Lake getting fish and crabs, eels and turtles, and they'd be down on the beach looking for pipis and shellfish. They'd go down to the red gums and get the grubs out of the trees and to the river to get cobra out of the logs. You'd never see any mince meat and sausages. It was kangaroo hanging on smoking rails.
> (Tony Perkins)

The material transition from bark to tin to brick represents the symbolic transition that took place in No Mans Land. Before Tony left, the people had lived almost entirely from the beach and sea. On his return they went to the shop to buy food. Their houses had evolved from bark to tin to the modern brick homes that they live in today. They had also begun to notice the devastating impacts of increasing coastal settlement on their land. Coastal development had begun to intensify, and sewerage from local housing seeped into the small catchment of Corindi Lake. Their beloved Lake was dying. 'You could see things dying off in the Lake but no-one was interested, as long as they built their house or road, or put a pipe in there to drain everything, that was good enough.' The intensification of their lives in No Mans Land meant that they knew the Lake intimately, they had been taught to look after it by the Old People. They had a strong sense of identity with the Lake because it had been so essential in their survival, and they believed it should be protected for everybody.

> It could be used for everybody but it should be restored, brought back. It should be really looked after, that place. That's how everyone survived, from that Lake, it's a really important part of it. It's probably the most important area

where we were pushed into this corner and the Old People were made to survive from that area, to get through. It took them a long while to teach our age group right from wrong but that area was where they could settle down and move forward then. (Tony Perkins)

For Tony, this became the imperative to find a new way of looking after their places.

In 1987 Tony established the Yarrawarra Aboriginal Corporation. The organisation was named Yarrawarra, after yirrawarra, meaning 'meeting place'. Like Arrawarra, the meeting place marked by the middens where the Old People camped and waited to be welcomed into country, Yarrawarra is a contemporary meeting place for bringing outsiders into country. Tony describes the purpose of the organisation as being to 'show the real value of Aboriginal culture and history … on the coastline of NSW'. Gumbaynggirr people had long been a 'hidden race of people' with an invisible story. Now it was time to tell their story to everyone, 'to get the message out' as another way of caring for country.

> The reason why we decided that we needed an organisation like this was to show the real value of Aboriginal culture and history that virtually was never known about on the coastline of New South Wales. How we've had to go about that was to first establish an organisation and then start very slowly getting the Elders of the tribe from this area to work as a clan group to work out what information we could give regarding the tradition of the group. To put together educational programs and on-site stuff to show that there is still an Aboriginal existence along the coastline. We can't continue to be a hidden race of people and we've come to terms with the fact that there is only one way to get this message out. (Tony Perkins)

They formed the Garby Elders group to make decisions about sharing their knowledge of country. Their group is named after gaabi, the swamp wallaby who lived with them in the swampy wetlands of the Lake. Their knowledge and authority is inextricably intertwined with the Lake and their place in No Mans Land. In the new contemporary context they had to decide what knowledge to release and what needed to remain hidden. It was a decision that involved a sense of loss as giving away knowledge is giving away power, but they believed that it was a necessary step to protect their identity and their places.

For Tony it was a process of continuing his grandfather's work of cultural translation, of working out how best to pass on the knowledge of this coastal country in a rapidly changing world.

> I spent so much time with my grandfather and grandmother and I think what I am trying to do is carry that role, that message that times are changing so fast and we have to speak out now. A long time ago we'd keep it all in our heads and we'd pass something on that way. Now we're better off researching everything, recording everything, getting it all down. I noticed it's a new way of doing it, putting it down on the tapes or the video and keeping it like that.
>
> It's very sad but we can't wait around for the right person to pass things on to. It's been a hard decision for us to make because our Old People couldn't see what we're doing today – the video camera and computers. They wouldn't know we had to make up our mind to go that way. (Tony Perkins)

They made the difficult decision to pass on the stories and knowledge of these coastal landscapes in a different way. There was an imperative to get the message out so that others could learn about how to know and protect this country. In the space of just over a generation they had moved from transmitting cultural knowledge about country through initiation, to passing on selected aspects of knowledge to particular individuals, to recording oral stories and places using modern technological equipment. It is this movement from one mode of telling to another, the processes of cultural translation, that we follow in this text.

~

Singing differently

We began our project with a bush tucker feast to meet the Elders. Auntie Marie Edwards, Tony's aunt, was the oldest and well into her eighties. She came to live at 'the Old Farm' at Red Rock as a young girl with her large extended family. From the Old Farm the family moved up and down the river to Red Rock beach, camping and catching worms for the holidaymakers. Auntie Marie told us how the Old People used to call to the dolphins in language to bring the fish in. Her father, Clarrie Skinner, could hear 'the jewfish choppin'' from their house a mile from the beach. He would disappear into the night and come back with three big jewfish. She told us how to collect pipis from the beach and make curry pipi gravy. Every time she and I met after this she asked me whether I had found any pipis yet and told me where the good ones were.

Uncles Bing, Bruce, Keith and Michael arrived at the feast together from the camp across the road. The four of them grew up together by the Lake and have lived there all their lives. Uncle Bing is the oldest and the keeper of the Gumburr, the protector spirit who lives down at the Old Camp. Uncle Bruce is a fisherman and a good cook. His house is where everyone congregates and the fishing rods are ever ready along the verandah for 'off-pay week'. He is generous, warm and friendly, and keeps everyone on an even keel. Uncle Keith Lardner is Clarrie Skinner's son by his second wife. I often see Keith by the Lake in the early morning, deep in quiet contemplation. He has a small tent down at the Old Camp so he can keep a protective eye on things. Uncle Michael McDougall wears a bright yellow T-shirt with LIFESAVER written across the front in pink. He tells us the story of how he found the old banksia canoe buried in the mudflats by the Lake.[3] The place on the boardwalk where the canoe story is told bears his name. These people are the Elders of today whose oral stories we recorded for our research. They grew up with the Old People by the Lake, learning their stories and their language.

> Yeah, well we used to sit down and listen. We had nothing else to do you know, we just used to go fishing a lot, sit down and listen to the men talkin', the Old People. Me grandfather and father, Uncle [Clarrie Skinner], Keithy's father, and Michael's father Abraham McDougall, and me old dad, all

them fellas, a lot of the Old People, yeah. They never used to talk in English or anything like that, it was just pretty much listening you know, used to all talk in lingo. (Bing Laurie)

Bing, Bruce and Keith are the only Gumbaynggirr Elders of today who speak the language they learned from the Old People. They learned the language because they grew up in No Mans Land as a place of resistance where some elements of Gumbaynggirr culture could continue. But, even for them, speaking language was a complex and fraught matter. They would invite me to the bachelors' quarters to record their stories in language. They would be sitting around a flagon of McWilliams Tawny Port and their language stories poured forth. I told them I could not record their language stories when they were drinking and this resulted in a stream of good humoured abuse. They said they could only speak Gumbaynggirr language when they had been drinking. Language speaking and drinking were profound and entwined acts of resistance in No Mans Land. It is only very recently that there has been a change in their approach to speaking language: Uncle Bing now welcomes outsiders to country in Gumbaynggirr language, and teaches language to the Gumbaynggirr community from Corindi Beach.

There are only a few Gumbaynggirr words in the place stories we recorded at Yarrawarra. On the whole the materiality of Gumbaynggirr language (the embodiment of places and things through language) has been translated into English through a process that happened over the three generations of people who lived in No Mans Land. The English language, however, has been bent to hold the traces of Gumbaynggirr meanings. In Uncle Bing's storytelling, the materiality of language is so strong that at first I was often not able to understand his stories, even though they were told in his English. His stories were so closely tied to the place and to the meanings of the Old People that for an outsider their meanings were quite opaque. Over time I learned to clarify his meanings while I was recording his stories. To make sure I understood I would repeat what he said for the tape recorder. In this way we proceeded slowly to an understanding of his language.

The material translation from Gumbaynggirr language in No Mans Land has been a slow process of bending English to express Gumbaynggirr cultural meanings. Each speaker has different individual inflections of language, depending on the age of speaker and their degree of exposure to Gumbaynggirr stories, as opposed to a white education. For our purposes in this text, verbatim transcription of oral stories is the only way to remain true to the language's materiality. It is the oral stories that hold cultural meanings and enable new meanings of places to be made. By including these stories as they have been transcribed from their oral form we make evident the processes of cultural translation. Reading these stories requires the reader to enter into the process of cultural translation, to listen carefully to the traces of the voice that remain in the written text. It is slow learning that requires slow and careful reading.

In all of our work together Tony recorded his remarkable knowledge through oral storytelling. We recorded the whole body of work that underpins this book in stories and conversations with each other. Tony chooses to remain essentially oral. He can read and write but has never wanted to become a writer or a reader of written words. When I am seeking feedback on his stories turned into written text I read them to him and record his oral responses. Both Tony and I are acutely aware of these politics of representation. We are aware that writing from the space in-between Aboriginal and non-Aboriginal voices and identities is a risky business.

~

The work of language and cultural translation is the work of the 'contact zone'.[4] Over many years of collaborative place research with Aboriginal people I came to realise that specific local places, such as Yarrawarra, offer us an in-between space for the intersection of different and often contested stories. In the contact zone it is important to hold these different languages and stories in productive tension rather than assimilating one into the other. It is 'uncertainty that marks this space out and continually remarks it'. The main function of the contact zone is to preserve 'the intervals of difference', even to the point of suspending meaning.[5]

Halfway through our research we recorded a series of conversations between the mixed Aboriginal and non-Aboriginal research team about the politics of representation. We recorded these conversations in order to more closely understand the work of the contact zone in our project. Tony places our research partnership with Yarrawarra firmly within the contact zone of a long-term and ongoing struggle for the protection of his people and their places. Our timelines and terms of engagement were clearly formed within this history. What was new about this research partnership was Tony's decision to continue the struggle through these different means, through a focus on representation.

> We see it as, for us, a new method in getting our message through. Whereas we tried the other avenues back in the fifties and the sixties and the seventies, we tried all those avenues of holding all the information, we tried the retaliation in the way of marching in the streets, being locked up because of riots, but the political power there was too great, you couldn't defeat it, so you had to turn yourself around, and use another angle.
>
> The only way we can fight against that political power is now through, to come out with the knowledge, the power knowledge within Aboriginal people and let that go so that it is recorded. That's why we attached ourselves [to the research], to gain the power behind our statements. It's probably – using a stone axe which was the tool years ago, well it's another form of tool that we're now using to lever away a political power. (Tony Perkins)

Tony clearly understood the purpose of our research as a political tool, a tool to help Aboriginal people 'gain the power behind our statements'. He explained his understanding of our collaborative research processes through his 'border work', making clear our different perspectives. From many conversations about the politics of representation we identified different sorts of border work that were critical to our negotiations in the contact zone. Border work was precarious, risky and sometimes difficult emotional work for all of us in what we came to call the 'discomfort zone' of cultural contact in our research. Some of this border work involved maintaining boundaries, such as making clear important differences and protocols between Aboriginal and non-Aboriginal ways of doing things. But much of the essential border work of collaboration involved moving between and across the boundaries of difference. We found the discomfort zone to be a creative space where the tension of difference has the potential to produce new understandings and new possibilities.

My learning in the contact zone was most difficult in regard to our shared colonial history of massacres and stolen generations. In telling and listening to these stories we faced the abyss of our different positioning within these colonial histories. My work with Tony about the massacre story was perhaps the most difficult and also the most productive. With careful and detailed work we recorded the massacre story over many years, each time moving closer to understanding what it meant for him to tell the story and what it meant for me to listen. It was important to understand why this act of telling and listening to the story, that for Tony defined the space of the contact zone, was so significant. To erase our differences in the telling and listening would have been to deny our different positions in relation to that colonial place story. It was only through entering that space of difference so deeply, with all of the ethical responsibilities, that each of us is able to speak from the place between Self and Other, between Indigenous and non-Indigenous. Even then, we each speak from that place so differently.

~

Coming to know the landscapes and stories of coastal Gumbaynggirr country was a matter of crossing many boundaries for me. My home of twenty years was in the New England town of Armidale on the northern tablelands of New South Wales at the western edge of Gumbaynggirr country. Although I grew up in Sydney, I was birthed into the landscapes of New England through my work with Aboriginal people there.[6]

To go to Yarrawarra I moved from the sparse, dry landscapes of the New England tablelands, down through the wild gorge country to the flat warmth of the coastal plains. Driving from Armidale to Corindi

Beach there are scenes that I have photographed in my mind's eye as I drive towards the coast. At first exciting and exotic, these places have become lovingly familiar, holding me in the transition to that other space. The first one that I wait for is the sight of layered peaks of violet, lavender and blue mountains beyond the green paddocks of Dorrigo. In the far distance the layered mountains merge with sky and on a clear day I imagine I can see the sea in that indecipherable space on the horizon. Winding down the mountain the air breathes blue eucalyptus and curled fronds of tree ferns reach onto the road. The first view of the sea as I drive up the Pacific Highway towards Yarrawarra is always exciting. In some ways it is a return to the beaches of my childhood holidays but in other ways quite different.

When I arrived at that place for the first time the meanings of these landscapes were largely opaque to me. I began to learn the place by walking McDougalls' Run, from Woolgoolga to Corindi Lake, to feel the measure of its beaches. The Old People measured out their country by the distance of their daily walk: half a dozen beaches, headlands, estuaries. They called the strip of coastline between Red Rock and Woolgoolga McDougalls' Run. Michael's father and uncle, Herbie and Abraham McDougall, were two of the Old People, brothers and initiated men, who came to settle in the area around Corindi Lake. The story goes that one of them camped on Red Rock headland and the other on Woolgoolga headland. When they visited each other they walked up and down the coastline between Woolgoolga and Red Rock, defining the extent of their local country in terms of the walking distance between the two places. In doing this walk they were also carrying out their responsibility to protect the places and the people, talking to coastline as they walked.

> Because all that strip right along – well that's McDougalls' anyway, like McDougall, old Herbie and, that's their run. Well that's the only place they could walk, outside, there's a strip runnin' from Red Rock right through to Woolgoolga headland here, there's another like sort of a cave thing under Woolgoolga headland there. They used to go from there right along and they called it the McDougalls' Run 'cause that's the only place they could walk in the finish, right along that

strip, and it's the only piece of land that was ever left, No Mans Land. One of them used to come over 'ere [Red Rock], used to stay on the other side of that headland here, and the other bloke used to be out that way and they'd walk between each other. It might have been a protection thing, you know, 'cause those times it was more like a protection for everyone else, like their presence bein' around like a protector. Keeping an eye on the land and everything along the way, they were talkin' to different places, they used to talk to a lot of different places, very special things they'd talk to it. (Tony Perkins)

I remember one morning when I walked McDougalls' Run as if it were today. All is movement and sound. Birds are calling all around, sound of waves breaking on the beaches, movement of walking along beach and over headland. This morning the tide is coming in and waves are breaking towards the top of the beach on soft dry sand. I walk along one beach and climb up over the headland then down onto the next, legs aching as feet sink into sand, trying to work out the rhythm of tides to see if I can walk to Corindi next week. Even when the waves go back my feet sink into the freshly wet sand, not like the firm sand at low tide. On some beaches patches of grey pebbles make a shaley sound, swish swish swish. The pebbles are cold and smooth, moving in layers each time a wave washes over. I have to hurry now because if the tide is really high I won't make it over the estuary at Arrawarra Beach where the people stopped and camped. I wade across the estuary knee deep, along the beach and over another headland, until I enter the hidden opening where Corindi Lake meets the sea. At Yarrawarra everyone wants to catch up on the beach gossip: weather, fishing, tides, estuary. We talk and I learn. As I walk the beaches I learn these places in a different way.

This writing is about the process of coming to know. It is about how white people can learn to live in this country differently. Through many years of working closely with Aboriginal people I have learned to think through place. I call my work 'oral place story' rather than oral history. Oral history implies the recording of oral stories that tell us about the past. Oral place stories tell us about the relationship between places and people in the present, layered through deep time.

In these times of rapid environmental loss it is now more urgent than ever that we listen to these stories about how to learn and inhabit our places differently. Writing about place and identity in Australia is characterised by this necessary engagement with the relationship between Aboriginal and non-Aboriginal people and place.

As a non-Aboriginal Australian, working with Aboriginal people and their places requires me to open myself to the materiality of those places as well as to their stories. In my journal writing I can trace my place learning and my growing responsiveness to place. I had to learn a new way of seeing and a new way of writing to move outside of the academic writing genre to embody place in my work. I learnt that I am required to put myself bodily in the places of these stories. This learning demands an attentiveness to place from the whole body: 'the body, and not only the ear, is a trembling flame, a vibrating surface, ruffled water. The body does not photograph the world, but filters it across permeable membranes'.[7] The weather, wind, rain, storms, sunshine, the beaches, sand and water, and the rhythm of tides and cycles of seasons are all part of this attentiveness to place. It is place learning that derives from a deep, embodied intimacy. This place learning gives rise to a different sense of self, an understanding of self-becoming-other in the space between the self and a natural world, composed of humans and non-human others, animate and inanimate, animals and plants, weather, rocks, trees.

Through this engagement the landscape itself became another subject in the research as I recorded my growing responsiveness to place. Place – the actual physical location – seemed to provide a third space, a safe place for all of us in work that might otherwise have been politically fraught. The actual physical place existed outside all of us, prior to our existence and continuing beyond our individual lives. In this sense it was the third partner in our research. I continued to write in journals that recorded my response to the places, to the research process, and my evolving ideas about Gumbaynggirr coastal knowledge. The journals continued into the second phase of the research when we moved to Nambucca Heads in southern Gumbaynggirr country, eighty kilometres south of Corindi Beach. Here we worked with Uncle Ken Walker and Gary Williams at the

Muurrbay Aboriginal Language and Culture Co-operative to learn about their place stories.

Often the learning recorded in my journals was ordinary, like my walks along the beaches. At other times it was extraordinary, like my record of driving with Uncle Ken Walker to the story places in his country. I wrote about the sense of the whole of this coastal landscape coming alive with new meanings:

> All the mountains and shapes of places are spoken into being as Ken stories them. 'That's a good jewfish place' and 'that's the place where you catch yellow perch'. It's a mixture of the everyday and the sacred. Mythical stories of Yarrahappini, the place of the koala Dreaming, and the fog Dreaming place at Smoky Cape. Every part of the landscape comes alive. It's too fast to be driving in a car, it's a knowing that comes from walking and being in a place. Ken takes us to a rough granite rock platform to feel an area that is smooth and shiny on the edge of the sea. We rub our hands over the rough granulated surface then on cold smoothness. People sat here, he tells us, in the shade of casuarinas sharpening stone axes by the edge of this azure sea.

I responded to all of these places in my journals for ten years until, when leaving New South Wales to move to Victoria, it was these coastal landscapes that I grieved for most strongly. I had worked with Gumbaynggirr people throughout this time listening to their stories until they became part of me through the rhythms of the language of place. For ten years I was involved with people in making stories, books, maps and collections of photos that gave us all great pleasure in the creation. These are being used to make big changes and it seemed as if that was enough. The challenges of writing from this space between Indigenous and non-Indigenous, the politics of representation, were great. I didn't know how we could write this book but I was haunted by Tony's imperative to 'get the message out'. Then, one day in 2006, I listened to a performance of Stephen Leeke's *Voices in the Landscape* in an old and crumbling whitewashed church in West End, Brisbane. In that performance I heard what I needed to know to do this writing.

Once a Greek Orthodox church, the building was itself a reminder that we are a country of immigrants. It was a bright, hot Brisbane day in early summer. Inside was dark with muted light through stained-glass windows. We waited on hard, upright wooden pews, clatter of voices and feet on wooden floors. Then all fell silent as we were transported on voices that spiralled through the domed ceiling towards the heavens. There were songs that evoked beaches of my childhood: 'On the banks of teased and sun-washed seaweed/ There would be frail sea eggs and sponges'.[8] Others, like *Kondalilla*, sounded the landscape in voice without words, holding in tension a falling waterfall in the wet season and the parched stillness of the dry. A guttural didgeridoo disrupted the lyrical as Aboriginal poet and storyteller Sam Wagan Watson delivered *Die Dunkel Erde, The Dark Earth*, a tribute to his mixed German and Aboriginal creative inheritance.

The performance revelled in mixing genres, traditions, instruments and sounds. It was energised through difference. Always sounding the landscape, Aboriginal and non-Aboriginal voices, song, music and text opened up a space for a different sort of writing. It gave permission to break through restrictive proscriptions around the work of representation while at the same time celebrating an ethics, a passion and a compassionate love of the Australian landscape with its deeply embedded Indigenous stories. It also gave me the metaphor of singing.

In Aboriginal creation rituals, people and place are sung into being each time the ritual is performed. In the ritual performance of these stories the landforms and water, the plants and animals, are sung into being in particular places. Individual songs and story places are connected across the landscape through songlines. Singing the country is an essential part of nurturing country. Singing is knowledge. In *Crying to Remember,* Fiona Magowan says that in Yolngu culture 'those who sing, know' and stories 'are often told in song as a means to make sense of the world and everything in it'. Knowing songs is equivalent to knowing country, and it is through song that the world has meaning. These song stories are dynamic and work in a contemporary sense to create and re-create connections between people and place and people and people.

> Storytelling is, therefore, embedded in ancestral creation but animated by contemporary action, such that the cartography of country is also a cartography of the mind. Places are spoken or sung into being through the imagined worlds of the storyteller, singer and listener, the places chosen partially on the response of the listener as the legitimator of the emergent narrative.[9]

These songs are not only about singing the country for Aboriginal people; they are about singing the country for all of us. They require a singer and an audience, a teller and a listener. Fiona Magowan points out that the choice of places that are sung depends on the response of the listener to the 'emergent narrative', the story that singer and listener make together. When she asked the clan leader if she could learn women's songs he replied, 'You must first learn my songs [manikay], my uncle's songs, my mother's mother's songs and my mother's songs from me in that order and then you may learn women's songs'.[10] Learning knowledge about country has a proper order and there is much to learn. Moreover, singing demands a response.

> To be located within the story-paths of memory is to be able 'to know, speak, act, invite, deny, share, and ask' as individuals and groups come to be situated in a complex of authorial relativities, and where not to sing is tantamount to a declaration of war on one's neighbour, and not to tell is to deny connection – an affront to the relationship.[11]

According to this ethic of country we are left then with no choice but to sing the songs, to tell the stories and hear them as listener and respondent. But singing is not such a simple matter when it is a metaphor for the creation of a written text. My question then, for this text, is how can we sing our coastal landscapes differently?

We need to make songs that are sad and painful, a requiem for what has happened in the past. We need to sing songs that are joyous, that celebrate the survival and rebirth of Aboriginal peoples. And we need to sing songs that express our love, that beat with the rhythm of our hearts for this country.

CHAPTER 2

Crying-songs to remember

Massacre

Dawn light is hazy as I walk through moist she-oaks with dewdrop needles in the shadow of sand dunes. On top of the dune a single golden flower catches the first rays of the sun. The long beach is crashing foam waves, too rough for swimming, so I walk with a slight shiver over the headland to the little beach, quieter and protected in the curve of the headland. At the river's mouth the red rock shocks my senses, lit blood red in the pink light of dawn. I float in shallow waves and contemplate the stories of this place. 'Blood Rock', they once called it.

M'grandmother was tellin' me
about the time
her mother was lookin' after a baby
between Blackadder Creek and Cassons Creek,
she said these policemen come along on horses
all the men were there, and the women
they were washin' and that sort of thing
and she said they shot the men there
then they chased 'em down through to Red Rock

the men was swimmin' across the river
and up here where they started and down there
the water was red
just red with the blood
where they shot 'em.
She grabbed the baby and the women hid
in the rushes on the creek banks.
She told me that was the worst thing she ever seen
they just came along and started shootin'.

The sudden intrusion of the policemen on horses into this intimate scene of daily life is shocking. The people were dispersed, never to return to that camping place. The bodies of the men shed their blood into the river at Red Rock when they were shot as they swam to escape. Their story is inscribed onto the landscape in the colour of their blood, and in the name they gave to Red Rock: 'Blood Rock' they called it.

Tony Perkins told this story in our first interview, sitting in a demountable building at Yarrawarra, with Blackadder and Cassons creeks on one side of us and Red Rock on the other, close to the trail that the massacre story etched indelibly into my brain.

This massacre story was to become central in the interpretation of all that was to follow, a lens through which to understand the place and its people. Tony and I revisited this story many times and in many iterations, understanding it also as a lens through which we could establish a basis for exchange between a white female settler-researcher and Tony as a voice speaking for the place, a representative of the Garby Elders, and manager of the Yarrawarra organisation.

This first scene of the massacre story lives in the landscape. It was told to Tony by his grandmother as a story of her mother's experience. All the way through the story Tony reminds the listener of his great-grandmother's presence. The story evokes the details of her daily life. She is there at the creek looking after a baby while the women are washing. It is set in a very particular place, located for the listener by the white farmers' names, Blackadder and Casson, that have named the creeks. It is there on the map. This was their camping place in a time when they moved freely through this landscape.

The story creates a relationship, albeit an uneasy one, between Tony, his grandmother as the original teller, the place, and me as the listener. It challenges me as a white researcher. What are you going to do with this story? But it is not primarily about me, it is a lesson about how to begin to listen to this place and its stories that Tony wants to communicate to a broader audience.

My first response was to ask Tony what this story meant to his grandmother. 'What sort of sense did she make of it? Was she bitter? What sort of feeling would she tell the story with?' He replied by telling me about her gestures as she told the story. 'She was always a person that sort of waved her hands a lot when she spoke. And she would talk fairly loud when she was talkin', an' always had her hands goin'.' He said his grandmother told them the story so that they could learn about the bad things that happened, so they would learn to listen with respect to those who were left behind.

I had fallen in love with Red Rock some years earlier, before I had begun working with Tony, before I had even heard of Yarrawarra:

> The beach is so rich in colour and form it seems to invite only a short ritual presence. At the southern end, just south of the confluence of river and sea, is the red rock, liver-coloured bodily extrusion, as dramatic in form as colour, marking this sacred place where river meets sea. What Aboriginal stories about this red rock are washing in these waves? On one side of the rock, a small sheltered beach, with silver grey casuarinas dripping towards silver white sand, curves in a quarter moon to a jutting headland. On the other, the bank of the river, extruded red and white, curls and crumbles with its fragile colonies of banksias, casuarinas and pandanus.[12]

I wondered now about my haunting sense of stories washing in the waves. Deborah Bird Rose says that country is rich in sentience. 'The Dreamings are there, of course, and so too are the dead people who belonged to the country in life ... Animals are deemed to be sentient beings, as are some trees, rocks and other sites.'[13] I had lived and worked with Aboriginal people in the Northern Territory and in many places in New South Wales, so I knew that there are always Aboriginal stories that I have not yet heard about all places. It would be expected that there were Aboriginal stories at Red Rock. I came also to Red Rock as a not-knower, but this feeling was different.

The place had struck me as overwhelmingly beautiful. A quiet holiday place with a wide sandy estuary, wildflower plains and wild uninhabited beaches. I was aware of the danger in the place where the river meets the sea. A strong rip runs out from the river around the headland and many have drowned there. Sometimes we would dive in and swim as fast as we could against the current to make it across the river when the tide was rushing out. Then we'd float down at great speed, coming in just before the red rock, always with a sense of danger. But it was the depth of colour of the red rock that clung to me. Always the shock of red, changing its intensity in different light and times of day. The landscape, however, does not yield its human stories until we are ready to hear them and we ask. Katrina Schlunke, in retelling another massacre story, writes about 'dumb places' where the quiet landscape has only two very gentle sounds, 'shallow running river over smooth river rocks … less than a gurgle … something like the resonance of your own circulatory system'.[14] We need human voices to sound these landscape stories.

Tony and I talked again, on another occasion, about his grandmother's storytelling so I could understand more about the quality of her voice in the interaction between storyteller and listener.

> I remember if there was any storm or anything comin', or if she was tryin' to get a message to you in some way, yeah, she used to get a really high pitch, and her arms'd be goin'. You know, like this. Oh it was unusual, it was, with the voice, and the same as down at the Old Camp. I dunno who passed away, it might have been Auntie Elsie Cowan, I'm not sure, but a lot of the old ones were there. And I can still remember them all outside the old hut there, near the bamboo, the same thing there, I still can hear it. It sounded like cryin', but it wasn't like normal cryin'. It was strange, like a cry but it was sort of all broken up. Some'd be sort of high, sort of raisin' the voice and they'd fade an' another one would come in and the same, like that. Yeah, I remember it like that. (Tony Perkins)

A chill ran down my spine, recalling the uncanny sound of wailing in the desert. Often the sound was preceded by a sign or portent, a whistling wind from nowhere blowing dust and unsettling the corners of the mind, and then the wailing, three days or more sometimes. I can remember it when someone died in Alice Springs, and the body made the 250-kilometre journey back to its place. The sudden sharp wind and then the sing-song wailing to help the spirit continue on its journey, to mourn the dead, sorry business. It was the song of the wailing that was the sound of his grandmother's voice telling the massacre story. This high-pitched singing, Tony says, is about fear.

> My grandmother used to sing if she was in fear of anything. She would sing, but a very high sound. Even though grandfather would sing, it'd be more – the only thing he used to sing to me about was how they used to sing the corroborees. It'd go a certain height but come down all the time. Very different. Women seem to have sung higher all the times because I think they had more fear or something. It's like if you get a pipi shell and you throw it, it'll give a whistle. Well that whistle has got a meaning, you see, it's got a meaning on why you shouldn't do that. Because that's a sound, it's not because you're throwin it, it's the sound. It doesn't matter what you do, the higher the sound the worse the message. And then you've got the death bird, of a night time. If anything's wrong, a high squeal comes through the sky. So the higher it is, that's more fear or the worse the message. (Tony Perkins)

Voice and sound have power, a power that belongs to the whistle of pipi shells, to the death bird's calls and to women's high-pitched singing. This is the voicing of fear, of foreboding and of sorrow in the landscape, sounded through his grandmother's telling of the massacre story. What must it have been like to live with this fear and how did it permeate the places where these events took place?

Fiona Magowan describes the crying-songs of Yolngu women as 'crying to remember'. There are no formal lessons in the art of crying. Young women sit next to their mothers and grandmothers during times of mourning, listening to the style and structure of their singing. Crying-songs are ritual songs for women to show respect for the deceased and provide a means for grieving personal loss. Women learn to wail little by little. Some songs are learned by listening, some from tapes and some from teaching.

While I was recording and pondering these massacre stories a young man shot dead thirty people at Port Arthur in Tasmania and burnt three other hostages in a guest house. Tasmania was reported to be shocked at its 'loss of innocence'. Australia mourned and the world cried with us. Each night as details of the massacre unfolded on the television we wept for the senseless violence and loss of life. The media talked of this event as the first time a tragedy of such proportions had ever happened in Australia. But this is Tasmania, I thought, a place where whole generations of Aboriginal people were wiped out. I remembered the story of Myall Creek, Cath Ellis's story about women being killed at Birdsville for performing ceremony, and the river red with blood at Red Rock. I wondered then, when will we ever make the connection between our pain and theirs? How can we learn to sing crying-songs to remember?

Tony suggested that I ask his Auntie Marie Edwards about the massacre story. Each time I asked her, gently, over a number of years, she would tell a little more. She would respond by telling me that Red Rock headland was a bad place, that the sea there was dangerous. The first time I asked about the massacre she told me a long story about a man who fell overboard from a fishing boat that went out in the dangerous place where the river meets the sea. She told me that his body was never found and his young son rowed the boat back from the sea, alone, against the current. 'It would be with the tide and that against him, you'd be just about movin', you know.' She warned me about the power of the water, the danger of the place. 'No dark people', she said, 'ever camped there'. That time she told me the massacre story only in the taboo, especially for women and children, against going to the place near the headland at Red Rock where her people were drowned. This taboo defined how she, and I, could talk about the massacre.

For many others it was also only the taboo that they spoke about. When we asked Glenda if she had ever heard any stories about Red Rock headland she said, 'I believe that's, um, that's only for men. Women can't walk on that headland. I've never been on there. That's where all the men go.' But none of the men, apart from Tony, spoke about this story in any detail either. I asked Tony what made the telling of the story so important that he would break the taboo and confront the intense emotions attached to the telling.

> I think it is important, it is very important. We hear a lot of history about everything else, you know, so I think it's gotta be told. That type of history, that's a history too and that's important to us. We gotta accept that it is part of the history of Aboriginal people from here, it happened. I think it is time that things are known, what went on. There's no-one got any grudges against nobody, all we want is that people accept what we say, what did happen, but there's no grudges against anyone. We know that even if there's any relatives here today belonging to them people, we don't hold them responsible for that, they weren't part of it, they probably didn't know anything about it and they are just things that happened in them times. It's just important that everybody should know. (Tony Perkins)

Neither Tony nor I had learned in school the history of the bloody relations between Aboriginal people and the new settlers who colonised Australia. There were never any books in any of the libraries of my childhood, or even my university studies, to tell me about these things. When I first heard about them from Aboriginal people they were told as silent, shameful and repressed stories, whisperings, the unspoken side of heroic exploration and conquest of a harsh land. Tony explained that in telling their story they did not hold any grudges, they just wanted to have the story recognised as part of the history of the place. Amazed by this remarkable generosity of spirit I asked him, 'Does it make you angry?'

> It does, there are some times – you know, like lots of times you can link up and you can find background for yourself but when you can only find halfway, and the reason why you can't find the rest 'cause over this period of time no-one will tell yer. It takes you all that time when you're growin' up and you become thirteen, fourteen, fifteen. Older people don't tell you where their brother is or where their uncles are, or

where their father was or anything, then when you get to a certain age they tell you what went on somewhere, then you think well that's the reason why you can't trace back where and who you're related to or anything. (Tony Perkins)

It was the missing family connections that Tony spoke about when I asked him this question. The missing brothers, uncles and fathers, represented by the gap in genealogies, in relationships and connections was not spoken about in the presence of young children. Tony was told the story in his mid teens, a kind of initiation knowledge given at the time he would have been initiated as a young tribal man. Even with the knowledge of this story, however, there remains a powerful silence about the lost relatives and the broken lines of family connection. Tony's anger is about these silences and he feels it for the nameless relatives who can't be traced.

Yeah, because – see we don't know who got shot out, that time, because there'd be lots of other relations but we don't know where our grandfathers' brothers and sisters and that are, there's no trace of 'em. There must have been more than just him and where was his mother and father and where was his relations? We can't find anyone related to him on his side and whether they were part of the ones gone, we don't know. If you have a look there's McDougalls there but where's all the relations from the McDougalls, they're gone, and there don't seem to be any trace of them today. We know you've got brothers and sisters and you've got aunties and uncles and they're all there but you can't trace from that time any other relations there. We always think that maybe that's the ones that have been shot out at that time. There's no trace of them. (Tony Perkins)

When we name all the people who lived in the camps at No Mans Land there is this same sense of people without blood connections. An extended family seemed to involve a core group of relatives and then a number of other people who are unconnected by blood but connected through their shared story. Tony tells me that each time they try to trace the relatives of these people they come to the same place. 'We always think that maybe that's the ones that have been shot out at that time.' When he talks about his feelings, Tony imagines the scene of the massacre and speculates on the morality of such acts.

> I do get angry at some things. I'm sure they could have worked it out in a better way back in those times. They knew our people were there with 'em, they knew that and when they give them selections out there, there must have been another way they could do it, not just give it away like that, put the owner in there then just come through and shoot anybody that's on your property. That seems a very uncivilised way. They talk about our people being uncivilised, but when you look at it I don't think you can get anything more uncivilised than just shooting people, especially people who never had the defence. They probably had never seen a gun in their life, and when you're only carryin' a stick with you, you got no protection whatsoever. It must have been an awful shock to see what a bullet could do I suppose in them times. (Tony Perkins)

The ethics of the relationship between Gumbaynggirr people and the new settlers relates back to land. As Tony puts it, there must have been a better way. As a listener to this story there is a point where words fail. I borrow these words from Katrina Schlunke, written in response to another massacre, as a refrain throughout the chapter to keep this sense of disjunction between experience and language.

> *I tell the story with the desire to make language, time and place stutter through it and I turn to the senses to try and keep us there within that moment where a body thought agonises. I hope that such stories change our worlds.*[15]

Creation

As the sun appears over the shadow of the headland it lights white-trunked paperbarks and white spoonbills sleeping on long black legs on the little sand island. In the broad curve of the estuary even the sea sounds round. Rosellas chatter in casuarinas, butcher birds water-chime their musical notes and a huge osprey, with fluffy legs and brown wings tinged with white, lands on the island. Five black cormorants take over from the white spoonbills who now dip long beaks into shallow water. High above, white seed-fluff clouds drift across the palest blue sky, reflected in the new deep-green of the river. The sun, now bright and strong, warms my back and draws out patterns of ripples and bird prints on the smooth skin of the sand island. On the edge, the curves made by water and tide are sculpted into body hollows in the rosy golden light. All are cradled in the big belly of the river with its ever-changing shapes of sand and water.

The only reason there's survival
was under Red Rock headland
is a cave that comes back out
all the way under Red Rock to Jewfish Point
the men actually got into there and came back up
and that was the only way that most survived
they came right back up past Jewfish Point
and that's the same place where
they use it as a birthing ground there.
You see all the clay floors
that's where they restarted
that's where they survived
coming back under the cave
then that become the birthing ground
they all started, like creation,
everybody's branched out, again.

The most extraordinary feature of the Red Rock massacre story is that it has a second scene, one of rebirth, a new creation story that followed on from the massacre. This story of rebirth has all of the elements of Plato's allegorical story of the cave and the labyrinth. The labyrinth is the passage of new birth, the passage from one state of being to another, the time without name. It echoes the caves of many special women's places in Gumbaynggirr country but the old women who spoke about the cave knew it only from a distance.

> A lot of them escaped from there through that tunnel. See there's two caves. The big cave was in the centre of the headland — and up there — up near Martin's Point was another one. Somewhere up there it was. I didn't know where that one was. I knew where the one was down there 'cause we used to go across — across the creek at Red Rock at low tide and we'd walk right out and look back into the face of the cliff. But you see it's more prominent, the red, with the sun shining on it. Directly across from the cave and on the side of the river, you look back. Go out as far as we could in the low water, at low tide, and look back in. That's the only way you could see it unless you climbed down. I was so disgusted about it [the massacre story]. Oh, forget about it, it's over and done with as far as I'm concerned. But you think about all those things later on in life. (Colleen Jarrett)

Auntie Colleen, now living far away, still remembered all the details of the rebirth story. She told us about two caves connected to the story, one on Red Rock headland and the other at Jewfish Point. Jewfish Point, she said, was the place where the Old People came into a new beginning. The cave under the headland was a place where they could not go, but from across the river they could see the cave in the sunlight at very low tide. She remembered the cave itself was red, red standing out in the sunlight. Only the old men, with deep knowledge of the protective spirits of country, remembered being inside the cave. In their stories it was a fearful place where only the very brave dared to go.

> Well I can walk there, walk there now, Red Rock headland, can't harm me. McDougall used to walk in there, Michael's father [an old initiated man who passed away long ago]. He walks in this cave. I remember, it used to be lower then, water used to be lower then. It's an old ice age — sea must've been risin' a bit see. And you can walk all the way in there. That's as far as it go out, yeah, to Jewfish Point. It go, it even go way in, near the black-point tide, tide comin' out. You'd be flat out — how you gonna get in there, big water all the time there, in and out, crashin'.

He used to climb the other side there. Oh he wasn't a
frightened man, a great big, great big man he was, Uncle
McDougall, yeah, round right in the other part, and then
climb down the headland y'know. Wouldn't take us in the
hard way. He reckons it goes a long way in, you can even see
behind you, it's right behind the water, y'know. All the crabs
rattlin' in there. He's out of there before the tide come in, he
said, old fella. He a game fellow he was, he wanted us to go
in there and climb up on the side. (Bing Laurie)

The cave is a terrifying place of death and rebirth. It is an ancient cave that belongs to the time of the last ice age. For Uncle Bing the rising seas increase the sense of danger. Even at the lowest tide, 'the black-point tide', the waves will be crashing in. Only Uncle McDougall, an old initiated man, could take the young men into the cave.

Deborah Bird Rose says we should start with origins. The Dreaming is the quintessential time of the liminal. In traditional creation stories all of the forms of the land and everything in it come into being. Each time these creation stories are performed in particular places the place and all its creatures are made anew. I have heard many new creation stories told by Aboriginal people to mark the re-creation of their peoples after white settlement. Patsy Cohen told the story of the five black matriarchs who birthed the new generation of children at Ingelba.[16] Four women in Coonabarabran told me how Mary Jane Cain made a new beginning for her people at Burrabeedee.[17] None of the stories, however, was so stark or so classical as this one about the abrupt ending of a way of life in the Red Rock massacre, the escape through the cave and the labyrinth, and the new beginning at the birthing grounds for the northern Gumbaynggirr people of Corindi Beach.

They called the place of this new beginning 'the Old Farm'. A space of some twenty or thirty years in real time elapsed between the massacre story and their arrival at the Old Farm. The time of the labyrinth, the passage between the cave and the birthing ground is a time without narrative. It is not a story about real time. It is about the cyclical and ongoing creation of people and place through storying them into being. 'Song evokes place, place evokes song, together they constitute relationships through time. Performance in place unfolds in time and draws other times – recent past and creation events – into a shared performative present.'[18] This group of northern Gumbaynggir people recreate themselves through the telling of this story.

Auntie Marie was a young child when her family arrived at Red Rock in the 1920s and Tom Richards, a local white settler, invited them to live in 'the old shingle house' by the river. Auntie Marie, and Celia Harvey, Tony's grandmother, both told Tony about the women travelling from miles around to have their babies at the birthing grounds at the Old Farm.

> Just this side of Red Rock, that's where the birthing grounds are. That's the birthing grounds for this area. My grandmother, Celia, used to do all the deliveries of the children. She used to do up all the women, they used to come there. See they used to walk miles, they used to go there, so the children were born. You'd see them comin' from Nana Glen, walk from over from Nana Glen, Glenreagh, right around, Moonee even, they used to come. All the women used to come up and this is where they used to stay and they used to have the children there. There used to be camps set up and that was a birthing area, on that ground there. (Tony Perkins)

Even though the birthing grounds were on private property and they had not lived there for over sixty years, Tony's grandmother and his auntie took him there to tell him the story in that place. They taught him how to read the signs of the clay floors that marked the places where the women gave birth to their babies. They showed him where his mother was born. 'I used to be here myself, when I was a young girl, when your mother was born. I was asleep in the hut just over there.' For the older women it was a place of remembering. For Tony, the massacre and rebirth story became the conceptual framing of the experience of his people. These stories locate Tony in relation to the whole story of an ending and a new beginning. The telling of the story became a new ritual in that place.

> I've been back to that birthing ground, I've been there twice. You can see the well there, you can see where they dug down, you can see all the floors. Straight across from it there is a tree, a tree with the bark taken out like a big canoe there, just across from it and the honey tree just next to it, runs up there on a bit of lean like that, you can see the toe holes goin' all the way up. When I was shown properly, and taken there, you can see all the raised floors, you can actually see where they are. There's clay, like it's all grassed over but you can see the raised areas where they carried the clay from the creek, carried it up and raised all the floors where each camp was built. And the one, the raised floor that's furthest to the east, is where the children were born, there. Auntie Marie showed me the one floor that you can sort of see raised where, she said that's where they used to be born there, that was the place. (Tony Perkins)

There at the Old Farm the birthing grounds were told as part of all the signs of their lives in that place: the well, the toe holes in the tree where they collected native honey, and the scarred tree where bark was removed to make a canoe. The birthing grounds were told in their precise detail. The ritual of storytelling in place ended with a story from Auntie Marie about her memory of the birth of one of the babies. The baby was Clarice, Tony's mother.

> She told me that she could remember one night when she was only young, my grandmother said to her 'You gonna have to go to sleep early tonight', and she didn't understand first up, and she said 'Well what's wrong?' and her grandmother said 'Oh never mind, but you will see in the morning'. And next morning she woke up at the other camp and when she woke up the grandmother, grandfather come out and said to her 'Oh the reason why you had to go to sleep early was because you had to wait for your sister to come along this morning'. And they took her over and showed her which camp it was. (Marie Edwards)

Auntie Marie and I talked often in her little unit on High Street in Coffs Harbour about her days at the Old Farm. Although she was then in her eighties, when she told me stories of the Old Farm it was as if she were back there in a vivid present as a young girl, erasing the space of fifty years and the modern unit around us. She talked about all the women who came there to give birth and how her grandmother had delivered all the babies.

> Yeah, we always had a place built up, made of bamboo for when they got pains or sick. And my Grandmother, we'd just go out and sing out to her, and she'd come over, big fire burning and deliver the babies. They used to put up their tents. They had special places for their baby and they'd go back in their tents. My father, he had this tarpaulin put up out there near the lemon tree. And I said 'Who's campin' there?' And he'd say, 'I'm gonna camp out here tonight'. Oh we had this fire, that's where my mother had my sister, that's Tony's mother. And we went to sleep I suppose and I went out the next morning when we woke up and my father said, 'You got a baby sister' and I said 'Sister? Where did it come from?' And he said 'Walking down the road!'
> (Marie Edwards)

Auntie Marie laughs at her childish innocence as she tells the story. She loved to tell the many stories of their lives at the Old Farm, how they built their shelters, collected food, made music and sang, lived, loved and gave birth by the Red Rock River. In the telling she reclaimed the place from the terror of the massacre. Her stories evoke a richly happy time, despite the sparse conditions of their new existence. The story of the old shingle house created a sense of warmth in the memory of falling sleep by the fire in the loving circle of grandmothers and aunties.

> We had an old shingle house, big old place. No rooms in it, just one big one. Mother had a bed up the side, but we used to all sleep in front of the fire. A big fireplace, oh it'd be wide as

that. And my father's seat over there. Us kids used to put our foot to the fire and we'd all sleep up this way. I dunno how we slept on those hard boards. Just slept, it was all just bags and whatever, and then the blankets over us. And further over my grandmother and my auntie. They lived further over. They made a camp out of a bark hut. (Marie Edwards)

Food was plentiful in the abundance of the river and the sea. She described her Granny fishing every day in the quiet of the river just near their camp. A bit further down the river, near Jewfish Point, they caught jewfish and mud crabs. Then even further afield, there were other stories about catching food at the beach.

Old Granny Armi, all day she'd sit down at the creek, Red Rock River. She'd go down there, she'd sit and she'd be pulling in the big bream, fish all round her. Just down the front. Then they'd go to Jew Point to fish up there all day, they used to catch big jewies up there, or anywhere up that river, or they might go get some crabs, so after you go past Jew Point you see all that weed, you see all the crabs landing where you can see 'em, spear 'em, bloody big crabs, used to be beautiful. (Marie Edwards)

Some of Auntie Marie's most vivid memories were about their friendships with the campers who came down to Red Rock in horse and sulky for the Christmas holidays. Tom Richard's daughters, Estelle and Doreen Richards, came to Yarrawarra one day to record stories with Auntie Marie and her daughter Vi, of their holiday times at Red Rock. The four women all talked at once, laughing and remembering their times together. There were so many stories and so much laughing that even with two tape recorders at each end of the table, it was hard to transcribe. There were stories of Clarrie and Celia, of the red dress Marie wore to the dance, and the places they went to at the beach together. Marie remembered how they camped at the back of the dunes near the bowling club and caught worms to sell for bait.

> Always down there at the beach at Christmas time when the people came. Like, my father'd say we'll go down 'cause we'll make a bit of money with the worms. We used to walk right up to Station Creek. Big tins like that, and the milk tin we used to only get a shilling off. But that was good money, we made good money, sand 'em all, put 'em in these tins. There was jam tin ones, a bigger one was, what two and six, or something, you know. But that's as high as it went. Well they used to always come up to the camp and say 'Have you got any worms, Clarrie?', or 'Anybody got any worms?', and so on. (Marie Edwards)

Laughter and singing were born again at Red Rock as the Old People made music and sang. Their singing and music are immortalised in stories and photos taken by the Richards family of the Red Rock band in the 1920s. The photos show a group of Aboriginal men and women dressed in their Sunday best, with all sorts of different homemade musical instruments.

> Well that's things they were makin'. Yeah, homemade harp. That's a auto harp, yeah, they used to make like different instruments. Yeah, you got, at the back here, they used to make their own, like stick in a box, sort of thing, and they'd only have one string on it, and just move the stick back and forward, and tighten it or let it go, and they'd just pull the one string, you know. The fella who's playing that one there, he's got a stick in his hand and he's got the broomstick there and the box there. You can either play it like a violin if you want to, the same thing. You can either make it like a base guitar out of it, or play it like a violin. If you want to make a base, you don't use a stick and just tighten the broom handle and just pull it, like a base sound. They used to use a lot of reeds, and that made the string to make a sound. They used to make a banjo, yeah, with a skin stretched over it. They used to use a lot of skins from different things, like a possum skin, or a kangaroo skin, whatever. (Tony Perkins)

Songs and music had always been part of their tradition. They mixed the old ways of making music, such as drums made of skins, with the new instruments of the settlers. They played at dances and at Christmas time they played from tent to tent for the holidaymakers, who would give them cake and wine. They'd leave in their flat-bottomed boat, playing and singing all the way back to the Old Farm.

> Pa Laurie and my brother and Jimmy Runner and Uncle Herbie, they used to play the leaf and sing. And they'd go from tent to tent, them days. Father used to play the leaf. Anyhow, he – they'd go tent to tent and they'd be waitin' a piece of cake and wine. By the time they got to the last one, they was pretty ripe. They'd be cooee-in' and singin' everybody, oh, even the men an all in the tents. Oh the good old days! Oh come up Clarrie, they'd say, and have a party. They built themselves a flat bottomed boat. They'd leave Red Rock with the music playin' and the Red Rock people used to say 'Oh Clarrie's gone home, they're all gone home, they're singin''. They'd sit at the back and one at the front playing the gumleaves and one fella singin'. You could hear them comin', here they come, they'd be cooee-in' and playin' and singin'. (Marie Edwards)

For Auntie Marie these were her best and happiest memories. Despite all that had happened to them they began to live again at the Old Farm. It was the place of the rebirth of their people as well as the literal birthing grounds where the women came to have their babies. There they made new friends, played new music, sang new songs, and wrote a new creation story for themselves.

> *I tell the story with the desire to make language, time and place stutter through it and I turn to the senses to try and keep us there within that moment where a body thought agonises. I hope that such stories change our worlds.*

~

Resolution?

In the evening the sand island and river are emptied of their daytime colours. The hollowed curves and folds of the late afternoon sun flatten out and the knoll of mangroves and grass on the little island are now only an outline against the dark curve of estuary. The river reflects shadows of trees and the last light of the sky. Ripples of feeding fish and small stones on the bank are thrown into sharp relief by the lingering glow of the setting sun. The cormorants, black wings dry, have flown, and the noise of birds grows less as the ocean roar takes form and shape behind the dunes. Straight across the river three hills recede into the night sky. The middle one, Green Hill, sitting in perfect symmetry: 'You must never go there.' Haunted. We listen still and quiet beside the ripple of the river as the tide comes in and a new moon appears in a pale green sky.

In memory of the victims and survivors
of the Blood Rock massacres.
Understanding their sacrifice
will make us stronger.
We as Gumbaynggirr people
have survived many conflicts
over ownership
of our traditional lands,
Including a massacre
where many were driven off the headland at
Red Rock (Blood Rock).
Gumbaynggirr descendents, especially women,
Still avoid this headland.
The significance of this place
And the rebirthing of our culture
Will never be forgotten.[19]

I wonder if there can ever be a resolution to such a story? I think about this question as I drive from the New England tablelands through Judith Wright country and down to the coast. It is another hidden story, closer to home, that Judith Wright wrote about in her poem, *Nigger's Leap*. In her biography of Wright, Veronica Brady wrote about the effect of this hidden story on Judith, who imagined this early dawning of a nation's consciousness.

> The story of 'Nigger's Leap had sunk much more deeply into her life than [her father] would perhaps have liked; and was to influence it to the end'. Though it is the kind of story most of us would prefer to forget or 'shuffle back into a violent and miserable past', for her 'that dark cliffhead with the depth of shadows below it in the gulfs, is still a potent place'.[20]

Brady goes on to talk about the twin strands that ran through Wright's life: her love of the land and her sense of being haunted by the history of our relations with its original inhabitants. Judith could not, Brady writes, 'divorce knowledge from responsibility'.[21] In her poem Judith Wright, like others writing at the same time, imagines the disappearance of an Aboriginal presence: 'Never from the earth again the coolamon/ or thin black children dancing like the shadows/ of saplings in the wind'. We now know differently. Aboriginal people have survived throughout Gumbaynggirr country to tell their own story. This gives us both the privilege of listening to the story and the responsibility to respond.

I asked Tony during our recorded conversations about what it was like to tell me as a white researcher about the massacre and why it was important for me to hear this story.

> I see it like this, like you're sort of helping us get through what we've been trying to cope with for a lot of years, you know, to get everyone to understand what went on. Because our message sometimes doesn't seem to come across very clear and strong. I don't know why that is, we've been unable to link up, you know, Aboriginal people find it hard to link up with people like yourself who get that understanding of what went on so that we're both carrying the message. In the past they thought themselves so silent because why tell anybody, because you're gonna tell them and they're not gonna look at you anyway, they're not going to believe it or they're not going to bother tellin' anyone else. (Tony Perkins)

Tony was very clear that it is important to tell this story, but that it is equally important that the telling is listened to. It had been hard, he said, to find people who want to listen to this story. Every story requires a teller and a listener. To sing a crying-song to remember requires a singer and a listener who has a responsibility to respond. If the listener does not respond to the story and pass the story on, the teller is rendered silent. The crying-song cannot be sung.

> I think that's the important part, because I think the thing is we're not afraid to — I'm not afraid to communicate about it and that's been the most important part of it all the way along, the sharing what went on and instead of us hiding that away, we've got someone else to listen to it and to carry that same message, what we're sayin'. I hear lots of things here today. I sit sometimes in the club and I hear different things being said about Aboriginal people, you know, they're always whingein' and wantin' this and that. (Tony Perkins)

For Tony, the responsibility of the listener is to carry the same message and to get the message out. He describes the scene of a possible telling, the local club or pub where he hears negative things about Aboriginal people, the usual talk of country towns. He knows it is not a place where his story can be told and listened to.

> All we want you to do is listen to what we're talkin' about, that's all we want you to do. I hear 'em say I don't know how much land they want. I think to myself you know how much, it's both ways, goin' back in the past. I don't know whether some of the people talkin' but maybe some of their relations they took up a selection too, you know how much land they want, they never paid for it either. Yeah it sort of works both ways, but then you can see what I'm saying, sometimes I might only be one person sitting in that club and my voice wouldn't go very far inside maybe five or six hundred people sitting there. I'm better off being quiet, sitting there listenin'. And I think that sometimes that's the frustratin' part, havin' to sit and listen, join in the conversation that says how you will be treated before you start. (Tony Perkins)

Before Tony had even begun to tell his story he knew the inevitable negative response, so the story was silenced. Many local people disputed the events told in the massacre story, but this is not just a local problem. In Australia more generally, we have been busy with the so-called History Wars in which we argue about the validity of such stories. In the deep silence of denial and repression it was even difficult for a white person to talk about a massacre. For an Aboriginal person in a 500 to one minority it was impossible. Advocacy and witnessing, however, are the crucial basis of responsibility and they do happen, even at a local level.

> You know a lot of people dispute it but there used to be a fellow there by name of Ossie Casson or Jack Casson, and he knew them – before he died and he was fairly old bloke when he died goin' back a long time now he'd be dead, he even said himself that he was told that he could have joined up in that hunting party when he was only sixteen and done the same thing and he was living there all his life, when Ossie Casson's father used to be, he was an old, old man, and his name was old Dagwood Casson, and they were livin' there at Cassons Creek and before he died he told 'em, he could have went with that hunting party if he wanted to when he was sixteen so he said that – he'd become very, very good friends with everybody down the Old Camp after that. (Tony Perkins)

The story of old Dagwood Casson is an important one for Tony. As a white man Casson knew the story and made friends with the people down at the Old Camp. It was not until just before he died, a very old man, that he spoke about the massacre story and the fact that he could have joined the hunting party as a young man. This validates the massacre story for Tony because it is a story about relationship between white and black. But ultimately it is the fact that for the people the story is so deeply inscribed in the colour of the red rock that makes its claims beyond dispute.

> Oh yeah, a lot of people dispute it but I can't even – grandmother told me, she told me whereabouts and everything, where it all happened, she told me the water was red, it was red

runnin' there at Red Rock, yeah because she told me that it was just red, the water was just red, and it was on the rocks, it was everywhere, like where they was. Everyone called it Blood Rock, that's what we always knew it as. Not when I was little, when I was told afterwards. (Colleen Jarrett)

In her book *Traumascapes*, Maria Tumarkin explores places of trauma in Bali, Berlin, Moscow, New York, Port Arthur, Sarajevo and Pennsylvania. She migrated to Australia from Russia and begins with a story close to her heart that calls forth 'thick, layered histories of spirituality, grief and empire', the story of a nation and nation-making. Tumarkin came to see her study of the relationship between trauma and lived geography as a study of haunting.

> Haunting not as a metaphor but as a presence underpinning the world in which we live, its histories, webs of social relations and everyday life. Traumascapes, of course, were haunting and haunted places. Yet they were not poetic or metaphorical terrains, but rather concrete material sites, where visible and invisible, past and present, physical and metaphysical, came to coexist and share a common space.[22]

This is so for the traces of trauma in the physical landscape of Red Rock. The massacre and rebirth story live on in the place. This haunting, however, embodies transformative possibilities. In being haunted we are brought to a moment of recognition when we become aware that things that appear to be dead, past and finished, have a definite place in the world. Tumarkin writes that the sense of haunting that lies in the places themselves gives rise to 'a deep unstated awareness of things in our social world that get under our skin without us quite grasping how, and why, and to what effect'.[23] Even though at every one of the places she visited the trauma was past, she felt it was still there waiting for her. This made her crave writing as the only way to become close to those places and the transformative possibility that was held within them, 'the pain, the memory, the enchantment and the future'.[24] In this sense it is essential that we tell our crying-songs to remember.

For the northern Gumbaynggirr people of Corindi Beach too, the place of the Red Rock massacre embodies possibilities for the future. 'All of us are very sort of – not wary of probably, but very protective of, doesn't matter who it is the whole lot of us think that it's got high sort of significance to Red Rock.' It is a place where the story can be remembered and told. In the past, the Old People used to gather at Red Rock to tell its stories in all its different places.

> And they'd all gather there and they used to tell us about the – 'cause they had all these different spots, they used to talk about – like the Red Rock itself, the headland, and then they'd come along and tell us about across the river at Green Hill, they used to call it. Then they used to come, they used to call that Jew Point, there, then they'd come round the corner further and they used to call one lot there, just up from Jew Point, they used to call that Dirt Rock there, then you'd come up a bit further, you'd come around further, straight across from that, a bit up straight across the river, they used to call that Black Rock there, then they used to go further up and they used to call that Red Bank up further where the Old Farm is, that's how we knew of all the different places. (Tony Perkins)

There were fishing places and dancing places, living places and special places. Each place had its particular stories, its particular qualities. And each time they would retell the story of the Red Rock massacre. These storytelling gatherings suggest something of a ritual-in-place beginning to form. The story of the massacre and rebirth was also told to young people in their families. As Tony said, it was when they came of age that they were told the story as something of an initiation ritual. At this age they began to understand the story as having deep meaning in terms of their Gumbaynggirr identity.

> It wasn't somethin' that they'd [talk about], or even did a interview about that close up, you know. Only was for the younger generation to know and to let us all know if they wanted to. I think that's when I started gettin, you know, really realisin' I was a Koori, really dig deep. And it all comes back to when I was at m'teenage years, over here at Corindi. I become very aware then, who I was. (Glenda Perkins)

People remember the shock of hearing the story and consider it a responsibility to pass it on to their children. Glenda worried that when she told the story to her son, it would be just a story, separated from the place and the events. She worried that the deep emotions of trauma that accompanied the story for the Old People would be forgotten because the story needed to be told in the place, and thus embodied in the telling.

> Yeah, I remember her [Gloria's mother] telling me that, and it's always been embedded in my mind. And I couldn't tell you exactly where that happened or what part – but that sort of stood out in my mind for a long time. Don't know if she told me to remember that for the rest of my life, or whether it was something that shocked her too. Shocked her, and she remembered it, I mean, I still say that, and this is my generation and I'll say it to him [my son], and he'll probably say it to his [children], you know, and pass it on. I don't know whether we should stop saying it, or, you know. As I said, we can lose the feeling as time goes on and it just becomes a story, but to our people at that time it was reality, it was an emotional thing, it was horrible, you know. It is just a story now without the feeling, and my son will probably lose the feeling of it although he'll know the story. (Glenda Perkins)

On my last visit to Auntie Marie she was waiting anxiously and the signs of her illness and recent operation showed. Her voice was shaky and wavering, not as strong as it used to be. Still, the old *joie de vivre* shone through from time to time. We talked about Red Rock again: as she said on the phone, 'Are you still on about that?' To her it was old ground we had already covered. This time, however, for the first time, she told me ever so gently the full story about the river and the killings, how the river was red with the blood. She said they were warned as children never to go on the headland. They were told the cave would suck them over the edge and, she surmised, that the body of the drowned father of the first Red Rock story she told me, must have got sucked into that cave. I felt I had passed a test, without fanfare, just from being around for a long time. She also talked about the birthing grounds, not so much about the grounds themselves, but she told me about the many babies that were born there. Then she insisted on giving us lunch, corned beef, mashed potato and pumpkin, and homemade pickles. She showed me photos of her latest great grandchildren. I left with three pairs of hand-knitted bedsocks to keep my feet warm in the Armidale winter. The stories of trauma were absorbed into the everyday lifefulness of food, babies and warm feet.

In telling the massacre and creation story so courageously for a non-Aboriginal audience, Tony has invited us into the dangerous space of the contact zone. In this space, he asks us to listen and then take action, to 'get the message out'. But this is not such an easy thing to do. As Mark McKenna writes, 'the dispossession of Aboriginal people, both historically and in the present day, lies at the heart of Australian consciousness and identity, and is connected to every aspect of our past'.[25] We have 'a preference for forgetting'.

> ... the overwhelming desire of human beings in certain circumstances to prefer not to know, to forget and 'move on', the constant struggle in public culture between coexisting narratives of acknowledgement and denial, and the intensely political nature of public remembering – all surface in settler Australia.[26]

How do we mark these stories in our places, and how do we remember rather than forget? How can we sing our songs in such a way as to respect the complexity of singing our contemporary country into being?

Peter Read, reflecting on an educational process in which he worked with Aboriginal people to present a dramatic account of a massacre to a non-Indigenous audience, spoke about our intense love of this country. 'Reconciliation,' he says, 'at once becomes much more complex, much more painful, much more traumatic. This is as it should be.'[27] Maori storyteller and activist Patricia Grace responded to a question from a non-Indigenous member of an Australian audience who asked: 'What can we do?' by saying 'Know your own history'. I took this to mean that we should know the history of our local places and understand how, as non-Indigenous people, we have benefited from the privilege associated with these acts of bloody violence. In Tony's words, we 'know how much land' because we already own it. Peter Read completed his re-enactment of the massacre story by asking participants to imagine how they could rearrange a symbolic table to share the goods more equitably. And Mark McKenna writes about 'a conversation of hope' in which we 'connect the frontier to the crucial question of explaining who we are and who we have become as a nation and as a people'.[28] Tony asks that we listen deeply and respond, then help his people to get the story out.

In 2002 Tony Perkins and other members of Yarrawarra Aboriginal Corporation and the Corindi Beach community marked the headland at Red Rock with the massacre and creation story. They placed a plaque on a memorial cairn, telling the story in written text, at the edge of the taboo place, halfway up the Red Rock headland. To the south a vast stretch of uninhabited beach, to the east the great Pacific Ocean, to the west the belly of the Red Rock estuary and the river winding silver around the birthing place at Jewfish Point. In this act they sing their song for their traditional lands as survivors of the massacre, celebrating their rebirth and continuity. The Old People continued their new lives in No Mans Land at Corindi Beach, creating a new story from the space in-between.

> *[We] tell the story with the desire to make language, time and place stutter through it and we turn to the senses to try and keep us there within that moment where a body thought agonises. [We] hope that such stories change our worlds.*

Sustaining inspirited places

It was a sacred spot, they say it is.
I remember my grandmother
talking about Jewfish Point
it was a favourite spot Jewfish Point
well to me that's where
all the Old People used to gather around
'cause they just kept going there
and as kids they took us there

*so we sort of grew up going down there
for a Sunday, or an evening or a day.
just going to Jewfish Point.*

Ten years later I returned to Red Rock to tell this story. Red Rock is now the name of a small beachside holiday place between the estuary and the sea. I visit first, as always, the red rock itself, sitting at that point where the river meets the sea. Just around the bend of the river, the red ochre crumbles from the river bank, red on fingers, red on the back of my hand. It's the colour of red ochre and the colour of blood. Tony said, 'they used to get all the ochres and paint themselves up and trade together there, have their ceremonies and dances. My grandfather told me it was the prettiest thing you ever seen, how they painted with the different coloured ochres, the white, the red and the yellow.'

Leaving the red rock I climb through silky needles of silver casuarinas up the wooden steps into the salt wind of the long beach. Stretching down as far as the eye can see there are beaches and headlands as far as Woolgoolga, the extent of McDougalls' Run. Arrawarra headland, the rainmaking place, dips towards the sea in-between. It was here, in the scrubby dune bush at the back of this long beach, that we looked for signs of the camps where Clarrie Skinner and Jimmy Runner brought their families for summers at Red Rock. They sang for the holidaymakers who came in their white tents and they caught worms for their fishing. Over the dunes the scrubby bush gives way to heathlands where Gumbaynggirr people collected wildflowers for Christmas. 'They used to get big bunches of flannel flowers and Christmas bells and Christmas bush, the red gumleaves. That'd be placed everywhere in the house, in the old camps, they'd put that in there.' I remember Christmas with a bunch of wildflowers from the heath and a gift of silver bream from the sea.

Halfway up the headland I stop and read the plaque that marks the place where time and place changed. 'In memory of the victims and survivors/of the Blood Rock massacres ... And the rebirthing of our culture/will never be forgotten.' Powerful and inexplicable events leave their marks in the landscape. Glenda says, 'We can lose the feeling as time goes on and it just becomes a story, but to those – to our people at that time, you know, it was reality, it was an emotional thing, it was horrible. It was just a story now, without the feeling, you know, and my son will probably lose the feeling of it although he'll know the story.' The Red Rock headland is inspired with this story and keeps it alive.

The ancient cave, born in an old ice age sea, is a place of struggle. 'Grandfather wouldn't let me go down, 'cause that's where they – they were – the white people shot all the black people there. Most of them died down there. That's why they call it – that's how it come to have that name, "Blood Rock", because of the blood that was spilt there.' It is also, paradoxically, a place of survival. 'A lot of them escaped from there through that tunnel. See there's two caves. In the centre of the – the big cave was in the centre of the headland and up there, up near Martins Point was another one.' The Old People escaped through the cave and lived in the darkness of no time: 'Old Teddy McCrystal, the oldest man out, he said they just herded them up, pushed them all over, he was only a kid at the time'. The journey through the labyrinth to the new birth took years, 'He said there was a ledge there, 'n' he got underneath it, he was there for, 'n' he laid there, I don't know how long, till they went away'. They wandered with no name until they came back to the place of the new beginning. 'Must've been a terrible time' they told me.

I climb through banksias clinging low against the wind to the top of the headland. From here the world is laid out below me, silver patterns of lacy waterways lit through shimmering clouds. The shape of the estuary is ngaalgan, the ear, for deep listening to its stories. I have taken these stories into my body, walked, eaten and played them in this place. I know the red eyes of the prawn that shine at dusk in the curve of the estuary, the octopus that got caught on the fishing line and ran on gangling legs across the park. Wild asparagus tips, red postman flowers, and bright pink lilly pillies; eating place. From the belly curve my eye scans the line of the estuary until I reach the point where I sat with the Elders, Bing, Bruce and Keith, in the quiet and stillness of Jewfish Point.

Bruce is no longer with us, but he is walking, talking, singing with the Old People. I can feel him there still. There on the salt flat in the first dewdrop light of dawn where the gnarled old mangrove tree guards this special place with its crooked limbs. It was there that people came to Jewfish Point with their families to picnic – and to remember their exchange with the brolgas. 'I always remember those beautiful birds – native companions, on the other side. Always in one special place.'

I follow the fingerline of the river up past the Old Farm where the traces of clay floors mark the birthing grounds, where Nan fished in the river, and people grew pumpkins and corn and potatoes. Where Clarrie sang in the old flat-bottomed boat all the way home from Red Rock. Then further up where the river branches off into Blackadder and Cassons creeks, where the hunting party first intruded into a very ordinary day. I cross back towards the sea, where Nan walked daily at dawn to do the white woman's washing and home again to Corindi Lake. Here there is just a tiny indent on the coastline into a small and insignificant estuary. This estuary is Pipeclay, girriin, or the Lake, the place where the people could live again. Beyond the fences, in No Mans Land, the Old People lived and died, spoke language, kept their sacred objects and told the stories of far away places inscribed in the marks on their bodies.

CHAPTER 3

Making home in No Mans Land

Them times
you find a lot of camps
along the back of the beaches
or headland
along the edge
of a creek or lake
'cause they all jumped over
the other side of the fence.
No Mans Land
that's what they call it.

The story of our research in No Mans Land began in a circular clearing on a small tongue of dry ground shaped by a mangrove-lined estuary. Hidden from the beach by the dune, a single dark-green Moreton Bay fig tree gives even further protection. On the ground, tucked against spindly casuarinas and paperbarks in small bundles or caches, are the objects that have been uncovered in this place they called the Flanders Camp. Pieces of metal and old glass, a smoky lilac bottle, some old china shards flecked blue on cream like the china of old electric jugs, and a coil of soft metal inserted into the tin lid of a jar. By the fig tree, scattered across one of these bundles, are the brilliant red, blue, green and gold feathers of a newly killed rosella. I do not know what all this means but just sit in the stillness on the edge of the estuary listening to the hum of the sea and taking in this scene.

To come to Flanders Camp, also known as the Fig Tree site, I have walked along the desire lines of the boardwalk suspended above the swamp to enter this place where landscapes, people, archaeological practices, place and organisation are all foreign. The bush tucker walk is a different way of mapping a place. It invites us into the hidden places of No Mans Land where the material remains reveal traces of its story. The boardwalk was constructed for Yarrawarra's ecotourism enterprise to open up the story of this place. The beginning of the track is soft grey sand winding through native grasses and the wide spreading branches of swamp mahoganies. As the trees change the sandy track becomes a boardwalk sculpted between close-growing paperbacks whose raggedy white trunks catch the early morning sun. Trees, bushes and landscape tell their stories. Toe holes carved into a tree mark the place where Jimmy Runner collected wild honey; scars on others show where the people collected bark for shelters. Bush tucker is plentiful. We eat geebungs and chew the aniseed taste of new red tips of the sarsaparilla bush that people used to ward off a cold.

It was along this track that the old men first brought me to tell me about Corindi Lake. At the sight of the Lake they all began talking at once, a collective story of fishing, catching prawns and mud crabs, digging for fresh water and building their shacks by the sea. No Mans Land provided an immediate source of food, water and materials for shelter. When people of today tell stories about No Mans Land, it is the camps of the Old People they remember scattered around the Lake.

> There was a lot of families stretched from right around the Lake system, on this side of it and on the sea side of it, because they were on both sides. When you look at who lived down there, back to well before the fifties, you had the Lauries there, and they had their hut there, that's where Bing was born, there. Then you had, there was lots of camps all

the way along. There was Doug and Jack Long – they lived there. Then you had Elsie Cowan lived there too. They were – I would've been only about seven or eight or something like that and they were Old People then. They were the Old People. And you had Fred Laurie, 'Pa' Laurie they called him. You know, he probably was a man in his sixties or more at that time when I was about eight, nine, probably 'round that age and I can remember all these Old People. The Flanders were there, that was old Tommy Flanders. He actually built all of the huts that they lived in. Then you had, you know going around further, you had Taylors, they lived there. (Tony Perkins)

The Elders of today who were born in No Mans Land are the grandchildren of the Old People and they remember the camps around the Lake and the Old People who lived there. The massacre and creation story told in the previous chapter is symbolic of the space between the time before and the time after white settlement. The time before is told in the stories of the Old People and written on their bodies in the scars of initiation. The time in-between is the liminal space with no narrative. The time after can be read in the material translations of No Mans Land.

The Old People

There was Jimmy, Auntie Lil, Uncle Herbie and Ted
Old Granny, Teddy McCrystal and Clara
Uncle Mac and Sadie, we used to call 'im Mac
never called 'im Jimmy Runner
and Herbie McDougall, used to call 'im Kooiya
Old Granny Skinner, we used to call her Armi.
We always didn't know their first name
when we was kids
'cause that's what we knew them as.
Bennelong, I think it might have been,
yeah, Grace Bennelong, Clara's mother's name

she was the queen of the tribe
many years ago
but she never spoke [of it].

By the time the Old People settled in No Mans Land at Corindi Lake they had acquired the new white names that overwrote the landscape along with the fences. The Elders of today recite the mixed-up names of the Old People, as if in this naming they are calling up these complex stories of the in-between. Remembering the names of the Old People is a collective song but speaking, like naming, was a risky and complicated business. The process of inheriting names was about much more than taking on the names of white property owners. These same property owners often fathered children with Aboriginal women who were then outcast in white society, a shame that could not be spoken. More than this genealogical silencing, however, they were forbidden to speak the Gumbaynggirr language. 'If you were caught speaking the language in those days there'd be problems for you with the white man.' Speaking in language even carried the threat of death. 'The whitefellas around here said we weren't to talk lingo outside the fence or they'd shoot us.' Whether this meant physical death or a symbolic cultural death, the intent and the impact was much the same: to wipe out Aboriginal cultural identity and practices. The speaking of language was the key to cultural survival. On the other side of the fence in the in-between space of No Mans Land, however, the Old People continued to speak their language of place.

> I still remember all the Old People. I still remember seeing them down on the Lake area, of a morning they'd all be sittin' alongside the old huts, and they'd never sit flat on the ground, they'd always sit, you know, and their knees'd be up in the air, sort of like a squat. And you never heard anyone talking in English. I still remember it, all the time they were talking, talkin' to one another, but never used English. It was just amazing some of the things that, you know, when I think back, to what it was like. (Tony Perkins)

The surprise for Tony of this detailed embodied memory of the sounds of the Old People speaking in Gumbaynggirr is in both the trace of language and its loss over the next generation. All of the Elders of today remember the sounds of the Old People speaking language, but few learned to speak it themselves because of the severity of the prohibition. The oral stories of the Old People are the only way to transmit the collective story of the extraordinary material translations of everyday life. We can only know the stories of the Old People through these translations into, and of, the English language. Their stories, like the bending of the English language, belong in the in-between place of No Mans Land. They are often mysterious with elements that are incomprehensible. They participate in a spirit world that is unfamiliar to me and that we will explore in Chapter 5. They are also embodied, material, individualistic, funny, funky and uniquely of the place and time.

There are a few key individuals whose stories stand out: Clarrie Skinner, Jimmy Runner, Old Tom Flanders, Arthur Taylor, and the brothers Herbie and Abraham McDougall of McDougalls' Run. They represent each of the five main family groups who came to live in No Mans Land. The stories of the women are more shadowy; it is of the characters of these men that I have the clearest sense. I have a strong sense of Clarrie Skinner, for example, and I feel like I know him through the many stories from Auntie Marie and Tony. I imagine him as a very strong man, powerful in his cultural knowledge and a leader in sculpting the ways that traditional cultural knowledge could be passed on in this new context. I know him through the stories of the previous chapter – as a musician and partygoer, much loved by the holiday-makers of Red Rock for his music and singing. Sometime in the late 1920s the extended family group moved to No Mans Land. There I learn about him through the stories of Corindi Lake.

> He [Clarrie Skinner] used to be sittin' in that house what he was livin' in, what grandfather built, the slab house. An' it had a big, this fireplace was nearly as wide as this, eh? And it had a big open fireplace an' he had sort of seats around the side. And he'd be sittin' there and he'd be tellin' us stories, and he'd go outside and he'd come back in, 'I hear 'em

choppin' down there', he said, 'I'm goin''. Yeah, and look at that moon, where that moon was. Away he'd go.

Then you'd hear him then, whistlin' and we used to go, he usually had one or two, 'Come down an' give me a hand', he'd say. He never eat fish, never eat it, but he was always catchin' it. He'd go down an' get a bag, might have two bags by the time you get there. Oh you're draggin 'em home!

When he'd catch his fish, he'd dig a hole and cover 'em over so the moon wouldn't get on 'em. He reckoned the moon'd send them bad. He'd always cover 'em over with a bag in the moonlit nights. (Marie Edwards)

This story tells a great deal about Clarrie Skinner and the materiality of their lives. Auntie Marie powerfully recreates this scene from daily life in No Mans Land as if it were in the present. The storytelling is interrupted by the sound of the jewfish 'choppin' in the distance', something only Clarrie, with his extraordinary attunement to the calls of the place, can hear. We are also told, mysteriously, that Clarrie never ate fish. Why? Whether it was a forbidden totem or he simply didn't like fish, we do not know. Added to this is the mystery of covering the fish to protect it from the moon, which strengthens the sense of Clarrie's connection to beach, tides, and the cycles of moon and sea.

Jimmy Runner, like Clarrie Skinner, was an initiated man, a language speaker, and cultural knowledge holder. Also known as Uncle Mac, he was the keeper of the rainmaking place at Arrawarra. A good fisherman, he taught Bing and Bruce to fish, and provided for his family in the days when 'keeping the family fed was hard'. The stories of Uncle Mac also portray him as an innovative man, a leader in cultural change. He was a larger-than-life character well known in the local village for his love of music and dancing, 'one of the mainstays in those hula hula dances'. Many local white people remember him fondly, one even having constructed 'a Jimmy Runner memorial fence'. People loved him because he was quirky and funny and made people laugh. There are two stories in particular that capture these aspects of his character. One tells how he swam across the river at Red Rock with his hat and his watch on his head, chasing after a woman who lived on the other side. The other is a fishing story with a twist.

> There was a lot when the jewfish was running, they all go out there. We's all fishing there, and one of the boys comes past me, and he said, 'Jimmy's getting drunk up there Frank'. I said, 'Oh come off it', I said, 'he hasn't left that beach,' I said, 'I'm watchin' him, we'll keep him here'. 'Well, he just seems to be happy', he said, and away he went. So anyway, I could see him laughin', 'How ya goin' Jim?' 'Oh', he said, 'gettin' a few bites'. 'Come on Jimmy', I said 'how you gettin' 'em', I said. 'You getting carved up, mate,' I said, 'but how are you doin' it?' He's laughed. Had his line wrapped 'round a bottle, and no wonder why nobody could work out why he wasn't leavin' there. Oh, yeah, he was a character in his own way, Jimmy. (Frank Duroux)

Old Tom Flanders, like Clarrie Skinner and Jimmy Runner, was also an initiated man and spoke several languages. He was reluctant to pass on his traditional cultural knowledge to his sons because he knew they were not going to be initiated. He did, however, introduce new skills of working in timber and forestry. His father, Jack Flanders, used his traditional knowledge of the bush to work as a tracker and timber-cutter. He passed on these new ways of working with timber to his sons.

> Well, my grandfather, years ago, used to be a tracker. One of these fellas, also very good knowledge of the bush, and he was a timber-cutter himself, Jack Flanders. He was from around Bowraville, came into becomin' timber-cutters, and, you know, cuttin' sleepers, poles and things, so they knew about all timber. What tree to use, what tree not to use, some things we use, what we wanted inside, only use cutters, and that softwood and a bit of iron, and things like that, you know, the main building was true hardwood. (Jerry Flanders)

It was Old Tom Flanders who brought his family to live on the edge of the Lake at the place we came to know as the Fig Tree site, or Flanders Camp. He brought with him the things he had learned from his father about building and timber and built a bark hut.

> So over in the corner over there where they first got it staked out, that was our first camp there, where that Fig Tree is but we moved from there, and the house we lived in was almost right near the old well was, dad, he dug that. The house near the Fig Tree, I remember that, it was a small, it [the floor] was just tramped down [earth]. It was just solid, and that was made outta bark, like sheets eight foot wide, by about three inches thick, what they cut themselves. Some of the sheets eight foot wide by ten foot long, and doing a six-man job getting up on top of that house. (Jerry Flanders)

This sort of changing knowledge of place – of trees and timber, of technologies of building with bark – were all part of the knowledge passed down through the men in this family. In No Mans Land it was these material translations of the Old People that allowed a bridge to be built between the past and a possible future. In this way the Old People literally inhabited the space in-between. They dwelt in the contact zone taking what they needed or wanted from white culture and adapting it to their daily life in No Mans Land.

No fixed address

My grandmother used to get the saplings
that would just bend, skinny long stuff,
she'd stick a bit in the ground,
bend it over like that
and tie them in the middle.
Then she'd get the ti-tree bark
and lace it in right down
to the bottom.

That used to stand for months
it could rain for weeks
not a bit of weather'd go in
just the way they tie these saplings
and worked the bark in it.

The shell middens tell us about the original camping places of the ancestors. They give northern Gumbaynggirr people a sense of continuity with a deep past in these coastal landscapes. There were shell middens on the exposed foredune at Corindi Beach and around the Lake. Everyone knows where the shell middens are and reads them as signs of people living there in the old days. Angela remembered being told as a child that the shells were left by Mindi, one of the creation ancestors, as he walked back and forth along the beaches eating pipis and shellfish and leaving the shells behind as a trace of his presence.

> Mindi just used to go along the beach eating the pipis. He used to sit, and I mean he was a big man, and there'd be lots of shells, and that's what they'd say, oh well Mindi's been here, you know, like that was what they'd say. Yeah, but that's what they used to tell us when we were kids, you'd see a big pile of pipi shell or something like that and mum, they'd always say, 'Oh look, Mindi's been here'. (Angela Brown)

Tony asked for two middens to be researched by archaeologists in our project, one at Arrawarra that was being washed into the sea and another at Red Rock. The midden at Arrawarra told us that it was a gathering place where big feasts were held between 900 and 1300 years ago. The majority of the midden was made up of shells from many different kinds of shellfish from the nearby estuary, beach and rock pools, the most common being turban shells, or gugumbal. There were also river stones knapped to make sharp-edged flakes to use as stone tools, and bones of many types of fish and animals.[29] The archaeological story of the midden supports the stories of Arrawarra as a meeting and camping place.

The midden at Red Rock was located by some shells on the edge of the track leading down to Jewfish Point. Below the surface of decaying leaves there was 'a layer of stone artefacts almost like a pavement across all the squares'. These were carefully removed 'and a dense layer of shell, animal and fish bone, coloured ochre stones and more stone artefacts appeared'.[30] This midden, dated at over 3000 years old, was unusually ancient for fragile coastal environments subject to weather and climate change. The presence of a large amount of ochre in a variety of different colours – white, yellow, orange and two types of red – and different types of stone in the tools, supports Tony's idea of Red Rock as a 'market place', a place where people gathered together to exchange material resources.

The scarred trees are also read as a sign of continuing activities and cultural meaning-making in the landscapes around No Mans Land. The scars on trees show where bark was removed to make shelters, canoes and containers. Tony says that the pattern of scarred trees in this area shows that the Old People once moved freely throughout this coastal strip from Corindi Beach to Red Rock.

> That's why you see all the [scarred] trees. Even though the scarred trees today are around different areas like private property, it was all Crown land runnin' from here right through. They just lived, like they would've kept movin' from right through on both sides, right through to Red Rock and everywhere.
> (Tony Perkins)

Through the signs of the middens and scarred trees, people in No Mans Land continued to have a sense of living their whole territory, throughout the beaches, creeks, swamps and bushlands of northern Gumbaynggirr country. They continued to live in the place as they always had done, only now moving and dwelling in smaller and smaller circles. If they stayed in one spot for too long they believed that they would become ill. When the land became worn out, when someone died, or sometimes just in response to the weather, they moved to another camp site.

Like they shifted a bit when they were down there. Everyone never camped in the same spot all the time. Even Bruce and Bing's parents, they'd continually move. They'd move from the one camp, they'd pull it down and they'd move it across the other side of the lake or further up the lake. They'd never stay in that same spot. They'd sort of, over years they'd go up and then they'd move back. I just think it's like a habit. Years ago they roamed from one campsite to another in a bigger fashion. I think it was the same thing. Like even in a small area when they seen things gettin' worn too much in one place, they'd move to another site and let that sort of grow more. Just move all the time. (Tony Perkins)

This continual movement and the nature of the shelters they built meant that it was hard to find material traces of their dwellings. The Old People continued to make traditional shelters using the materials at hand around Corindi Lake. Our earliest photo from No Mans Land shows a simple bough shelter at a site that became known as 'Armi's Camp'. In this photo, Armi (Clara Skinner) and Maggie Blakeney are photographed in front of their shelter, with Ted McCrystal in the shadows at the side. The shelter is barely distinguishable from the surrounding bush. Auntie Marie described how Clara, her grandmother, built this bough shelter. The bent saplings and ti-tree bark, the weather and human need for shelter, are intertwined in this story. A sapling shelter lives lightly on the land and leaves no trace as the natural elements of these simple structures disintegrate into sand and bush. Their human dimension is evident as Marie demonstrates the technologies of their making by interlacing her fingers to show how they were made and how they kept the weather out, even when it rained for weeks. Keeping the rain out featured in all of the stories of shelters. The sapling shelters, however, were only for sleeping or sheltering from the weather. All other activities took place outside.

Even as their huts became more elaborate, many of the activities of living in this place happened outside. Fishing and gathering shellfish, hunting and gathering bush food were continuous with cooking, eating and storytelling by the camp fires.

> Out of the front of the place where you walked in the door, out from it, sort of joined on, the fireplace – they'd have a fireplace there, just open fireplace like on the ground. Then they'd have this stick across. This big lid sort of across the top of it and they'd hang everything over it. The fire never went out – they used to just throw logs on there and during the day it'd just smoke or until they wanted to light it up again sort of. But I used to remember 'em they went and got wallabies or fish or eels or whatever they got, they'd clean 'em, and like the wallabies they'd cut the legs, and they used to hang 'em over the top of this crosspiece. And during the day the smoke – like it'd hang there, might have been for a week – but it was smoked, all the meat was smoked all the time. Nearly every camp they had it, this fireplace, and it went all the time and the smoke used to keep the flies off and at the same it used to stop the meat, the fish from goin' off, 'cause it'd be smoked. That's how they done it.
> (Tony Perkins)

The fireplace was an important source of warmth, cooking, preserving food and telling stories. Washing, similarly, took place outside and many people have memories of days spent doing the washing, bathing and picnicking at the swamp or creek. Bing remembers when they used to go to the swamp with a big old copper, boil the water with a fire underneath and go fishing for eels and turtles in the swamp. Glenda has similar memories of washing days.

> We used to go down the creek and do our washing, you know on the rocks, where the creek is. We used to wash clothes down there. And we had a copper down there. Light a fire under the copper. Boil the water and wash the clothes by hand. And then when you'd finished with the hot water that'd boiled the clothes, you know, it was always lovely and warm, and still frothy. We'd take the old tub, the big old tubs, we'd carry it over into the middle of the bush where the lantana is and we'd have a bath [laughs]. A hot bath in

the bush there, in this beautiful warm water, big old tub. Oh yeah. (Glenda Perkins)

Inside and outside were permeable and dwelling in place was to dwell in the whole landscape of No Mans Land. They moved through the place in all of their daily activities and from place to place in their dwellings. They left little trace of their activities there. When Marie and I looked at the photo of Armi and Maggie outside their sapling shelter she said, 'they used to get the old broom and sweep all 'round, used to be beautiful'. They used to sweep the dirt around the shelter to keep it clean and clear of weeds. Tony remembered in detail the materials they collected for making the dirt floors in the huts and then sweeping them smooth and hard with the same bush brooms.

> They'd go out in the bush or out round the bush paths and they'd bring all these white ants' nests back. Then they'd get the clay, like ended up white clay or reddy looking clay out of the lake and they'd put it on the floor and they'd crush this white ants' nest into it, then you sprinkled water on it and swept it. They used to make these brooms out of those spiny prickly ti-tree-type leaves. They'd break all the branches off and they'd tie 'em onto a stick and they'd sweep the floor with 'em. That used to be the broom they used to use and the floor would go really hard. They'd sprinkle it every day with this water and you sweep it and the white ant's nest in this clay used to really make it hard. (Tony Perkins)

The clay floors were the only traces left of the birthing grounds of the Old Farm where Tony was taken to show him where his mother was born. At the Lake, however, there seemed to be no trace of the sapling huts, clay floors, termites' nests and bark that made the shelters in No Mans Land. At Flanders Camp the only obvious marker was the fig tree. Tony said that planting a Moreton Bay Fig tree was a custom to mark the place of a camp.

> It's a symbol, yeah. Because no matter where they lived around here, every time you come across the fig, that's the

mark of, we can always pick up where all our Old People actually went and lived 'cause everywhere they were there was a fig, growin'. That was their first thing that they would do, was put the fig in, so that they'd have their identification point. (Tony Perkins)

Auntie Marie also said that in the old days her mother always planted a fig tree to mark the places where they camped. 'Mum'd always – wherever we shifted they always grew a fig tree in a stump. That was the Aboriginal law type of thing. Wherever you see a fig tree in a stump you know the Aboriginals stopped there.' When Old Tom Flanders set up camp with his family at Corindi Lake, it was a lantana bush that marked the spot because it provided a windbreak. A little further down the Lake the remains of a fireplace and a well showed where he had camped before when he came up to Corindi Lake on fishing trips.

We lived in a tent there actually. Lived in a tent, and there was no fig tree there [laughs]. It only had lantana growing around the edge of the Lake there, like a windbreak. But Daddy's old camping ground was – he used to camp there before we ever went there. Oh, yeah, there was a little area down further from us you could see where they had a fireplace. We had a well – up from the Lake there's a well – you know where we used to get the water for drinking and that. (Tom and Gloria Flanders)

Whether or not the Flanders planted the fig tree at the Fig Tree site we don't know, but Old Tom Flanders soon moved his family to higher ground because of the wet weather. 'When we got solid rain, it used to get a bit mucky. So that's why we moved around to the other point and got the bark house. Yeah, because it was up off the ground.' The new bark hut that Tom Flanders built at the point was equally elusive, so the story of the bark hut began by describing the scars that remained to show where they removed the bark.

When we lived in a bark house – those trees out there, I think I showed you somewhere they had a big scar on them

swamp mahoganies, where we took the bark off them.
There's a couple down near the houses out there, there's one
– oh, where Bingy and them live. There's one just out on that
end on the eastern side where Brucey is, there's one straight
out the back. There's one there too, big scar on the swamp
mahogany where a big piece was taken out. That's where
we barked some of them out there. And there are probably
some more – that are dead and burnt in the bushfires.
(Therese Flanders)

Because of this intimate knowledge of the place and the history that can be read in them, the scars on the trees are highly significant for northern Gumbaynggirr people. It is a way of reading their memories in the place. While the remains of the bark huts are gone, the scars are a visible reminder of their connection to that place.

When Bing and Bruce described the places where their houses were built, they were always by 'the rose bush' or at 'the bamboo'. Bing often refers to the fact that he was born at the rose bush house and Bruce tells the story of planting the bamboo at their other camp. 'That bamboo, yeah, came out from the Clarence River, you know. It's growing everywhere now. Just cut it off and stick it in the ground and it'll grow. It's taken hold over near the present camp there now across the Lake there. Wants diggin' out really, you know.' Exotic plants become place markers because, like the fig tree, they are distinct from the bush around them. The dune scrub with its casuarinas and banksias, paperbarks, ti-trees and swamp mahoganies, continues to grow all around but these introduced plants stand out. The rose bush and the bamboo became the new place markers.

From the archaeologists' point of view, understanding the material and spatial practices of people in No Mans Land was confusing and complex. They could not pinpoint exactly where the camps were, how they were constructed or who lived where. They were continually perplexed in their quest to map the dwellings at the Lake by the absence of material markers of the shelters and by the seemingly endless proliferation of stories about who lived where. In relation to Armi's site, for example, they concluded that:

Working out who lived at Armi's camp site seemed a confusing and sometimes impossible question. Many people camped in the vicinity of a small inlet on the north side of the lake, now overgrown with bamboo. Jimmy Runner, Sadie, Val, Bing, Jeanie and Bruce camped several times at the rose bush just near the bamboo. The Taylor family lived there at one time and Bing, Bruce and Keith had their own teenage camp there.[31]

It was the same story at all of the camping places. When people were asked about the lack of material evidence of their dwellings, the men continued to insist on their ephemeral and transitory nature. Paul Taylor said 'They never made them too good, because they moved. Three or four years, maybe, and that was it, they'd pack up and leave.' Bruce and Bing explained that when they moved from the bamboo back to the rose bush house they 'Took it, pulled it down, moved over there then. Place was pulled down, put up near the rose bush there.' When I asked Tom and Gloria Flanders why there were no material signs of the substantial bark houses that their father had built so carefully, Tom laughed and said, 'They'd be gone with the wind. They'd deteriorate, rot away, white ants, they'd vanish within fifteen years.' Nothing was built for permanence.

Within the space of No Mans Land people continued to live lightly on the land, building shelters that either disappeared with time or moved with them when they went to another camping place. They imagined the whole of the space around Corindi Lake as home, with fireplaces outside their huts, the swamp where they did their washing, and the beach where they fished. They moved around and within the space of Corindi Lake relating intimately to all of its places and beyond. The landscape continues to be read for the material signs of the ancestors and the Old People, through the middens, scarred trees, symbolic fig tree markers, and through introduced plants such as the rose bush and the bamboo. In this way the place markers evoke a storied past and continuity in peopled places. In these stories the landscape is not imagined as a singular, pristine, unmarked wilderness, but as a multitude of places teeming with the signs of life.

The patched-up house

The house was built outta big slabs
where the crack part
the rain come in.
Old People use' to have
wall to wall newspaper pasted,
flour they used to use,
never had glue in those days.
We use' to go to Pipeclay
get some white clay
to whiten the walls.
Real thick and strong then,
use to make the place look a bit new [laughs].

When Old Tom Flanders moved his growing family from the Fig Tree site to escape the wet, he built a more sophisticated house at 'the Point'. Here they had a view of the sea between the headlands that marked the entrance to the Lake. He took all the materials that might be useful, leaving only the rubbish that remained to mark the place when it was uncovered for the building of the boardwalk. At their new place they no longer had a dirt floor and a single room. They were proud of the new bark hut their father built.

> There was two rooms, there was one room here [drawing with finger] and one room there and the boys all had this room and mum and dad had this room, and I slept on the floor, because I was the only girl at the time, and then the two younger boys, they slept with the boys in the other room. You had steps even going up to it, made out of logs we had, and you had the push-out windows with a stick, and you put the stick on the thing. But my father was very clever in measuring like that he was, he was self-taught and he measured more or less by a string, or by a piece of wood, of how long a foot was, or an inch was, 'cause he helped build houses in Valla where the old sawmill was over there. The

> other thing was there was no chimney or anything, because there was a tent outside, and in that tent was the cookin' area and where we ate. (Theresa Flanders)

The tent came with them from the old place and it was added to the new structures built from bark and timber. Old Tom Flanders had learned to measure, to make window openings with shutters, and to divide their hut into separate rooms for the boys and girls. They imported these new building technologies and materials into No Mans Land, adding them to whatever they had recycled from the past. As the bark huts became more elaborate, so did the practice of collecting bark.

> Yeah, because that house that Dadda had built out of bark, it didn't even leak, eh? None of them do if they're – you know how you handle a bark when you take it off a tree, if you handle it wrong it'll get a split, you'll get a leak. When it doesn't split it's right. You can either split it up for a sheet, depends if you got it too big an oval it will crack and leak. If you split that down the middle, you get two big sheets about that wide. It depends on the, you know, width of the bark – if it's a big piece like that you'll have to split that down the middle. See it's torn from the tree. And it won't leak, only thing is it's that heavy! Twice the weight or three times the weight of an ordinary sheet of corrugated iron. Now especially it depends what type of eucalypt you got it off, too. The big black butts, they're about that thick, it's that heavy when it's raining, it saturates it. (Tom and Gloria Flanders)

Old Tom Flanders knew exactly how to split and place the bark so that the roof didn't leak. For Bing and Bruce, the leaking of their old bark huts was a source of great hilarity. Bruce laughed when he said their house used to 'leak like a waterfall at times'. Bing described collecting the bark from the swamp mahoganies, heating it on the fire to press it flat and the crisscross way the bark was laid to prevent it leaking.

> Oh it use' to leak a lot, sometimes it use' to leak, the roof was all bark [laughing]. Oh same old lay the bark down and lay another one over this way and another one that way, yeah, straddle 'em, watch them other ones don't leak sort of thing. Big bark that tree, right along the land over there, swamp mahogany. It easy to bark, we use' to make a big fire and throw him on the fire, and put something, you press him out really flat, as long as it's heavy you know, keep it flat. Yeah, use old fencing wire to tie it. And all the tin and bit a posts on top of that, keep that down. Yeah, got windy, oh cyclone, use' to be cyclone then. The old house use' to stand up to it though, I reckon if we had one of these houses down there, it would blow the tiles off 'em. In them days, oh the wind used to blow, when the cyclone, when you get cyclones, we used to get a cyclone. (Bing Laurie)

Keeping the rain and weather out was a continuing feature in all of the stories of their shelters, very much part of life at the Lake. Unlike the new brick houses, their huts were built in response to the weather rather than against it. The bark huts were constructed on spots of higher ground and when that ground was flooded they went to stay with relatives or moved to the shelter at the Racecourse to wait until the waters drained away. The rose bush house where Bing was born was described fondly as 'all bark hut' with the chimney made in the traditional way, facing north away from the prevailing southerly winds.

> It was a big old house there we had board floors, all boards we had, not the ground one, well the two of them had floorboards, others we had just all dirt, you know, ground dirt. Oh, well big fire kitchen there, close the door that way, well when Old People make a fire, the chimney hole they face that way. The southerly blows back, always facing north, make a fire, yeah. We had a dirt, you know, a little hump, make a fire in that. When it gets too high with the ashes we just shovel 'em out, shovel out. All high up on the side there,

on a wire you know hang up big bar across, hang the billy there, old oven, old camp oven. (Bing Laurie)

While on the outside the bark hut was tied down with wire and poles against the cyclones, on the inside it was patched up with tin, newspaper and clay to cover the cracks where the weather could come in. Bing called it 'the old patched-up house', the quintessential material expression of the in-between space of No Mans Land. The white pipe clay, which gave Corindi Beach both its names, was transformed into a building material. Corindi Beach was known by the people as 'Pipeclay' after the new settler practice of making pipes with the fine white clay. The white clay, previously used for ceremony and to keep the spirits from visiting the children, was now used to patch up the houses. A new coat of white pipeclay gave them a new house.

All of the furnishings and utensils inside the houses were similarly made from recycled and local materials. Beds were made by stitching hessian bags over a frame made from forked sticks and poles. The recycling practices of the patched-up house were also used for making mattresses, bed covers and clothes.

> In those days they used to have a big chaff bag so Mum used to keep that and that was unpicked and then you had this great big square from the chaff bag, well then Mum, what she'd do with that, she'd take it out to the copper and you'd have the caustic soda and you'd get that water boiling, put the caustic soda into it so that all the fibre from the chaff – that would help take whatever there was away from it. And that was just thrown over the fence, or bushes, wherever you could find and lay anything like that out. So then she'd sew that together – well then, what you had was your mattress. And then we had to go out and cut this grass. Once that was dried out that was stuffed into that bag then, so you 'ad your mattress which went on to your bed. And that was the way of living in those days – to keep warm and you had your mattress, and part of that was used also for covering in

the winter. What did they call it? [Laughing] The wagga? (Gloria Flanders)

We only know about the white clay, the waggas and the furniture from these stories, but the objects from the little bundle lying against the tree on that first day at Flanders Camp tell us more. There was one of an especially intricate construction. It was a coiled piece of tin made from what looked like the top of a sardine tin rolled around some rope and placed in a hole in a jam tin lid so that the rope was held dangling into the jar. Gloria described the fat lamps Old Tom Flanders used to make at the Fig Tree camp.

> Dad used to make all the fat lamps. In a jam tin – made a little funnel and then [what] you added through the funnel was a piece of felt, and that would be attached through and make the wick comin' out, yeah, bit of rag, or rope you could do 'em. Only got to soak 'em. He used to nearly always have felt, 'cause it was a lot better for burnin'. Sash ropes are good because it's compact hemp and it's woven stronger, sash rope. Make the little funnel out of tin, he made it out've. Tin, the lid of a jam tin, you roll that up. But see, we used to go down into the tip and you'd get stuff from down there and say, 'Oh, we'll take that'. (Tom and Gloria Flanders)

Gloria travelled from the Flanders Camp to the convent school in Grafton, 50 kilometres each way, and studied by the light of the fat lamp at night. She laughed when I asked her about the fat light. 'That was no problem, we thought it was great. Great just to have a light, eh? Let there be light!' There were many stories about fat lamps. They were best when burning kerosene but when the kero ran out people would substitute fat from animals or fish they had caught and cooked. Some forms of discarded metal, like the soft lids of sardine tins, were superior, and there was lots of discussion about the different sorts of materials that were suitable to make the wick. The different qualities of rope, felt, gabardine and canvas were compared. The trick was to have the funnel narrow enough so that the wick was fine and did not burn too much kerosene. Bing offered a comprehensive description of the subtle art of making a fat light.

> Inside a jar, any kind of jar, a long as it had a lid on it, bore holes in the lid and make a spout sort of thing there, and put that wick, put the wick inside of it. Oh, old sardine tins the front part, you know real soft aluminium, tin like that, and it was easy to roll up. Or some might have pipe, little brass pipe, or some old brass pipe. Don't want it too thick 'cause it, don't want to use a lot of kerosene [laughs], it sucks the kerosene too quick. Sometimes they use' to have, just stick the wick up through the lid and squeeze it through the hole yeah, let it burn then, 'cause you gotta have real soft, or the right draft for it to, you know, can't start. Something like a towel, soaks the kerosene up. If you had a different kind of rag like any silk or that it will just burn the cloth up that's all. Had proper sort of cloth, towels sort of thing. Canvas was the one that was mainly used, canvas 'cause it sucks it up, yep.
> (Bing Laurie)

Glenda told us how they solved the problem of the wick. Old Ma, her grandmother, always wore 'long dresses and hats. I mean, that was ladylike, that's what you did – back then, she had cupboards full, always had a hat'. The hats were made of felt, which was a superior material for making a wick for fat lights. 'When our kerosene lantern – we'd run out of wick, we'd sneak into our grandmother's room and get a little bit of felt hat – did a wonderful job, the old felt hats dipped in the kerosene – had to wait on sufferance. Oh God, yes, beautiful hats.' Everything had multiple uses. Once all the kerosene had been used the empty kerosene tin was recycled. 'The half kerosene tins, well they used to cut 'em, like from corner to corner and open it up, and you'd sort of have it like a tub there, like a sort of a dish sort of thing.' The flattened tins were used for building huts. 'They'd cut 'em down the corners and got a sheet of tin about that long and about that wide. They actually built a hut out've them they got so many.'

Singing the coast

The people who lived in No Mans Land were the ultimate recyclers before the word recycling was invented. It wasn't only about making do because they were poor but it was a form of pleasurable inventiveness and improvisation. Many of the objects at Armi's camp came originally from the dump. There were fragments of dinner plates with pretty flowers, a speckled enamel saucepan, a harmonica and lead from a telephone pole that was used to make sinkers. Bruce, Bing, Michael and Keith would go to the dump every day to see what they could find. At night they would return with their loot in a wheelbarrow constructed from bits and pieces from the dump.

> Oh, we used to go to the Red Rock tip, Red Rock dump. We got a lot of things from there, sheet irons, ovens, things like that, y'know. Me and Keithy and Bing, we used to go there with carts, down near Jewfish Point there, that dump. There was three fridges, and only one fridge worked out of the three [laughs]. All gravel road those days. Oh, I couldn't do it today. We used to walk, down dinnertime, come back, go down again. Yeah, nearly every day we used to go down there. We find some good stuff down there. Old tape recorders, wireless, things like that. Sometimes we find old crockery, sometimes some good crockery there, you'd put in a box on the side of the road, Keithy come along and grab it, cups and things, plates. Good stuff, really good stuff. Wheels, we used to make, put wheels on a cart, or wheelbarra, something like that. Oh, yeah, we always cut wood, yeah. We had the wheels there for 'em. Sometimes you find some good clothes there, some nice clothes. Used to put 'em on the side of road, wouldn't throw 'em in the dump, in boxes. (Bruce Laurie)

The dump provided an endless source of building materials, household utensils, crockery and clothes. It also provided them with entertainment. Michael described an old AWA wireless and Bruce said they found a record player and some old Hank Williams records. They couldn't wind the record player up so Bing used to make the records go round with his fingers. It was the dump that gave them their first guitar.

> They used to have a rubbish tip at Red Rock, back this side of Red Rock. And Bing found a guitar there in the tip, but it was burnt, and he brought that home and he sort of patched it all up, and that's where he first started there. Yeah then he used to sit by himself and learn how to play it. No-one ever showed him how to play. He did it all by himself.
> (Tony Perkins)

Following the tradition of the days of the Red Rock band they made lots of other musical instruments from the materials at hand – boards from the beach, fishing line, and empty food tins.

> You couldn't buy a guitar then 'cause there was no money to buy nothing. So, all us young fellas we used to get a piece of just flat board, just flat board, and you know just put a hole, like four holes in the end of it and just put a stick in the end of the board, and the same at the other end, and just put fishin' line, four strands of fishin' line up on the board. Then we'd get a square camp pie, meat tin, and put it on the end of the board, make a hole in it and put in on the end, and you'd get more sound when you start strummin' the strings with the fishin' line. And that's, I watched him start off there. Keith was the same, he was with us and that's where it first started like that. (Tony Perkins)

Together they formed a band called the Sea Foams and played to raise money to help local charities. They sang the Gumbaynggirr song[32] in the old language but with new meanings. From all of the elements of old and new materials and technologies, people cobbled together a life in No Mans Land. They built patched-up houses and made patched-up objects with materials recycled from the local dump. Patched-up houses are like patched-up writing. The process of constructing this text is like building a patched-up house, from all of the bits and pieces that make up a story of the in-between. They are cultural translations stitched together from the materials at hand, shaping new forms from old, creating new conversations and new meanings.

The Old Camp

How we come to do the Old Camp
it was rainin', couldn't dry yourself
this old bloke Jimmy Mackay
built a sort of galley
we ended up building onto it,
never leaked there.
We had a big room to ourselves,
had everything real neat,
when it rained never got wet,
fire keeping us warm, lovely and warm.

Every time we come to Yarrawarra we visit the tin hut that still stands in a protected place behind the dune at the back of the beach. Each time its shape changes as different people move in and live there for a while. People call this tin hut the Old Camp. The Old Camp today is a physical presence that tells the story of cultural translation, a symbolic reference point for the time. It reminds me of the tin humpies I saw in the desert, especially the women's camp where the old women would sit with their special things and tell stories of country. Their tin humpy was shape-shifting, growing larger and contracting as people moved in and out. It was a living, organic being, and a place of memory like the Old Camp.

To enter the Old Camp you walk across a bridge and through a thicket of bamboo where the Gumburr lives. The Gumburr is the spirit protector of the people and place. It is as if that little bridge represents the crossing over, the risky movement between two cultures, and the Gumburr protects them. Jimmy Runner had a permissive occupancy of the whole area around the Old Camp and moved there in the 1960s with his wife, Sadie Laurie, and their family: Jean, Val, Bruce and Bing. When Jimmy Runner moved his family across to the Old Camp the first thing they had to do was to build the bridge over the northern arm of the Lake to reach the sheltered spot behind the dunes at the back of the beach. Like all their other building practices, they made the bridge with materials at hand, this time driftwood washed in from the sea.

> Keithy built that bridge there, near the bamboo. High sort of bridge. We had planks that we found on the beach, fork like that in the tree and he decided to put a pole across it like that, and he had four poles 'n' a plank, walking up the plank! We had some big planks down on the beach years ago, big seas.
> (Bruce Laurie)

Keith, as the eldest of the three and the one with the most skills in building, was responsible for making the bridge to help them across to the other side. The move itself was a collective enterprise. As with all of their other moves around the Lake, they carried everything they could recycle across to the Old Camp. This time they used the cart they had made with materials from the dump. They cut bloodwood poles to replace the old ones and began by constructing a roof to give them shelter from the rain.

> When you moved from one side to the other, from this side of the Lake, took everything that we had in the old place. Take it over there, build it up, pack it up again, what we had there, table and chairs, y'know. Pull down the building bit by bit and other sort of spare timbers to start with. Just before we pull the house down, like iron for the roof. Yeah, Keithy got the cart on. Four-wheel cart we used to take it across that. We used to take across all the timber and irons, and things like that. Yeah, we used it straight away, used it all up, sort of bit by bit. Put the posts up and roof on, start on the wall then put things inside that roof, and take things over, bit by bit. A bit of ground in case it get rain, so it won't get wet, y'know.
> (Bruce Laurie)

Soon there were other structures and temporary shelters that grew to house the extended family at the Old Camp. Noeline remembers that Old Pa Laurie 'used to camp in an old car on this side of the Lake', and Uncle Abraham McDougall 'was in that kind of other car, a wagon beside the Lake'. It was the wet weather that led to the construction of the tin hut that still stands as the one remnant of the Old Camp.

> How we come to do the Old Camp, it was rainin' so you couldn't dry yourself much so this old bloke named Jimmy Mackay, with his wife used to stay with us, he built a sort of galley there you know for us to wash in when it was wet. So we ended up building on to it. Never leaked there, we had a big room down there to ourselves. We had everything real neat and all that, when it rained it never got wet, y'know. Fire keeping us warm, lovely and warm. (Bruce Laurie)

Bruce moved into the Old Camp with Norma, his young wife from Coonabarabran, as their first home. There they had their own room, it was dry and the fire kept them warm. I sat with Bing, Bruce and Keith on an iron bedstead with a knitted patchwork quilt. There was carpet laid over the dirt floor and shelves for books and kitchen things. The fireplace was built in the old style with a tin chimney facing north away from the southerly winds. A sense of warmth and wellbeing permeates the stories about the Old Camp today. Norma remembers how food was shared and there was always enough to go round for anyone who came to visit.

> When Val was alive, she use' to cook, you know, all share around what they eat and that. Or anyone come there, there was always somethin' to eat there. Val was a good cook, dampers, scones, oh a lot of things, pipi gravy and damper mainly. And she liked her turtle then, she loved it. Turtle and crabs and things, she use' to go and find them. We use' to do our shoppin', when we get a bit low on that, we use' to go out to the sea then. (Norma Skinner)

When the food from the shops ran out they continued to live off the sea and estuary as they had always done. Bruce also grew vegetables – pumpkins, tomatoes, lettuce, onion, capsicum and chillies – watered by carting water in 4-gallon drums on the cart made from the tip. One of Bruce's many photos shows Johnny Laurie with his surfboard in front of a raised garden with sides of corrugated iron bursting with vegetables. Other photos show Bing and Val with pin boards covered with rock 'n' roll idols and Bing and Bruce playing the guitar. Noeline remembers the Old Camp as a place where they sat around the campfires at night listening to stories of the Old People.

> Just bein kids an' sittin' 'round camp fires at night an' listening to the Old People talking, tellin' stories, of their past. And you know I was interested, to sit there and listen, about life. How they used to travel from here and walk all the way to Station Creek, or further up, if they had to go further, along the beaches, and where they camped. And like they used to get the food and how to, I dunno, how to gut them. Fishin' trip, and hunting. (Noeline Dootson)

The Old People told stories about the days when they wandered throughout their country hunting and fishing, singing and dancing. The Old Camp was a place of memory and story. The stories that the grandchildren listened to were about particular places that they came to know and practices that they would learn. The grandchildren were taught how to fish and collect food. They had to learn the skills of survival in No Mans Land.

> They told us about those things, but as I got older I'd go fishing with them, and, oh they taught us a lot, Debbie and I, we sort of grew up with it. We used to follow 'em, up the beach. And they'd walk for miles and miles, ages. And we'd be there nearly all day, and in the end you just get in and helped them, and we sort of, we learned from the smaller ones, the smaller worms, they'd let us have a try with those … Oh catch pipis, get pipis, just diggin' 'em up in the sand. And then fishing with a hand line. Yeah, well our lines were on a milk tin. Down here, straight down, and onto the beach. If there was a strong wind it was no good, they usually died down in the evening. Low tide and high tide, goes with the moon. The tide comes up with the moon, when the moon comes up. (Noeline Dootson)

The Old Camp was a place to learn survival, to learn the rhythms of moon and tides, wind and weather. The sense of the Old Camp as a place of important cultural learning is very powerful in Margie Lardner's stories. Margie and her sister Sylvia were taken away by 'the Welfare' as young children. Her story begins with the denial by her foster family of her identity and place belonging. She does not dwell for long in this story of the 'stolen generation', however, and quickly moves on to tell the story of her return to the Old Camp.

> I didn't know where I come from 'cause [my foster family] had told me that I'd been found in the bush and nobody wanted me. So Link Up ended up findin' out I had come from up the coast somewhere and what they did, they took a passport photo of me and sent it right up to Tweed Heads. So I remember when I lived with [my foster family] I got into trouble with 'em, which is all the time. I used to see an old man, used to come to me, and in his hand he had this flower, it was purply pink flower. And I'd always see water nearby. I found out it was the pigface he was holdin' in his hand, yeah. That old man was my dad, Clarrie Skinner.
> (Margie Lardner)

Margie's real connection to the place was remade through the image that came to her repeatedly in her dreams of an old man holding a purply pink flower, with the water nearby. Through this image she recognised the pink pigface flower that grows on the dunes, and the face of her father, Clarrie Skinner. Although Clarrie Skinner and her mother had passed away by the time of her return, people at Corindi Lake recognised Margie and called her by her nickname, Gusha Gusha.

> I hadn't seen them, I was only a little girl so I couldn't remember anything. Bingie was the first one, when I walked in the door of the house, at Barkhut Road, Bingie started yellin' out, 'Here comes Gusha Gusha!' And sorta, I went all funny, I didn't remember them. Uncle Mac, that's Bingie's Dad, he gave me the name 'cause Gusha Gusha means near the water. When I was little I used to always cry to go with Dad and them down the beach all the time, when I was tiny.

In the beginning was the mother place.

I find most meaning in the everyday, in the marks on the sand.

Bing Laurie 2000

Bushtucker walk
winding through
swamp mahoganies and paperbarks
invites us into
hidden stories
of No Mans Land

Red Rock band, 1930s. They made musical instruments from materials at hand – boards, fishing line and empty food tins.

Clarrie and Celia Skinner and family eating watermelon on holiday at Red Rock in the 1930s.

I follow the fingerline
of river
where traces of clay floors
mark birthing grounds
where Nan fished
and Clarrie sang
all the way home from Red Rock.

Sapling House, 1920s. 'They used to get the old broom and sweep all round, used to be beautiful.'

The Old Camp, 1998. There they had their own room, it was dry and the fire kept them warm.

The Lake was our
survival
crabs, prawns, fish
it was all
in the Lake.

Clarrie Skinner and jewfish, 1930s. When he'd catch his fish, he'd dig a hole and cover 'em over so the moon wouldn't get on 'em.

Milton fishing, Corindi Beach, 1998. On off-pay week the rods that sit in a row on the verandah of Bruce's house 'have all gone fishing'.

Collecting pipis, Corindi Beach. We went pipi collecting with a group of grannies, aunties, young women, children and dogs, all down on the beach.

Preparing curry pipi gravy with johnny cakes. 'We used to throw 'em in the coals with damper, that's all.'

Bing, Bruce and Keith
in quiet and stillness
of Jewfish Point,
Bruce is no longer with us
he's walking, talking, singing
with the Old People
I feel him there still.

On the salt flat
in the first dewdrop light
of dawn
gnarled old mangrove tree
guards this place
with crooked limbs.

Val on the Island, 1930s. 'I was the last born on the island.'

Val and family on the Island, 1940s. 'The island itself, everywhere you look is memory.'

Val and Rosina on the Island, 2003. 'Us young girls, we used to do a lot of moonlight swimming in those days, so beautiful.'

Islands in Nambucca estuary. 'The island created a place for us people, for our generation to go there, to feel safe and know that we belong there.'

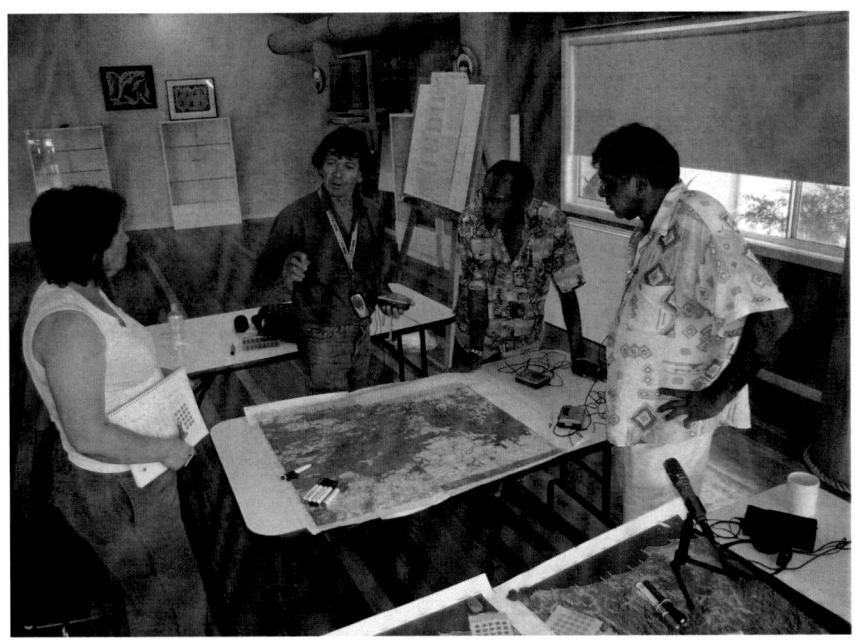

Deep mapping; Tony, Ken, Gary with Meg Goudling, 2004. 'You'll never get the jigsaw puzzle back but there's enough there.' (Gary Williams)

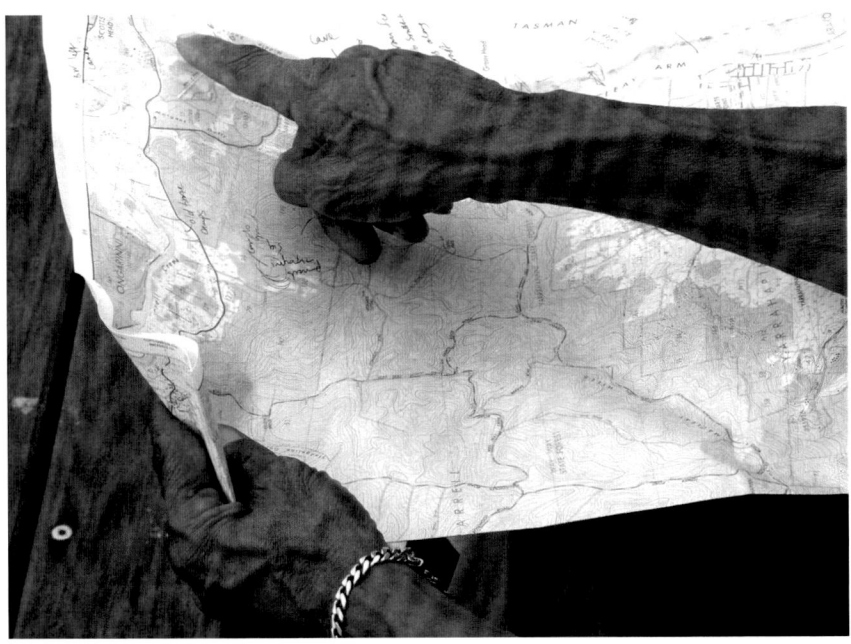

Mapping at Scott's Head, 2003. The work of reconnecting story to country involves reclaiming language, story and place.

We call it *Nunguu Miirlarl*
kangaroo special place
an increase site
when kangaroo was scarce
they went up
and done their dances
on top of the mountain
so the kangaroos
would come back.

The two sisters
completed their circle
making the sea and sand
of our coastline we call 'Australia'
they met up again at Moonee Beach
swam out to the ocean
crossed their yam sticks
at Split Solitary Island
and went up into the sky
into the stars we call Janagan
the Seven Sisters
where the story ends.

> So they used to put me in an old sugar bag and carry me down to the beach there so that's what it means, by the water. Auntie Sadie and them used to yell out 'Here comes Gusha Gusha now', and they reckoned I was only little, runnin' through the long grass down there. (Margie Lardner)

By telling her this story they gave her back her connection to the place and the people of No Mans Land. In calling her by this name, Bing was evoking her relationship to the Old People and a special story about her relationship to her father when she was a little child. When Margie returned to the Old Camp she was an adult with children of her own. She could then begin the long slow process of learning about her place and community. This learning was inextricably tied to the landscapes and structures of the Old Camp.

> We ended up comin' out to the Old Camp down here. Me and the boys come down and stayed with my cousin Vallie and her husband John and the kids. They started tellin' me then all about Dad, and who everyone was in the family and that. It sorta, I mean, it's a lot tryin' to get into my brain, you know, I was tryin' to think of everyone and who they were to me. There was me and all my cousins, which were across the road. There was one, two, three, four huts then, were down there. Sally and Jean used to have their own hut. No-one was separated, all the families were together. When the time come to go shoppin', we'd all go in and do our shoppin' and then we'd come back and we'd take it in turns. Some'd carry groceries. Wheelbarra, any way we could, we'd take our groceries down to the Old Camp. (Margie Lardner)

Margie had been fostered in a nuclear family in Sydney so had to learn extended family relationships and a collective way of life in No Mans Land. She remembered the four huts down at the Old Camp where all the relations lived in separate spaces but she learned that 'the families were not separated'. They lived together, sharing chores like shopping, washing, collecting wood for fires, and collecting and cooking food. Margie had to learn how to find fresh water and dig a well, how to do the washing using a wood fire, and how to collect the wood for the night-time fires. She also had to learn to catch food for survival – fishing, gathering pipis and gugumbal at the beach, and eels from the swamp.

> We used to go on the beach a lot and do a lot of fishin'. That's what I liked the most, goin' fishin' and pipyin', go and get gugumbals off the rocks. My little fella, Davey, he's been brought up on all the seafoods plus he'd eat turtles, eels. Sally used to take us when Davey was only a little fella then, we used to go up around near the racecourse there and there's a hole of water there, like a little sort of dam or a lake. We used to go and catch eels there. Michael, he used to go down to the bush, he'd say, 'Well, I'm goin' huntin' now', and he'd take my boy Derek and Sally's daughter Leah. And he'd take 'em huntin' with him to catch a kangaroo. And he'd do it every so many weeks or somethin', he'd catch a kangaroo for us. (Margie Lardner)

For Margie this cultural learning, especially of language, was not always easy. 'Sometimes I get in limbo with 'em, I'm gettin' pulled one way and I'm gettin' pulled the other way and it's really hard to explain to them somethin'.' The Old Camp, however, gave her a sense of home and belonging that enabled her to learn about her place and identity. 'I loved it down there and I found myself back, it was like I belonged, that was my home, I belonged there you know.' For Margie it was a place of sharing and community. They shared their physical survival in the activities of collecting food, wood, and water, and afterwards sat down together and yarned, telling the stories that kept their cultural memories alive.

Therese Flanders lived at the Old Camp during the time that Margie was absent. She moved away before Margie returned and I interviewed her in her house at Evans Head. She expressed very similar feelings to Margie. Like others who have moved away, Therese felt a strong sense of connection to the Old Camp and what it represents in their lives today.

And it's the sense of belonging. There's no – they're not like, sort of, you know lost, or they're only lost for a little while, even if something serious has happened in their lives. But they're brought back into the fold. So you looked after each other and there was no overlapping. If someone had more here than that family there, it was shared. 'Oh, take this over to Auntie So-And-So and Uncle.' So you grew up with all that sharing. Then it's up to them if they want to stay there, or if that is what they're looking for. But the word we come across was 'belonging'. So down there, even though you had all those families, the belonging was one family, one family. (Theresa Flanders)

There are many photos of the Old Camp that capture its multiple shape-shifting lives, but there is one in particular that is hauntingly beautiful. It is a photograph taken from the outside, the patched layers of corrugated iron now faded deep red overlaid with mottled rust and lines of nail holes from previous use. The timber struts of the roof are echoed in a row of elegant shadows on the tin. Just visible over the flat roof is a blue, blue sky, and the green foliage and lemon brushes of coastal banksias. Softening the blank tin wall, a lace curtain is blowing in the breeze and casting its own margin of lacy shadow against the tin wall.

At this particular time Noeline was living in the Old Camp and had made it into a home. As Jimmy Runner's granddaughter she keeps the tradition of the Old Camp going. She 'cleans up' around the old place, leaves camp ovens and cooking utensils there so people can use them, and plants fruit trees. She moved into the Old Camp for twelve months because it was like going home. 'It was nice and quiet, and being able to walk away from people, and go home. If you feel like sitting down and thinking and you don't want – need someone interrupting you. That's what I liked about it.' When Keith's tent appeared down at the Old Camp, I asked Noeline whether he stayed down there too and she said, 'I think he sits there and watches us, watching what we do. 'Cause every time I seem to go down there cleaning up, he's always sitting back somewhere watching.' Other people go to live at the Old

Camp in times of worry and stress, when they need a break, or when they just want to fish, collect shellfish, and live more simply.

I love the image of the corrugated iron outside of the Old Camp with its curtain blowing in the breeze, the sense that life still goes on in there and I am an outsider to this place. Later, I am invited inside with Keith, Bing and Bruce, the darkness lit by patterns of sunlight shining through the lace curtain, to listen to its stories. The Old Camp is the last hut that people lived in down at the Lake. They lived there until 1988 when they moved to the brick houses closer to the road.

The Old Camp is a symbol of the material translations of No Mans Land that allowed the people to build a bridge between the past and a possible future. There were once several shacks and dwelling places in that spot, now only one tin hut remains. The tin hut stands as the material expression of the Old Camp, the last place where people lived before moving into the modern brick homes. It has come to symbolise all that the old days represented to the people who lived in No Mans Land. It houses their memories, and is a physical reminder for people who are connected to the place but now live far away. It is a place of story and memory, a place where people can learn about their identity in place and community. Most of all it is a belonging place where people have a collective sense of home and community. It is the story of these translations that allows us to learn how their new life was built from the past.

CHAPTER 4

Eating place

Just along the beach, beautiful blue beach in there
mullet come just in the mouth
of the Lake
a terrible lot of them, mostly big sea mullet,
walk along the beach for pipis and things.
We ate lilly pillies, wild cherries, raspberries, five corners
and just along the beach you get them little white berries
we used to eat those,
geebungs, another one, roly-polies, gooseberries
you're never short of things to eat.

Southern Gumbayanggirr people lived on prawns, crabs and fish from the estuary; turtles, swamp hens, eels from the swamp; pipis, gugumbals and abalone from the beach and rock pools; mullet, tailor, mackerel, whiting, jewfish, bream, trevally from the sea; kangaroos, possum and porcupine or echidna from the surrounding bushlands; and turtles, eels and cobra from the river. In-between all of these places people ate native fruits such as lilly pilly, wild cherries, nyum-nyums and pigface as they walked on their tracks through the dunes and coastal heathlands. When people tell stories about eating all of these things they talk about them in terms of the places where they come from, the local food ecologies.

Sharing food and telling stories about eating from local places, or 'eating place' as we have called it, is the most common of everyday place practices. In his welcome to country, Bing invites us to 'Darruyagay, biyambaygu yuraal Yarrawarra', 'Be happy and eat food at Yarrawarra'. Welcoming people to eat in one's country is an important way to share what it means to live in that place. Yarrawarra Aboriginal Corporation established the bush tucker walk to teach visitors about local bush foods, and they developed their educational activities around the concept of yuraal, local food knowledge. Stories of gathering, preparing and cooking food from their local places were by far the most commonly told stories in our research. Offering food, and tell-ing its stories, is an everyday way of sharing cultural knowledge about place. In this chapter we explore what it means to know a place in this way.

Estuary

When we swam in the Lake along the sand
we could scratch very closely below the sand
in the water
and you'd see prawns lying in the sand
come up behind and grab them with our hands
catch the big king prawns
that used to get washed in
from the full moon,
on the high tide.

We began with food stories at the Lake. The Elders took me there for our first conversation and told me about all the food they ate from the Lake when they were growing up. That day it was a surprise of blue. We sat by a big sweep of blue water that curved around a changing shape of sand. The blue trickled out to sea in-between two banks carved by the Lake's flow. In the other direction dark-green mangroves hugged the blue and two white egrets fed in the water.

The Lake, as Yarrawarra people continue to call it, is a typical small estuarine system at the back of the foredune at Corindi Beach. The estuary is an uncertain body of water and land, fed by rainwaters from the local bushland at one end and permeable to the sea at the other. The salty part of the estuary near the sea opens to the tides and seawater. Here people caught crabs, prawns, oysters and saltwater fish. Eating food from the Lake was the most primal story of our project. The Lake was their survival, the unremarked centre of their daily lives.

> The Lake seemed to have been, like, it was more of a quick way, if you wanted to go a quick way for anything. The sea was more of a challengin' way. I used to get, 'cause you wanted, you enjoyed it, I think you enjoyed the sea food the better, for us, because it was more of a challenge to get it. Whereas the Lake was there, it's probably just as hard, but you knew, you knew they were in that area, what you were lookin' for. (Tony Perkins)

The Lake represented home, ease and safety. For children it was a safe place to play, to swim and to learn how to collect food from their local places. When the fish were gathering together to leave the mouth of the Lake 'we used to get mullet on the low tide. Sometimes Keith and Bing used to go along with an old bed, make 'em jump. See one bloke run with a wire whip, hittin' 'em and that. Big mullet, oh, there was big mullets in there. They were lovely too, beautiful.' The children swam and played in the safety of the Lake and grew up learning its rhythms through learning to catch its food.

Theresa remembered swimming along the shallow bottom of the Lake, just ruffling the shallow water with her hands to expose the big king prawns lying just below the surface of the sand. At night she learned to see their red eyes glowing in the dark. Night time was the best time for catching prawns because they swim to the light. At first it was the light of their fires, but later they had Tilley lamps. They made nets out of corn sacks and often cooked and ate the prawns at the fire by the Lake.

> Oh, prawns, used to go night time with prawns, make a big fire on the side of the Lake. Mum and me Uncle, they used to get in the water with an old sort of bag, like a net, and

wipe it up the thing and get all these prawns. Oh, good feed of prawns we used to, night times around there. The net was made out of bags, well, like old corn bags. Cut 'em open, and line 'em up together, and make one, they just filled 'em up with prawns. We used to put it in a bucket and take it home, boil 'em up. Next morning, or that night, they'd have a feed. Gee there's some good prawns from that Lake. The size of them big ones, they got that big in that Lake there. They come down to the light, and net, in the night time. We make a big fire on the side of the lake, see what you were doing, no torch. After a while we got a Tilley lamp, old Tilley lamp. It was a good time, good times on that Lake, good thing to eat. Clean you know. (Bruce Laurie)

There is an air of performance about the stories of catching prawns in the Lake. All the elements are there: darkness, firelight, people, abundance of prawns, and a good feed. They learned that the Lake would provide for them. They knew that the king prawns would be washed in from the sea on the high tides that came with the full moon. In this way they understood how the rhythms of the Lake connected with the cycles of the moon and tides.

Learning the rhythms of the Lake meant understanding its openings and closings to the sea. The only way that sea creatures could enter the Lake was when the mouth opened to the sea. The sea would break through the opening with king tides that came with the full moon, or in rough stormy weather with high seas. In times of heavy rain the floodwaters flowed from inland towards the sea, breaking the Lake's banks and flowing into the sea. The intimate details of these rhythms were learned through eating place.

Sometime you used to get a jewfish, 'specially when a big flood's on, that Lake gets a breakout, all that freshwater rush out. That's when the jew went up the mouth of the Lake when the breakout, there used to be jew then, that's when they feed round in the mouth over there, at the Lake. The water'd be dirty with that floodwater, that's when it'd be good for jew too. During the day anyway. (Bing Laurie)

The jewfish feed around the mouth of the Lake when its warm, fertile floodwaters flow into the sea. This can be seen in the 'dirty' colour of the floodwaters carrying silt and plant debris into the seawater. Other fish, prawns and crabs come into the Lake on the king tides and swim up to the warm backwaters to breed. They recognise the opening by the presence of the warm water at the mouth of the Lake.

> The fish'll come up in there. They'll come up in the Lake and they breed up in the Lake. Then the bigger ones'll, some will stay, but others'll go out and the younger ones will breed up in the backwaters in the Lake. Always been fish in there. You can get bream in there, you can get swallowtail in there, sea mullet'd come in there. They'd all come in, for breeding, yeah. All the prawns and crabs will come in there, you see a whole lot of 'em. A lot of time it takes the warm water, see where there's the water runnin' out, that water's a lot warmer than the water in the sea. And when the water's comin' out into the sea, it's warmer where it's runnin' through, and they feel that warmer water and they'll come up with the water into that warmer area. Only at a certain time, like when there's any high tide or that, when it's time for the eggs and that. (Tony Perkins)

Understanding the Lake's food means knowing the bodies and cycles of the creatures that feed and breed in the Lake. The Lake was teeming with creatures – bream, swallowtail, sea mullet, prawns and crabs – moving in and out with the rhythms of the Lake. The feeding and breeding rhythms of these creatures were linked to the other cycles: the rains that made the Lake open to the sea, the king tides that came with the full moon, the saltiness or freshness of the water, and the warm and cold waters. The people knew these changes intimately, catching their food within these rhythms and cycles.

> Crabs and prawns breed up in there. The young ones grow up in there then, then when the high tides come they'll

> go back out. Only time that, only times you want to catch prawns and crabs it's easy. It's just before you get a big storm, right, when you get a really big storm, when the sea starts risin, or a lot of run-off comes into the Lake, it'll break out. And just before a really big storm so there was a lot of rain, the prawns and crabs'd go right to the mouth of the Lake, where it's ready to break. Ready to go. That's the best time to go down, right to the front and get 'em. You go right to the head of the Lake, before it breaks out. They're the first things to go with it. (Tony Perkins)

When the fish come in through the mouth of the Lake and up to the warm backwaters to breed, they become docile in the still, quiet backwaters of the estuary. Then when the time comes for them to travel they become as one, joining together to form a school to leave the Lake and return to the sea.

> You never see the breeders till the certain time of the year. They're sort of docile, up there all the time, and they're done the trip up there breeding, but when it's time to come, different changes of water, and things like that, you know when to travel and you know it sort of come in a school, in a school till, it breaks open or big tide and they'll just, it's all go. That's a certain type of mullet, but the other mullet, some of them go, but a lot of other mullet that's with them there, they stay there, and so it's a different kind of breeding mullet. They used to just spear 'em then. (Jerry Flanders)

The swamp is continuous with the Lake. In the upper parts of the Lake where the fish go to breed the waters are still and warm, and at the farthest reach of the estuary the water flows into the land to form the swamp. The swamp had a different rhythm from the lower part where the waters were open to the sea. It was marked by the different foods that were caught there and the fact that the water was fresh. At the swamp, Bing says, they caught turtles, eel, water birds and freshwater fish. The swamp is also remembered as a place where they spent the day doing their washing and catching and eating the food there.

Eating place

> Years ago we used to go to the swamp fishin' for eels and turtles, take our dinner up there, do all the washing all day. Yeah, big washing with old copper, big copper. You just make a fire and that there. Swim in the swamp. Yeah, turtle, big turtle there. We used to cut some grubs out of the trees, ti-tree there, and take 'em line up with a lot on it, and throw out, you would of caught one then. Any line, not really a fishing line, not too big, not real big. Anyway you don't know what's gonna get hold of it, could be a big eel. Little hook for the turtles, very small hooks. Yeah, put the grub on it, and throw it out. You're gonna get a turtle or an eel get hold of it. Nice freshwater fish. Would be our turtle, swamp turtle, yeah, loved 'em. I could eat a dozen of them. (Bing Laurie)

The many stories of washing day at the swamp stretch out in the rhythm of the day's outing. The trek up to the swamp carting the copper and all the clothes, making the fire to boil the copper, washing, rinsing and drying the clothes, and catching, cooking and eating food were all part of the day's activities. In Bing's story, the swamp food is told in all its intimate bodily detail – the grubs from the nearby ti-trees, the different-sized hooks, the quality of the line, and the surprise of what you might catch. There were freshwater fish, eel and swamp turtles. It was the swamp turtle, 'our turtle', that Bing relished in these memories.

> Yella belly fella you just throw it in the fire, you don't have to clean him out at all. Long neck, you gotta clean him out. Cut up at the bottom, the back legs, take hold [of the] legs and pull the guts out of it, the long-neck fellas. But the yella belly, you eat a yella belly like he is, throw him on the fire, eat him like that. And that's the best way to cook 'em, on the coals. Yeah cook 'em up there. Oh the eggs are beautiful eggs. Used to love the eggs. (Bing Laurie)

To clean and prepare turtle for cooking they had to learn how to tell one type from another. The long-neck turtle 'had a poisonous sack in it, so that when they put it over the coals, that was the first thing when they lifted the shell was to go looking for this sac'. The short-neck turtle, or the yella belly as Bing calls it, had no poison sac so it was just thrown on the coals in its shell and eaten. This body knowledge of animals and food was part of knowing the swamp.

All of the different parts of the estuary offer food according to their own rhythms and cycles. The salty water of the Lake near the opening to the sea is easy and safe. It is a place where children can play and begin to learn through catching prawns and fish there. The Lake changes with night and day, the opening and closing to the sea, and the larger cycles of weather, moon and tides. Each of the creatures that inhabits the Lake has particular breeding, feeding and seasonal patterns that respond to these changes. People know the movements and rhythms of the Lake, and the cycles and seasons of its creatures, through eating food from the Lake. They are all aspects of the intimate place knowledge that comes from eating from this place.

Through this intimate daily knowledge they knew that the Lake was the place that was most vulnerable to the arrival of the new settlers. It was the first of their food places to be lost.

Beach and rock pool

Down the beach
all along the beach
getting pipis 'n' fish,
love pipis.
I like m'pipis just chucked on the fire
and when they open up
you just eat 'em, beautiful like that.
Mum used to make curry pipis
curry pipis and gravy and fried scones.

Shellfish live in the in-between space of rock pools and sandy beaches. We find gugumbals, periwinkle and abalone in the rock pools at low tide and pipis in the sandy–watery space as the waves come and go. We went pipi collecting with a group of grannies, aunties, young women, children and dogs, all down on the beach, walking, talking and moving back and forward in the shallow waves. Catching pipis depends on deep concentration and a sort of soft vision, being aware of the movement of the waves back and forth, the glassy smoothness of the watery sand, and the appearance of tiny air holes as the wave recedes. Each time the water flows back lots of air holes bubble up in the sand and most of these belong to crabs. Pipi holes are smaller and have their own special look. There is only a brief moment when a wave goes back to recognise the hole and grab the pipi from under the sand as soon as its air hole appears. The women are adept at finding pipis, feeling them with their toes in the sand.

> There used to be hundreds of pipis, you could go straight down and fill up a bucket in an hour, half an hour. Now you've gotta walk. I reckon, walkin' really slow, it took us about two hours to get half a bucketful. I was teaching the kids though, they love 'em. They kept just chuckin' 'em in the pan, chuckin 'em in. The little ones eat 'em raw. Haydon knows how to find them and he got a couple of big ones down there the other day. He knows how to find the holes. He carried it in his pocket, the pipi he found, he ate every one. (Noeline Dootson)

Pipi-collecting stories resonate with the rhythm of the meditative walking back and forth along the edge of the waves. Men and women both collect and cook pipis but mostly it is the women who collect them and they are regarded as the staple diet when the men can't go fishing. Children learn when they are very young while they are playing and collecting pipis on the beach with the women. Haydon was only four when we went along the beach collecting pipis. He carried the bucket and the dog followed him closely, quickly grabbing Haydon's pipis if he was too slow and crunching the hard shells to eat their salty flesh. Noeline remembers when there used to be 'hundreds of pipis' and everyone has a story about another place where the pipis are bigger, easier to collect, more plentiful. Adult pipis move around the beach and in the larval stage pipis wash on the currents in the sea so it is unpredictable where and when they will arrive next. Up and down the coast people catch up with the news about where the latest pipis are.

> So they used to go all, well they used to follow the beach along, you know, and pipis, pipis move around. Like you might strike a heap of pipis here now, and maybe a month, two months later, they're gone. Well they just move up the beach. So, well, if I remember there at Moonee you used to get pipis there that big. Gee, they were big ones! Well and they just left and over the last ten years, I suppose, they've all moved up near Ballina. They reckon they get 'em up there as big, just as big as about anywhere you get pipis. (Tunny Skinner)

Everyone has a pipi recipe too, and favourite ways of preparing and cooking them. I came across Noeline one day when she had just collected and cooked pipis down at the Old Camp near the beach. She likes them straight, she said, with the salty taste from the sea. 'Just on the fire in their shells, a little bit burnt. Brings the taste right out, and then inside it's just all cooked. If you put 'em on a barbecue, they're cooking in their own juice in the shell and then it pops open.' When I collected pipis with the women we prepared them to make curry pipi gravy. We sat around together talking and laughing while we painstakingly cut the small amount of white flesh from each bivalve shell until we had enough to make a big pot of curry gravy. Auntie Marie asks me if I've had a feed of pipis every time I visit her. She tells me where they've recently been found and who to ask to collect them for me. She gives me the most comprehensive instructions about how best to prepare and cook them.

> Yes soak 'em, let 'em soak, 'cause they sort of spit their sand out. Lot of sand in 'em. If you don't, and if you open them straight away and cook 'em, they're just sand, crushin' sand, you'd be eatin' sand, 'specially that little black part, you get that out, that's where the sand is, the little black part at the end of it. Yeah, just cut that out, and you've got all this other white stuff then. And then you can either cut it up or cook it. You can cut it in halves, or quarters or put the whole lot in there. Please yourself. Curry it, bit of onion with 'em and a bit of cooked potato. You won't get the flavour if you cook them first. You can boil 'em and eat 'em straight out of the

shell, when they open up. We always done that, or we used to throw 'em in the coals with damper, that's all. I'd cook a damper in the ashes, beautiful. We used to have ashes damper all the time, yeah, it's so lovely. (Marie Edwards)

You learn the bodies of pipis and how they are still part of the place where they live when you prepare them. Soaking them in seawater keeps their salty taste and you have to cut out the sandy black part of their digestive system. If you cut out the raw flesh the pipis take up the flavour of the curry better but it takes a lot of time. Everyone loves the delicate taste of pipis and the knowledge of preparing and cooking them is a source of pride for both women and men. They are stretched to go round a large mob by making a curry gravy and damper, 'to make it go round for the family'. Damper, fried scones or johnny cakes are always an addition to a meal of shellfish. Auntie Marie says the best is damper cooked in the ashes made with the cobs of the banksia trees that grow on the sand dunes. Banksia cobs burn hot, making a fine ash, and the smoke from the burning pods infuses the damper. The damper gives the taste of the dunes and pipis the taste of the sea.

Pipis also represent continuity with a deep past in this place. 'Up in the dunes there's some places where the wind has eroded the soil there. Banks that deep and pipi shells from there to the top. They must've just lived on them there.' People have been collecting and eating pipis here since time began and the creation heroes left their traces in the piles of pipi shells in the great coastal middens. The shells in the midden at Arrawarra were exposed when big seas ate into the coastline. The midden was made up of a dense layer of shells where Gumbaynggirr people had eaten shellfish in that place thousands of years ago.

Walking along Arrawarra beach the midden was at eye level. Most of the shells were crushed pearly white but the beautiful spiral forms of the turban shells retained their shape. Some whole shells shone from the sand below and spiral remnants hung suspended from the midden on fine threads of roots. People call these shellfish by many names: 'button fish' for the round doors that cover the opening to the soft flesh, or the language names gugalungs and gugumbals.

> I call them conks and button fish, gugumbuls, they just the same, just clean 'em, clean 'em and just throw 'em in the coals there, usually if they're unwrapped. Few rocks around like, you might make a big fireplace, used to cook 'em there. They call 'em gugalungs, I call 'em just conks. (Jerry Flanders)

Gugumbals, or turban shells, are very different from pipis and to find them we were sent to the farthest edge of the rock platform. It is midday and low tide and I can see that the tide is very low by the exposed bright golden colour of the seaweed on the very edge of the rock platform. Closer, the waves are already washing over the outer edges where the gugumbals live. At this furthest point of low tide the rocks are thickly covered in seaweed that feels slippery and fleshy underfoot. The waves are washing over the rocks and everything in the rock pools shimmers and moves. In-between each wave I focus on the tiny spaces that open up between the thick beds of swaying seaweed. I can see shellfish and other creatures of every size, shape and colour but as soon as my eyes focus, another wave comes. All is constantly shifting in patterns of water and light. Try as I might I cannot see the turban shells that I have been sent to find.

As soon as I switch my energy into being in this place rather than searching, I see lots of mottled pink, blue, yellow, and brown-coloured turban shells. They are covered in lichen and crusted with worm corals, hidden in tiny underwater hollows. On their coiled shells there are calciferous worms, pink and green seaweeds, and lichens that mingle and move. It seems they are not one life but many. Turban shellfish are formed by living in this very edge space. They wait opportunistically for the movement of waves to wash their food over them. We collect a small bucketful and ask Auntie Marie how to cook them.

> You chuck 'em on the coals. The meat starts to come out by itself, but you might have to pull the rest of it out. Just cut off the black bit on the end, the little green bit, about that much [a finger joint], that's supposed to be the male. And the other one's yellow, like an egg, that's the female, you eat that. We used to just eat them with damper. (Marie Edwards)

We have no coals to chuck them on but others tell us to drop them into boiling water.

The gugumbals are so much like a whole living environment that when it comes to killing them I want to have the water boiling hard and drop them in really quickly so that the moment of dying is small. I think about Shirley saying don't listen to the screams of the pipis when you put them in the pot. I put the lid on and the smell changes from seaweed to one of boiling meat. Margie says they are ready when the flat round door comes loose and the flesh starts to pop out. 'You have to pull the flesh out like pulling a plug,' she says. I pull and whoosh, the whole flesh comes out stretched out long and then coils back to its original spiral form. I lay them on a board to look at their fleshy bodies curled up into their little coils and have to work out which are males and which are females.

Sorting out which bits to eat is a challenge because their bodies are so foreign. There is nothing about them that is easily identifiable in terms of what you can eat and what you can't. So in the middle of it all I ring Tony again and ask him what do you do with all that dark gritty sort of intestinal bit in the middle. He says to wash it out thoroughly under the tap to get all the dirt and sand out. Once the turban is cut down the middle it opens out into a sort of butterfly shape. There are still parts of minute but perfect portions of seaweed and even miniscule baby limpets intact in their digestive systems. And as the water washes through, soft frills of the inner walls bob in and out. Once we have extracted the last bit of seaweed and grit, it is nice then to chop them up finely, making a lovely little pile of diced meat, much more of it than I thought. I follow Uncle Bruce's recipe. He says to drop them into boiling water and then to chop the meat finely. Mix with Keen's curry powder, a mashed potato, a beaten egg and an onion. Roll in flour and fry lightly and serve with fried scone or damper. If you cook them too much they'll go tough, like abalone.

Abalone, like gugumbals, Jerry tells us, can be found on the farthest reach of low tide. Their soft bodies are protected by a hard shell, and their flesh has the same frilled body parts that filter the waves to extract the small particles of food that wash over them. Their meat has a tendency to grow tough with cooking and people have particular ways of preparing and cooking them so they stay tender and delicate in flavour. Jerry says to just cook it on the coals but to watch it and cook it very slowly. Gloria has a more elaborate method of using gauze and a mallet.

> Abalones will do it on you, if you overcook abalones it's like a bit of boot to chew. What you do with your abalones, because the flesh is tender and soft, you get a piece of gauze and you put that abalone inside. Right? This is after you've clean it and everything so, so to soften that – say for instance you're gonna put it into egg and breadcrumbs and fry it like that, all you need is a little mallet and you touch that very gently like that [tap-taps]. Once you've accomplished that, then you just put it into the egg and breadcrumbs and oh, it's beautiful. Abalone and conk. They're very similar to eat those two, very similar taste they got. (Gloria Phillips)

All of these shellfish live in the places between the tides of beach and rock platform. Collecting shellfish from these places means getting to know these watery edge spaces. Preparing and cooking shellfish is also a process of learning about their bodies and the ways they are adapted to the places where they live. Eating them means taking part of this place into our own bodies and becoming part of beach, rock pools and sea. When shellfish are eaten, the hard shells that protect their soft flesh are left behind to make the middens that tell us about the great feasts of times past. The stories of the hero ancestors connect these signs to the time of creation when all beings are made and remade in the telling.

Sea

They go fishing there every day
most the time
it's mainly bream and whiting.
I love tailor
you get 'em round the headlands
they go along the surf beach

just a matter of throwing a line out
you used squid for 'em or just use a spinner
when you see 'em choppin' up the sea
or you see the seagulls diving all the time.
When that wattle is out
that's when the bream comes along.

The sea gives us both extraordinary and everyday stories of eating place. As Tony said, the food in the Lake was just there for the taking, while fishing in the sea was more of a challenge. The sea stretches beyond the horizon to places that are unknown. It is vast, powerful and unpredictable, and in creation stories it has a personality of its own. Fishing stories are heroic, taking their power from the sea, and fishing itself is unpredictable so is associated with mysterious and cosmic powers. Heroic fishing stories give a sense of continuity with the past. Auntie Marie told us how Clarrie Skinner could hear the jewfish choppin' a mile from the sea. He'd leave their shack and come back with jewfish as tall as himself. There are the stories of the extraordinary abundance of the great mullet run when people from the west would come to the coast for ceremony. And there is the iconic story about the power of Gumbaynggirr language to sing the dolphins in from the sea.

> Well the dolphins would be travelling the fish along, you know. And when they'd see them they'd sing out in the lingo. And the dolphins'd all come around in groups, bring all the fish in. And the fish'd all be comin' up in the waves flappin' and flappin'. They'd run down and get 'em, get what they wanted and the dolphins'd keep going again. But they'd cooee, they'd sing out in the lingo. Yeah, when the tide goes back see they're layin' there, and they just took what they wanted, bream, whiting, jewfish or tailor, snapper, or whatever. (Marie Edwards)

This iconic story about the Old People tells us about the relationship between the dolphins, the fish and the Old People. This relationship is mediated by the power of their Gumbaynggirr language to communicate with the dolphins. It is a story of plenitude and grace. The only thing the people had to do was sing to the dolphins and the sea delivered all they wanted – 'bream, whiting, jewfish, tailor, snapper, or whatever'. In a similar tone Bing sings in language to Baali, the Lord, to deliver him some fish when he's hungry.

> I only just go down now and sing out 'Ngura nganya, Baali', that means give me a fish. When I go fishing, 'Ngura nganya Baali', give me a feed, Lord, I'm hungry. 'Yaam nganya minandiju', I'm hungry, give me a fish. Yeah, every time I go fishing, when I see the sea, just before I throw m'line out, sing out to him, sing out to the Lord. Give me a fish. When you're really hungry, sing out to him you're hungry. He'll give you something, always come home with something, always something to get hold of. (Bing Laurie)

The sea gives them the gift of fish to satisfy their hunger. As well as heroic and special stories of fishing there are everyday stories too. People fished to survive and fishing was part of the fabric of everyday life. The most common fishing place was the closest part of the sea. 'That's the main part – we fished on the beach. Right down the front of the Lake there.' On off-pay week the rods that sit in a row on the verandah of Bruce's house 'have all gone fishing'. 'I still fish. Might even go this evening. I went down yesterday got a bream.' There are always stories of fishing, what fish are biting, who has caught fish, what they have caught and where they caught it.

> Lived off the fish mainly. Bream – we used to fish for bream and whiting and everything like that. Jew sometimes, you know. Go down at night time, straight over the bank, fish for jew. I remember me sister there, we went out one day, the mullet were there, 'cause they wouldn't let me go with them there one day, across the creek. She got whiting about that big – coupla big whiting, real big ones, huge, straight down where that camp was we was tellin' about the camp, straight over the terrace. Went down there fishin', me and Jean, me elder sister. I was pretty young then. Yeah nice one. Never ever starved down there. It was good. (Bruce Laurie)

When they caught large fish, like Clarrie's jewfish, there was enough to feed a large family. At Christmas time the meal was usually fish, or fish would be exchanged for kangaroo or wallaby for a change. 'Someone'd be down there fishing, and they caught a heap of fish, they'd take some around to everybody.' In times of abundance fish were shared or bartered for other food. 'I used to catch forty-six fish a day, a sugarbag full of tailor. I used to take 'em up to all around here, people I knew up there. Me old fella used to know a lot of white people up here, used to take up there and share it around.' In this way fishing was part of an economy of daily life and it was also economical.

They caught their own bait – worms, pipis, cunjevoi, prawns and crabs – and sold worms to holidaymakers for pocket money. Fishing lines were rescued from amongst the seaweed and driftwood on the beach. They improvised every sort of fishing gear, threading their fish on seaweed to carry them – 'we just put the seaweed through the gill and out through the mouth to keep a line of 'em on it' – and they made sinkers from the lead in old telegraph poles. No part of the fish was wasted, even the oil from the sea mullets was collected to use for fat lights. People remember the dailyness and centrality of fishing to their lives and the seasons of the year were measured by the great cycles and movements of the fish in the sea. 'Yeah, all different signs you've gotta watch when different fish is comin' through.'

> I tell you, here, one time ago, like, the sea mullet, when they come along, you get the white butterfly. They come and swarm, they fly through, and they say, 'Oh, the sea mullet's close'. Sure enough, a coupla days after, along come the sea mullet. I know people who could smell the fish. Funny, everyone got their own ways of doing little things, and that's one of them. And also that was another butterfly too, oh, and the dogwood, when the dogwood's out – they had their little signs, anyway. The flowers, or the animals, like birds or that, how they behave. Yeah, seasonal things. Tell how they sort of fitted in with everything else. The white butterfly, he was the one before the sea mullet, that's what I can remember plain. They used to come along thick, and as they'd fly, they'd fly north, just ahead of the sea mullet, just before winter they'd come in. Say, like, get out there then. They had all their

> little signs for things to come along. 'Specially, it's all right if you're at the beach all your life. This is all Gumbaynggirr area. (Paul Taylor)

If you live at the beach all your life you learn to read the signs of the Gumbaynggirr landscapes that tell you when the fish are coming. They tell you how the seasons of the flowers, animals and birds are linked to the seasons of the sea and everything is interconnected. There are signs for the weekly and daily rhythms of fishing. The Old People taught Milton how to read the weather. 'If they're all southerly you don't fish 'cause that's chopped the sea up. If it come from the nor'-east it's all right, or from the nor'-west 'cause that'll blow, comin' off the land.' Bruce says that the best time to fish is two nights before or two nights after the full moon and with the moon come the king tides. In the old days fish were caught in the fish traps at Arrawarra in the full moon in winter when there were two high tides in one night. This would have been the time of the greatest season of all, the time of the great mullet run.

> They used to travel, right on the first of April they used to get out here, could expect a mob the first of April. The bays were that black with sea mullet, you know, you could smell them from down at home there. You could smell the sea mullet. See it's that thick. They used to travel in schools, big schools – just black stretched right along the beach. You'd never miss mullet. Yeah, it was good fun getting it. And really big ones, you know, these were big sea mullets. Yes. Oh, it used to be good fun. You'd go up the banks and the bay's just packed and the waves could hardly break they were that thick. Especially low tide. That's the biggest what I've seen. Back in the sixties I suppose, be when Mum passed away, she passed away. And shark, just on low tide, you'd see the biggest sharks, following along there, school, they'd be stuck on the sand spit here and everything, yeah.
> (Bruce Laurie)

Eating place

Every year the people waited for the schools of sea mullet to pass the coast of Corindi Beach. The mullet run is always described in the most spectacular terms. 'The waves could hardly break they were that thick' or 'Like one permanent cloud on the shoreline for months on end'. There were so many fish that people could smell them as they travelled. Jerry says the smell of the sea mullet is like the smell of fresh seaweed. When they recognised the signs of the mullet run they would go to the top of the dune to watch them passing through.

> We used to go on the beach, me and Bingie and Keith, sit on the sandhill, watch, and see a big school comin' along, on the sandhill up there, round near the rock on the bay there, this side of the headland. They used to be that thick, the waves could hardly break. And sharks, big sharks'd follow, low tide, and they was that thick, miles long, just black with mullet. We used to jag 'em, y'know, years ago. When the white butterfly comes, one time they come on the twenty-fifth of April, but always come on the first of April. Get all the leaders first, go fishing at night, that's when the jewfish biting, even the tailor follow 'em along. (Bruce Laurie)

The excitement of the event is matched by the excitement of the stories. Jerry tells how the travelling schools of mullet are accompanied by a frenzy of feeding and fishing. There are jewfish and tailor to catch as well as mullet. The water erupts when it is time to feed, signalling that it is a dangerous time to swim. The tons of mullet are accompanied by sharks who swim beneath the schools, not visible through the black mass of the mullet. It is a time to respect the power of the sea and its creatures.

> It's a dangerous time to go swimming, from January to April and May, about the end of May, that's when all the mullets, trevally, other fish as well but mainly the mullet, which they let off a smell that's very distinctive, you can smell 'em the same as jewfish, the smell of jewfish. It also attracts sharks and

> real dangerous time, that's a lot of tons of mullet, you know, but underneath that, which you don't know are there, all you can see is a black mass, but they always got this big school of sharks travelling underneath 'em. They all, when it's time to feed, and you can see the water just erupt, and just go crazy, 'cause the sharks underneath it, following, this is a dangerous time to swim. When some of the stragglers they come in looking, some of them attack and they blame it on the people then, themselves, but it's not the people, it's just you've got to watch yourself, you know if there's mullet around, don't swim in the water. (Jerry Flanders)

There is a sense of resolution once the fish are caught and eaten. Stories of the different ways of cooking mullet and using their oil are about their abundance. Cooking the mullet is mostly a simple affair. Cooking was often done on the coals in fires dotted along the beach, echoing the past. The methods of cooking are about their oiliness, the taste of the flesh linked to the smell, the mullet run, and the seasons and cycles of the sea.

> Cook the fish in a pan you know and a fire. Didn't worry about it at all, those days. Or put them on the fire and boil them, make a curry soup out of them. Or you make, if it's sea mullet, just put him behind the coal, you know on the grid iron, sheet of grid iron or somethin, cooks in its own oil it's so fat. That's when they cook 'em on the fire, top of the fire, 'cause it tastes better than frying, it's too fat to fry. Oh they're beautiful when you grill 'em, over an open fire. We get the grid out of a fridge, you get an old fridge. Sometimes they put 'em on the coals, you know. Like just put 'em there, could be nice. I like 'em better – well fried are all right, but they're real greasy, you know, fried. Very oily fish those sea mullets. (Bruce Laurie)

In the old days the mullet run was a time of ceremony and gathering when large groups of people could be fed. They travelled from all of the nearby places to meet and celebrate life by the sea. The celebration continues today in the stories of the mullet run. Fishing and eating fish from the sea make the texture of daily lives. Fish were survival. The stories tell about the heightened sensory awareness of the sights, smells and sounds of the sea that fishing brings. Knowledge of the rhythms of moon and tides, the feeding, breeding and movements of the fish, the weather and of the great seasons and cycles of the sea are all part of knowing these local places through fishing.

Bush

We weren't short on a roo or two
or a goanna, porcupine or possum.
We used to vary the diet
if it was too rough to fish,
some of those southerlies used to blow down there
blow for a week or more
then ya couldn't go 'round fishin',
so ya go out and get a roo
that was your staple diet with damper
you lived on that till it blows over.

The bush tucker walk between Yarrawarra and the Lake wanders through the bush of No Mans Land. Closest to the road it's open forest with native grasses under the spreading branches of swamp mahoganies, bloodwoods and stringybarks. As the ground becomes more swampy the track becomes a boardwalk winding through paperbarks and ti-tree and cut to shape to fit their branches. In some places there are still some rainforest trees draped with coastal vines. These coastal bushlands are rich in bush tucker, usually thought of as plant foods, although many animals are eaten from the bush. These plant foods are casually eaten as people walk through these coastal landscapes. They are walking food.

> During the day when we was runnin' 'round everywhere, you'd just get whatever was growin'. Fruit or them little vines, eat all that, every day. Like we used to live on the

pigface, every day, you know, get a heap of that and eat it as you was goin' along, or wild cherries at the back there, or roly-polys, them little five-corner fruits. When you was on the beach if you get hungry you just go over the top of the headland, get some stuff when you was goin' along. Lilly pillies, all different sorts. Comin' back this way from Washaway you used to get purple ones there. You used to get a pink one and a white one. Yeah, 'cause that's where the wild cherry there, about half way to Red Rock, along there, wild cherries all along the back. And geebungs, wild raspberries, strawberries. It was mainly when you were walkin', you know, when you were walkin'. (Tony Perkins)

When people tell stories of eating these bush fruits they mentally walk along the tracks where they find them, locating special plants as they go. The plants are named by their fruits – geebungs and roly-poly bushes, five-corners, nyums-nyums and lilly pillies – that they eat as they go. The native fruit trees like the wild cherry, black plum and lilly pilly are special and known by the places where they grow. People remember exactly where they are and their walking tracks purposely intersect with them. Travelling through the bushlands to hunt was connected to the sweet pleasures of the bush. 'They'd go shootin' and go way out for honey same time. That was the goodest, best sweet, better than sugar plum, better than sugar, pick ya up, y'know, honey. They're the trees down there, yeah, only them old trees.' The scars of the toe holes on the trunks of the big old eucalypt trees show where they climbed the tree to collect honey in the bush immediately around the Lake.

People told stories about eating kangaroo and wallaby, possum, porcupine, goanna, flying fox, carpet snake and various birds from the nearby bushlands, although these were mainly stories of the old days. Hunting for animals in the bushlands was seen as an alternative to eating fish. Jerry said if the weather was too rough to go fishing they survived off roos from the bush. For Clarrie Skinner, the legendary fisherman who never ate fish, wallaby was his favourite food and Auntie Marie described how they roasted a leg of wallaby in the camp oven for him. Kangaroo and wallaby were shared as special foods at Christmas time to complement the usual fish and pipis.

> It was more like a time when you'd see everyone walking around to one another. Like someone'd come along the night before and he'd have a leg of wallaby there, sharin' it around to everybody. Food and fish, if someone's go and get the biggest bag of pipis, share it out, then take some round to everybody. Someone'd be down there fishin' and they caught a heap of fish so they'd do the same thing. Then you'd see another one, might be you'd see someone with a sugarbag over their shoulder, you'd know that they had a leg of wallaby, kangaroo in it. It was more or less a sharin' sort of time. (Tony Perkins)

A single kangaroo provides a substantial amount of food, so killing and eating kangaroo was a significant event. Kangaroo stories are told as a performance because they were much rarer than wallabies and more special. 'There's not enough around, but there's plenty of wallabies out the back.' Gloria told the following kangaroo event story as a childhood memory. In this story, everyone is hungry and they are waiting for a feed when their dad and uncle appear with a kangaroo.

> We were all hungry. Yeah, and they were all around the camp fire there down at our place, see, and Auntie Sadie come over and she was saying, 'Oh, they should be back soon'. And Uncle Jimmy, he was the first one we seen comin' through the bush there, and 'Oh, there's Uncle Jimmy, eh'. 'Oh, he's still comin' now, my girl. I left him, I got too tired.' Then they were talkin' in the lingo then, my Mum and Auntie Sadie and old Pa Laurie too. He came behind Uncle Jimmy then. 'Oh, where's the old fella?' 'Oh, he's still comin' there.' Now [chuckling] someone's gonna run down lookin' for the old fella comin', eh. Still waitin'. Next thing, here comes Dad [Tom Flanders], and he can only just walk and this big bloody kangaroo over his shoulder, pullin' that along. Bit of a change from the seafoods I think. Ah, God, Uncle Jimmy whistlin', cuttin' it up. Dropped the skin off. Ah – the kids pounced on it then to put it onto the coals. Not enough around, there's plenty out the back – wallabies. (Gloria Flanders)

This story is the performance of the hunter. The characters in this story are the Old People: Jimmy Runner, Old Tom Flanders, Old Pa Laurie, Auntie Sadie, and Gloria's mum. They are all sitting around the campfire at Flanders Camp by the Lake. It is dark and Jimmy Runner appears from the bushes, playing a trick on the waiting children until Old Tom appears with a kangaroo over his shoulder. Uncle Jimmy whistles as he skins and cuts the kangaroo according to the rules of sharing. Michael McDougall also explained how he learned the intricacies of skinning and cutting up a kangaroo from the Old People.

> And they taught us how to skin a kangaroo. You turn him up side down, and start from the hind legs, and cut him open, skin him and that. Cut around the joint of the tail, and it's split down the tail and that, cut down, and just pull the skin off then. Yeah, right down to the shoulder blade, to over the shoulders, down to the head, and then take the head off, and open the belly up then. Yeah, they clean it and wash it, do all of that.
>
> They used to make drums out of it, just old ordinary drums, that you know, used to make, put it on a old cheap box and that. And make the sinew, making bows and arrows out of 'em, they make the bows and they had to get the arrows for them. Oh that's all, mainly, they used to do with it, oh and used to cut 'em up and used to get dry [the skin], just put around ya for night time, keep warm.
> (Michael McDougall)

When an animal was killed every part was dealt with carefully so that everything could be used. As well as Michael's story about using the skin and sinews, Gloria describes how every part was eaten – 'the ribs, and around the side, and tail soup' – and how her mother used to put gumleaves into the stuffing to vary the flavour. This kind of knowledge of eating food from the bush continues today when these local foods are still eaten. The knowledge about others, like carpet snake, possum, flying fox and 'parrot soup', are preserved in stories of times past. The most extended and detailed of these old stories were told about the porcupine. These were particularly associated with the Old People and a past way of life.

> I can remember eatin' porcupine with Old Ma, and Mum and Dad in that house. I remember Old Clarrie, Old Baba when he used to be ready to go and get a porcupine, he'd have a bag, and he'd have a mirror. He used to go down the front from us through the bush there, where all them houses are now, in a hollow log, and the way he'd know, he'd sort of shine it at the sun, and he'd look into the mirror and it'd show him what was up in that log, whether there was a porcupine there. And he'd put the bag on one side, and he'd make a smoke on the other and the porcupine would run out the other side into the bag. It was easy. You didn't have to have fifteen guns or whatever. Use a bag and a mirror. But, I mean, now things are changing. When I was growing up and Mum and that, there was no way any woman would be allowed to have a porcupine, or a piece to eat. It was men's food. (Glenda Perkins)

These traces of place, ritual, the Old People and food are important connections to places in the present. Bing remembered how his father hunted porcupine with his dog in the sandy hills down near Red Rock. He trained his dog by rubbing the smell of the echidna on its nose. Once caught, the echidna takes a long time to prepare. Tony described how Clarrie used to break the bottom of a glass bottle and shave the edges to make it knife sharp in the same way they made stone knives. They used this implement for shaving the quills off the porcupine. Bing's story of preparing the porcupine is remarkably detailed and complex, revealing the extent of care that the Old People went to in the preparation of food.

> Yeah, oh you put it in hot water. Big kerosene, old kerosene drum. Boil that up, boil it and keep dipping it in now and then you know, put him back down and prise the ones off, you pull all the fine part out then, all the [spines], don't take any guts part out of it. It's a hard way to clean 'em, I don't

know how, you know shove grass and everything in 'em you
know, clean out sort of like that, grass and all that we should
be, me sister used to knew how to do it, Valerie used to take
great notice of Old People cookin'. She knows how to clean
all them things like that, porcupine, mainly porcupine 'cause
that was really hard. Pull the tongue out and tie the tongue,
all the tongue use' to tie it in knots, just tie it and pull it right
out and tie it in knot. And then they get wire piece, not that
copper wire, never used copper wire, just used plain wire.
Get the wire, sew the guts, middle part up, and then he's
ready to cook. Oh just, you used to put it on that, you keep
your big fire going all night, you got a lot of big tins there,
old boards you know, just put that on that, make sure the fire
up, he get brown all night, keep turnin' over and over
all night he does, you gotta have patience for 'em things.
(Bing Laurie)

The knowledge of eating food from the bush was intimate body knowledge. The intricacies of preparing and cooking porcupine is slow food at its best. 'You gotta have patience for 'em things.' Bing's father would stay up all night cooking it long and slow, turning all night by the fire until it was cooked to perfection.

I ate old porcupine, he's the best of all of 'em, that porcupine.
Yeah, like the Old People cook it you know. You have to
have patience to cook it. All night me old fella would be
there alongside the fire, lay there all night, and watch it cook,
lovely and brown he'd give us, just like a little pick, beautiful,
Mum used to cut it open to the gut part, cut and take that
part out then. Beautiful, it's better, better than all meat. Oh
the juice is beautiful, beautiful juice, dip the damper in the
juice, beautiful. (Bing Laurie)

Each of the animals had their own particular rituals of hunting, preparation and cooking, depending on the nature of the animal, their particular habitat and the means of transforming their flesh into food. This close relationship to the bodies of animals and the places they inhabit is fundamental to eating place. Each of the animals was known in its body – where it lived, how to catch it, which parts to eat and which not to eat, how to cook it so that the pleasure of eating was the greatest. Their understanding of the nature of this animal–human relationship through eating place is most closely expressed in the concept of totem.

> Possum and all, I remember we got a possum there at the racecourse. Took about half an hour for them to drop out of the tree. I would never touch a possum. They used to cook 'em like that, an easy method without even skinnin' 'em, you chuck 'em on the fire – burn all the fur off 'em first. I wouldn't touch a possum because that's Dadda's totem – was a possum, whereas Mum's totem was a python. And I would never kill a python. But gee a lot of 'em dead on the road, they're di' of a night – dead everywhere, possums. Yeah, get killed – all on the road. (Gloria Flanders)

Gloria's brother, Jerry, adds to this story of the possum totem. 'Didn't get too many possums. Maybe one or two, that was my dad's totem, he was a possum. So it runs in my family too. So they're sort of more or less sacred to us, and can only eat one. They didn't mind us taking one, to eat.' In the full expression of this relationship between animal and human, the group of people who belong to that animal are believed at one level to be that animal, becoming the animal in increase ceremonies to protect the species. In the absence of ceremony, this translates for Gloria into her deep empathy for possums and for Tom to a sense of the possum as 'sacred'. This sense of the sacred is also expressed in the Garby Elders' identification with the gaabi, the black-faced wallaby of the coastal bushlands.

While the people continue to eat plant foods as they walk through all of this country, the stories of hunting, killing and eating animals are mainly from the old days. These stories and practices represent a different form of knowledge from the casual eating of bush fruits as you walk. It is a knowledge that comes from the connection with these animals that was ritualised in ceremony. These stories from the Old People preserve the traces of the ritual understandings through which the life force of these animals and their places is nurtured and protected. Traces of these practices live on in the stories of eating place, and also in the storylines and special places of the creation ancestors.

River

Down past the bridge used to get cobra
lot of oak trees used to fall in the water
rotten logs layin' in the water
you'd see the marks in the log
where the holes'd be
you knew they were there
bust the log on a rock to open it out
there's lots
you'd never starve in a day
got lots of thing to eat.

The Corindi River flows parallel to the coastline of No Mans Land towards Red Rock. There are river stories about the Red Rock River at the Old Farm, about Old Ma fishing in the river and Clarrie singing along the river in the handmade boat. The only time I have been taken to the river where it runs closest to No Mans Land was to see the Widow Tree. This tree is the place where widows went to grieve and I wonder whether it's connected to the place on the river where the massacre story began. It was here that the quiet everyday scene of washing at the river was so violently interrupted. Tony tells another story of washing day by the river, a day when all the family went to the river and the river yielded its plentiful food.

> Every Sunday you'd start, and then if you'd never got it all
> done on a Sunday you'd carry it over till the Monday. There's
> a lot of wild cherry all down the banks, used to go there
> and get a lot of them. Bush lemons used to be there. Used to
> catch all the – down below the creek some of us used to go
> to the other side, fresh sort of water, water was brackish, fresh
> up this other way, brackish down a bit further where it meets

the salt. Used to be a lot of fish in there then. You used to get
the perch where the salt and the freshwater met. We used to
get a lot there. You used to get a lot of eels underneath that
old bridge. We'd bring 'em home and throw 'em on the coals.
You'd get big ones there. Oh you'd get turtles in there, there
was a lot of turtles in there. (Tony Perkins)

Washing was an all-day affair, or even two-day affair, and while they were at the river they caught and collected the many foods to eat. Wild cherries, the favourite dark red fruit of one of the lilly pilly trees, and bush lemons – an introduced fruit gone wild – were picked from the banks of the river. There were eels and turtles, the same as they caught in the swamp, part of the same ecology as the river. But the real focus of food in this story is the fish they caught in the brackish water, the place where saltwater and freshwater meet. The nature of the river as a food place is produced by the quiet rhythms of the ebb and flow of the tide that brings the saltwater to meet with the fresh.

> Used to get a – sometimes if you're gonna test out if there's
> any fish in there, you get that, like a bulrush, like a reed, and
> you'd twist it till you got a sharp spike on the one end. Well
> you break it off, might be six inches long or something, then
> you bend it to make a circle out of it, then you'd push that
> through so that you've got a circle with the spike end through
> it. Then you let it float out on the water and as it goes out, on
> the water, it'll sort of expand and when it expands the sharp
> point'll come out, and it'll flick on the water, and see the fish
> think that's something fallen in the water and you can see
> the bubble come up and you know straight away that there's
> something there. (Tony Perkins)

Catching fish at the river depends on knowing where the saltwaters and freshwaters meet, and how each place in the river lives. These are the distinctive rhythms or pulses of the river. Unlike the sea, which is ever turbulent, the ebb and flow of the river is almost imperceptible. The still surface of the water responds to the slightest disturbance, like the flicker of a reed. The fish, in turn, will respond to that slight disturbance because it might be food for them, and the fishermen cannily imitate this ripple using the reeds that grow there, so as not to reveal a human presence.

> We used to get them cicadas, little baby sort of ones, and we used to put them on the hook and throw 'em out and let 'em float. You don't throw with heavy things, like you used to have a light line there an' you get something that'll still be flappin' around a bit, and you throw so that it'll land in the same part. The fish'd grab 'em. They'd come up and get 'em. 'Cause they think the first time that something fell there, so the second time they're thinking, when it's landed on top of the water, then they just come straight up and they grab it. Oh yeah they'd come out after it if you trick 'em into it, sort of, when they went to bite it. Perch, or the mullet. The mullet'll take it too, like that, same way. They're waitin' on it, you know, waitin' for somethin' to drop on the water.
> (Tony Perkins)

Catching the fish takes part in this rhythm, the line must be light and the bait alive and moving. Cicadas can be used for bait because they imitate these disturbances. Hunting ducks extends this participation in the same still, quiet rhythms of the river:

> The same with the ducks. Get in the water, and goin' slowly out, same thing, the duck'll sit there. You put a different sort of sound, it was sort of sung, or talked and sung, sort of thing. Well what they used to do, down here, the ducks was on a pond like that. They used to get in the water, right? Whether they was goin' towards the water and get in the water, they'd sort of sing to 'em, or talk, or half sing, talk and the duck'd sit there. Then they'd go under the water then with just a reed and breathe out of the reed, and then

they'd just swim along underneath and just pull a duck down
underneath. And he'd sit there. He wouldn't move while
they walked towards them, until they got under the water.
(Tony Perkins)

In order to catch the duck the Old People had to become the duck within the duck's habitat. They immersed themselves in the water, sang to the duck in duck sounds, and breathed through a reed so they could breathe underwater. Becoming part of the river in this way means to know the river in all its forms. The river was known through all the foods that were eaten there, the turtles and the eel, the waterbirds and the freshwater fish. The river was also known through the cobra.

Cobra, or sea worm, are strongly associated with the Old People and with Gumbaynggirr cultural practice because they are not eaten by white people. Cobra are eaten raw or cooked and used as medicine. They are difficult to collect now because the river is cut off from No Mans Land with fences that signal private property. In this sense the river is a place of loss and fond memories. In the old days cobra collecting, like washing days at the river, was an all-day affair when they took all the implements they needed for cooking and set off to walk down the river to the back of the Old Farm.

> Used to get the cobra out of the oak logs, back of the Old
> Farm there, when we used to just feel like goin' to get a feed
> of cobra. We used to all go and just packed a – just put the
> bags – the frying pan, billy can and that, grab an axe and
> flour and tea, sugar and put it in an old sugarbag, and used to
> go down back of the Old Farm. Grab a fishin' line as well,
> just throw a line out, fish there, leave the line set an' get an
> axe and get a tomahawk and go and get the cobra out of the
> oak tree then. (Michael McDougall)

Cobra grow in fallen logs, mainly the casuarinas or river oaks, that grow along the banks of the river. They were collected by using an axe to cut into the fallen logs, which must be partly green rather than dead; the cobra are part of a living ecosystem.

> Get cobra under the logs. In them times you could walk through these places. The main log to get it out of is an oak. Yeah, but not dead, it's got to be half green. So they live in a log, you see 'em movin'. Like make a little cut in it with an axe, then you just go like that, and they'd all just fall out. (Keith Lardner)

The best cobra grow where the saltwater meets the fresh, in the fertile brackish water where all life forms are most plentiful. The precise quality of the water is read by its turbidity, a little bit of mud but not too much. When the right spot is chosen the still-green rotting logs are found and chopped open in the right way to yield up the long silvery worms.

> Oh, you can see into the hole in the log there. The muddy – not real muddy water, sorta just ordinary brackish water, you know. You see the logs there, you just go and chop the log there, or bring it out, or you can just pull him out. When you're trying to do that they're likely to break. And you can put them up on the bag and spread 'em open an' then out comes the cobra then. Bang the wood onto the other woods, and out comes the cobra then. Or doesn't matter whether you cut it or not, you know, because there's that many in there. They look like a long sorta like a worm, like a sea worm but haven't got no legs, just like a worm itself but long and silvery. You can get 'em about five foot, somethin' like that, pretty long. Yeah, thicker than your thumb some o' them. They're beautiful. (Michael McDougall)

The biggest cobra are highly prized, growing especially large where the conditions are the best. These conditions include the mix of salt and fresh water, the stillness and movement of the river, the presence of the right sort of trees, the logs that are left to rot in the water for just the right amount of time. The way the cobra are collected is important so as not to cut or mash their soft flesh. In telling this story Michael imagines the 'beautiful' taste of the cobra after it is cooked. I can't even imagine eating them, let alone the taste, and I ask Michael to describe the cooking.

> You just fry 'em up with curry and onion. Fry 'em up. Beautiful really. We eat 'em down there. Used to bring some home in big old tins and cook 'em up when we got home here. You can eat 'em raw if you want to, but I'd rather have 'em curried up. I did a few times [eat them raw] but I don' like the taste of him raw. I like 'em when they're fried, fried just beautiful. It's hard to explain what it – no taste for it really – you can taste a little bit of salt in 'em, not that much though, gotta little bit o' wood taste in 'em, in the woods all that time you can taste that bit of wood in 'em. (Michael McDougall)

Like all their foods, cobra could be eaten very simply on the spot or taken home and cooked in more elaborate ways. For Michael, they are beautiful cooked with curry and onion, but what he likes most is the taste of the place in the body of the animal, the mixture of salt and fresh, and of the wood from the logs where cobra grow and feed.

At the most fertile place in the river where the salt and fresh waters meet the fish are best and the cobra grow their biggest. Like the other foods that are eaten from this place, the foods of the river taste of its particular flavours, the mixing of salt and fresh water, and the wood of rotting logs. The pulse of the river is slow and quiet and its foods belong in the same silent rhythm. Catching the river's foods requires one to be part of that rhythm, to become one with the bubble on the surface of the water.

All of the places where food is collected and eaten have their own pulse or rhythm that produces the bodies of the creatures that live in that place. These bodies have their own particular characteristics that are learned in finding, collecting, preparing and eating these foods. In this way Yarrawarra people take part of the place into their bodies, giving them an intimate connection to the place by incorporating it into their own being. In the intense engagement required to collect and eat food people learn the intimate embodied knowledge of their local places. This was the basis of ceremony. Today, through this, they know and care deeply about the health of particular places like the Lake. They learn to read the signs, the place speaks to them through their daily activities. This intimate knowledge from eating place is the basis of caring for country, and of understanding the health and wellbeing of country and the people who live there.

CHAPTER 5

Spirits in places

It's early morning, soft and quiet on the sandy track, walking past the camp. All are sleeping, even the camp dogs don't stir and the fishing rods wait on Bruce's verandah. On the gnarly trunk of a swamp mahogany tree I run my hands down the smooth scar where Old Tom Flanders cut the bark for his hut. Did his fingers feel the smooth inside place where my hands run down its strong-bodied trunk? Further down the track, paperbarks lean their raggedy trunks and catch the early morning sun on peeling paper skin, smooth enough to write a story on. My big toes wriggle into the toe holes as I haul myself up the tree where Jimmy Runner collected honey from the wild bees. Clutch and haul but can't quite make it up the tree. They say he tracked a single bee by attaching a feather to its leg to find out where the honey was. Out of the paperbark swamp the surprise of blue, always the surprise of this opening to the sea. My eye follows the curved line of estuary, past where the buried canoe lay, to the hidden place of the Fig Tree camp. The place where the fat lamp, flaked glass and pieces of patterned china were bundled under a scatter of gaudy parrot feathers on that first day. There, standing bright white against blue water and green mangroves are three white egrets.

What are the spirits of these coastal places and how can I get to know them?

I had not intended to write about spirits but the spirit presences that inhabit these places and their stories were insistent. Because we began with archaeology we had asked lots of questions about the material translations of No Mans Land. Then there were daily conversations about food and eating from these places so I began to learn by living off the land and sea. I had never specifically asked about spirits in places but when I looked at the body of stories there was a profusion of stories about spirit presences and the spirit powers of the Old People, about special places and initiation. I began to think of these as multiple 'spirits in places' in contrast to the more dominant idea of a singular, transcendent 'spirit of place'. The spirits that have come to inhabit this text are particular spirits with their own stories that I have become familiar with over a long time. They are related to a complex and evolving spiritual practice that dwells in the space between the time prior to, and the time after, white settlement. They live in the stories and places of the Old People, they are spirits of the in-between.

This writing about spirits in places begins from a place of unknowing. This is an ontological stance, in which knowledge unfolds through my engagement with the stories. I have a conversation with them in which I try to understand. Sometimes this conversation is mimicry as that is the first way one learns – by repeating what one hears. This is how I had to learn to interview Bing as his words and language were so foreign that even though he was mostly speaking in English it was almost impossible for me to understand the meaning of his stories. I had to repeat each small narrative section of his stories to know that I was following the sense of them. In an oral culture learning is like this. It is circular, repetitive and iterative. It builds up from listening and being there for a long time, hearing the same stories over and over. I want to parallel this experience of learning in this text.

It is challenging to write about this partial and incomplete knowledge. It is hard to write the sense of the missing bits, the importance of silence and of respecting what cannot be said. It is important to tell these partial stories in a way that they are not experienced only as absence but as fertile potential. I draw on the other sense that the spirits have always been there, immanent in my place writing. I am a writer of these places; that is the work I bring to this text. When I am in these places with soft vision I am surrounded by the spirits of the Old People, in all the stories I know. I have been introduced to them from the beginning, intentionally, as part of my learning. So, from the space between Tony's stories and my learning, I need to be able to give a sense of the profound meanings of this spirit world. I want to explore the absences and presences of spirits in places, and the remarkable translations that these stories of spirits in places perform.

Spirit presences

There's different times through the year
you could be peggin' out clothes
or just walk out on the front verandah
there's a breeze blowing
you just feel real close
this is when I really miss the Old People,
'specially all the grand-aunts and Mum,
it must be just the change of season
or something.

The breath of a light warm breeze caresses the skin at the coming of spring. Wave after wave of colour – pink, purple, white and gold wildflowers – transform the coastal heathlands and birds sing all around in sweet-smelling banksias. Through the paperbarks and down towards the beach the salt air calls to the warm currents in the blue-green sea. By the Lake all is stirring and Keith will be sitting there watching, waiting, for a sign. Someone might move into the Old Camp for a while to be closer to this awakening. The smell of their campfire will waft by on the early morning air. This is a time for feeling the presence of the Old People in that place.

While the spirits of the Old People inhabit all of Gumbaynggirr country and beyond, their presence is intensified around Corindi Lake because of the concentration of people's lives there. All of the stories that people told about living in No Mans Land – fishing, hunting, collecting shellfish, building shelters, washing, cooking – are permeated by the presence of the Old People. In each physical place of camp site, fishing spot, ceremonial place, the spirits of the Old People reside.

> Yeah she come back, just to come out here, die out here, she didn't want to die in town, so she wanta die out here at the old place. See that's where she died down at the Old Camp. This side of the Lake, you know, we had an old house there. If you go round that way, you'd get the feelin' that they're still there. Oh yeah, they look after us, they just watch us, keep us away from danger. (Michael McDougall)

The spirits linger in the places where the Old People lived, the places that draw them back when they are near death. They are felt in those places in the material signs of their life there, like the scars on the trees where they cut canoes or bark for shelters, the toe holes made for climbing and the objects left behind in the camps. Michael feels his mother's presence in the very particular place where the old house was, not only the spirit of his mother but the other Old People as well. Robyn Duroux feels her great-aunts' and mother's presence when she is pegging out the clothes, just doing the ordinary things of everyday life. It is by sensing their presence in the everyday that we can begin to know them as benign presences there to watch over us.

> And I'll go by myself, I'll go and walk over to the beach or walk away from people just to keep that feelin. It's so close. They feel so close, like you wanna see them walk there near ya. But I know too if I got a lotta worries – and I do get some, you know, pressures, with, oh I suppose just through life. I can go to sleep and I dream of the Old People, and they're so real. I get up and I'm amazed that they're not there. And I dunno, these problems just seem to sort themselves out you know, it's really good. I'm so glad I'm able to, you know. (Robyn Duroux)

They talk with the spirits of the Old People. When Robyn feels their presence in the touch of the breeze on her skin at the change of season she wants to withdraw, to be alone with them to enhance that communion. The close relationships she had with them in their lives are with her then and this helps her to deal with the pressures of her life now. The spirits come to Robyn in her dreams too and they came to Margie Lardner to help her make new stories and new connections. When Margie was in the foster homes in Sydney, Clarrie Skinner's spirit came to her in her dreams, carrying part of the place with him in the form of the brilliant pink pigface flower so characteristic of the sand dunes at Corindi Beach. Through this image she was reconnected with her people and her place. Once she moved back to the Old Camp it was Bing who took responsibility for much of her learning about the spirit world.

> I remember when I first come down here, he come to me one night. I didn't know it was him, I was in the caravan sleepin'. I jumped up and I kept sayin' to Bing that someone tall come into the caravan, he'd got big hands. And he looked at me and he said, 'Oh that's Uncle Fred'. And I said, 'Uncle Fred who?' He's goin', 'Uncle Fred Laurie'. I said, 'Well he's got a big hand whoever it was'. Just as I was going to sleep he'd appeared to me, yeah. But it, the feelin' you get down when you live in the bush, in the camp, you know, it's a good feelin' you wake up and the birds are singin'. It's a real happy place to wake up in. (Margie Lardner)

When people hear the birds singing they think of them as the spirits of the Old People.

In this way Gumbaynggirr places come alive through the presence of spirits in many forms and the spirits of the Old People are central to these presences. The Old People are the people who came to live in No Mans Land in the beginning, after the massacre and rebirth at the Old Farm. They are present in the contemporary landscape through memories, through family connections, through stories and through their spirit presences. Their stories are foundational in the sense that they bridge the time before and the time after white settlement. Their spirits inhabit this liminal space, the in-between space of the contact zone.

They are the men who are believed to have escaped the massacre, Johnny McCallum and Ted McCrystal, and the women who provided continuity through birthing the new generation of children, Celia Harvey and Armi. And there are the initiated men, Clarrie Skinner, Jimmy Runner, Herbie and Abraham McDougall, Arthur Taylor, Fred Laurie and Tom Flanders, who carried forward the knowledge of the special places. It is this knowledge that was translated and passed on from the Old People that enabled Gumbaynggirr people to live again in these places.

The spirit stories, like the characters of the Old People, are mysterious, haunting stories where only a small glimpse of their meaning is possible. Some of the knowledge of spirits in places can only be transmitted bodily in place, some is secret-sacred knowledge that can only be passed on in ceremony and is now only recalled in taboo. Passing on the knowledge of spirits in places was difficult in the absence of the ceremonies through which much of the knowledge was traditionally transmitted. Tom Flanders said that his father did not pass on any of this spirit knowledge to his sons because they were not initiated. 'He went through an initiation period when he was a young fellow, and then he seen all of these young – even his sons grew up and weren't initiated. And he probably thought, "Ah, they're not interested in it, I'm not goin' to tell any of them about that"'. Despite the breakdown of the traditional forms of teaching and learning, however, the knowledge of spirits in places continues to be transmitted in new and contemporary ways.

Each of the initiated men seems to be linked to particular spirit stories and special places in line with Tony's account of the passing on of different aspects of knowledge to different people at the time of contact. Abraham McDougall was linked with the headland at Red Rock and Pa Laurie with the brolga dancing ground at Jewfish Point. Jimmy Runner was keeper of the rainmaking place at Arrawarra. Arthur Taylor's spirit stories belong in the places where he camped at Corindi Lake but they also follow the path of his travels as he moved up and down the coast. Clarrie Skinner brought the initiation knowledge and practices back to the places where they lived around Corindi Lake. Bing said one day, when we were walking up the track from the Old Camp past a dead old gum tree leaning into another tree, 'That's where old Clarrie Skinner kept his property, old stone, it was as ugly as anything. When he died that tree died.'

Each of these initiated men had responsibility to decide how to pass on their knowledge of spirits in places and to teach the next generation how to respect the places and their powers. This knowledge was passed on to the generation of people who are Elders today, especially Bing, Bruce, Keith and Michael who continue to live at Corindi Lake.

> Well Bing seems to know more about the spiritual side of things and the different sites there, you know, like Arrawarra and things like that. Keith knows everything about the different plants, the different vines for the water, he knows the roots and all that. The only fella is Bill, my brother, he won't say much, but he knows a lot. He was told about different things, how to take the power out of somebody, when a person's just died, what you gotta do. But he won't say much about it and he knows a lot about it. He knows how to heal people, he was there, seen it. (Tony Perkins)

Tony described how Clarrie Skinner used the metaphor of the jigsaw puzzle to explain how the Old People had made a decision to pass on different aspects of knowledge to the different individuals of Tony's generation. The Old People watched over the young people to decide which ones to pass on these different aspects of knowledge to. Each of these people then had the knowledge inside them to ensure that important cultural knowledge was not lost. It would only be when they came together that the pieces could be connected and some sense of the whole would be revealed.

As the eldest of this generation of Elders still living at Corindi Lake, Bing is the holder of much of the cultural knowledge of spirits in places. He is the only person who has directly inherited responsibility for a protector spirit.

> I've got one down there, yeah, in the bamboo. That's why I don't like anyone muckin' around with the bamboo there, touchin' it. 'Cause Clarrie Skinner's the one that gave it to

> me. That's my property. This side them tin huts, with the little bridge crossing there is where the hairy fella is. I don't let the kids go there now. I go through there – everyone's allowed to go but got to be careful of a baby, carry a baby you know, might start talkin' to it, in case it will follow, come home with ya, stop there, little kid sick, it'll go mad. I start talkin' lingo to it, I just say, 'Yilaami wanaa yuunggu', that means 'Don't torment, don't do anything'. Yeah, got, well from me Uncle Clarrie Skinner. (Bing Laurie)

The gumburr is a spirit of the in-between. He lives in the dense thicket of bamboo that has grown so wild. It is the perfect place for a spirit to live, hidden in its impenetrable depths. The bamboo grows beside the little bridge that crosses the northern arm of the Lake into the Old Camp. The bridge is a liminal place, a threshold between the new brick houses where people now live and the physical and metaphorical space of the Old Camp where the spirits of the Old People are. Bing can only speak to the gumburr in Gumbaynggirr language as this is the language of the spirit world. The gumburr is a little hairy fellow. Though Bing says he has never seen it he hears it sing 'like a mopoke, jinijinu, jinijinu'. Bird calls commonly announce the presence of the spirits and it is sound that calls them up. In an oral culture, sound, singing, naming and language hold spirit powers.

Children are particularly vulnerable to the spirit world. In the many stories of the gumburr, Bing uses a repertoire of Gumbaynggirr instructions to tell the gumburr not to torment the children, to leave them alone. 'Wanaa ngirra, nguraalami!' 'Don't do that! Go home!' Because of children's openness to the spirit world, the spirits can enter them and threaten their hold on the world of the everyday.

> When anyone died like that, they'd get clay, they'd either get the clay that was down here, get the white, white clay, the white pipeclay stuff. Either that or flour, just get ordinary flour, and when the kids went to sleep they'd get the clay and they'd rub it on their face or they'd get the flour and put on their face. That was so that, you know, that spirit of that person wouldn't annoy those kids of a night time. An'

that'd only last like for three nights. After the third night
everything was right again. Only on the kids 'cause the kids
was the ones that was most affected by the spirits comin'
back. Even though the spirits wasn't there to harm 'em,
they'd come back to more or less show the kids you know
that they were carin for 'em, protectin' 'em. (Tony Perkins)

During the time between life and death the spirits are unsettled and may seek out the children as a way to return to the material world. The white ochre, girriin, which left its traces in the name Corindi Beach, was used in ceremonies and had the ceremonial powers of transformation. Through the power of the white ochre, white flour could be a substitute to keep the spirits away when painted on the faces of the children at night. Mothers remain vigilant to the signs of the presence of spirits that might endanger their children and they refer to Bing's spiritual knowledge to help them interpret what it might mean.

I can't remember who was there with us that night,
something woke me up and I could hear this whoo whoo
whoo, comin' through you know and it sounded like – it
was way over the other side of the men's quarters – and I was
thinkin' oh no, and then as it got closer, it was real loud but
one minute it's out the front of the house, the next second it's
out the back, and it was like circling around. When it went,
the girls went back, and they went to sleep, 'cause they were
muckin' around you know, they were being silly. Uncle Bing
can send it to ya if yer playin' up, you know or anything like
that. (Shirley Duroux)

Children are frequently disciplined with the threat of the spirits who will be out and about in the dark of night. It is instilled into all Gumbaynggirr children that they must be home and inside before dark or they are at risk of confronting the spirits. Children have no power over these spirits because they have not yet reached the age when this is learned. The power of the spirit world belongs to the Old People and was gained through initiation. It has been passed onto the Elders of today through stories. The powers of the spirits can be called up for many purposes, especially for healing. Bing will summon the gumburr by singing out to it in Gumbaynggirr: 'Yilaami! Come here!' and send it to heal someone who is sick, even if they are far away.

> If anyone's sick there, need any help there, I just sing out to it, 'Yilaami, yilaami'. It'll come straight away, just one word. I don't like singing out for fun, no making fun of it, 'cause it's not to be mucked around with. Take it very serious, like they told me. I can send him a long way. Sydney, somewhere, if I want to. If anyone's sick I say, 'Look after that fellow, look after that fellow in hospital', 'Nyaaga ngarri daandurr'. 'He's sick, look after him.' He can go anywhere, you know, anywhere, long way. That's what the Old People, it's happened in South Grafton hospital, the Old People out there used to see him laying under the bed part, sticking out from the foot of the bed part. In Grafton hospital, a long time ago, Old People there. (Bing Laurie)

In the precarious world between healing through spiritual powers and healing through western medicine the Old People were taken away from their places. It was necessary to call on the spirits to travel to those places and to be there with them. They travelled in their physical bodily form. The spectre of one of the Old People in bed in the Grafton Base Hospital with the little hairy gumburr poking out from the bottom of the hospital bed is so incongruous it is hilariously funny. But the gumburr was only visible to the Old People so it could stay there to protect and heal them.

Healing for Gumbaynggirr people involves physical, emotional and spiritual wellbeing and especially recognises the connection between the wellbeing of people and the wellbeing of their places. Tony remembered watching his grandfather healing a young child down at the Old Camp. His knowledge of healing was enacted through the power that he sang in Gumbaynggirr and transmitted through his hands. The healing powers of the spirit world were vast and extensive, relating not only to the people but to their places and all of the living creatures that shared those places with them.

~

For Gumbaynggirr people living in No Mans Land, the knowledge of spirits in places belonged to the Old People. It was passed on through ceremony, particularly initiation ceremonies. This knowledge today is passed on in stories, in special places, and in the spirit presences of the Old People. These spirit presences visit people in their daily lives at the Old Camp by the Lake. People feel close to these spirits and welcome them as a sign of caring and protection. Those who grew up away from the Lake have to learn the spirits on their return. The stories about the spirits in places are stories of the liminal. On the other hand, the Old People have importantly begun the process of translation through which we can begin to understand these stories today.

Spirits in places

Jewfish Point some nights
you hear all these birds
Old People talkin', walkin', 'n' birds,
mopoke sing out, night owls, curlew there
they can't stay away then.
Used to go with them Old People
we didn't care we had Baaba there
me Uncle, Clarrie Skinner
we 'ad 'im there with us
he was all cicatriced on the back
we weren't frightened then
we 'ad the Old People there.

At Jewfish Point all is in shadow as we throw our lines into the still water. Fish jump plop, plop, plop and there's a fireplace with charcoal remnants of someone's fishing fire. Two white cranes are on the far bank with a group of cormorants feeding and all around us the sound of birds waking. Everything is dewdrop wet so I light the fire with dry she-oak needles caught in the forks of trees and dry twigs from upright bushes to boil the billy. Soon the sun lights the green lichen-trunks of she-oaks making a circle around the edge of the salt flat. The salt flat is bare, its surface marked only by crab holes and crystal white of salt left behind when the very high tides reach here. I wonder: Did the people dance here in this circle? Did the pounding of feet make this bare space a place of ceremony and spirit powers? A single gnarled old mangrove tree stands silent guard in the centre of the bare salt flat. They told me that it was here they came for Sunday picnics and camped overnight with the Old People. In the night they heard the mournful sounds of the birds that were the voices of the Old People, but they were not afraid because they had Baaba with them.

The spirits and their powers were associated with all of the special places throughout the clan territory of the Garby Elders, the area of the northern Gumbaynggirr people who came to live in No Mans Land. For Tony, understanding the spirit powers begins with their identity in these local clan areas, now known by the names of towns such as Corindi Beach, Coffs Harbour and Nambucca.

> It doesn't matter where you go to, you talk to each – like well each town now I suppose, like it should have been clans, but you always find their power is different, you know some sort of might really believe their powers are in the animals or mountains or different things, and even the things they change into, you know the Old People in them times, when they used to change into different things with their power, different forms one talks about, yeah. (Tony Perkins)

Tony's grandfather taught him about the spirits in these places by singing to him. 'Clarrie Skinner used to sing about the clever people whatever they're gonna do – if they're travelling as an animal or a bird, it's like a power in 'em 'cause they used that for their power.' The Old People became 'clever', able to access spirit powers, through the ceremonies that were carried out in these places. The highest form of knowledge belonged to ceremony and was the deepest knowledge of country. The songs were just one part of the language of ceremony through which this knowledge was expressed. The sound of the song contained a part of the power of the spirits of the place. In singing about the spirit powers to Tony, his grandfather was communicating in the language of ceremony. In the absence of ceremonies the old initiated men continued to look after the powerful spirits of those places, singing their songs and telling their stories to teach the young about them.

Old Fred Laurie danced the brolga dance at the Old Camp as an initiated man. He painted himself up with white ochre from Corindi Beach and danced the brolga dance to teach the young men about the spirits of the brolga place. The dance, like the songs, holds some of the powers of the spirits of that place where the men changed into brolgas.

> They used to tell us about Jewfish Point there. They used to tell us about corroborees and that they used to hold it there on the flat. And the brolgas and that on the other side. They used to tell us about it, right across the water. And they used to have the corroborees this side and the brolgas'd be on the sand on the other side. And the brolgas, they'd learnt that, they'd learnt the corroboree. When I seen Pa Laurie doin' it, it was identical to the brolga with his arms like wings that's goin' round. And I think that's where the brolga learnt by lookin' across, they learnt then how to do that corroboree the same way. And I mean you when you see two brolgas dancin', it's identical to them, the corroboree goin', yeah. (Tony Perkins)

Tony said that in the old days they used to have their big gatherings at Jewfish Point. They painted themselves up with all the different coloured ochres and had their ceremonies and dances there. All the coloured ochres came from Red Rock so this was the place where they were traded. When Tony spotted a midden shell fallen from the bank at the edge of the track down to Jewfish Point he recognised that that was the place where they camped for the gatherings. That was where we found the big Red Rock midden, a very old midden in the shifting formation of coastal places, and laid down over a long time. Tony's generation 'never went there' because of the encroaching white settlement but Pa Laurie did the dance at Corindi Beach to teach the young men the story of the place. Bing and Bruce both remembered the power of Jewfish Point in the 'mournful' sounds of the Old People talking in the call of the night birds there.

> At Jewfish Point there'd be mopokes singin', night owls singin', curlews and different other birds singin' out there. You go there at night time and you listen to them birds sing out there round the river they're everywhere. Some birds I've never heard that sound near the river, that curlew's mournful, a mournful bird that fella. (Bruce Laurie)

There are many spirit places at Red Rock. The headland where the last events of the massacre took place, Jewfish Point where the brolga dancing grounds were, and the place where the river runs out to sea are all believed to be powerful because of the spirits there. All of these places are also infused with the trauma of the massacre story and the spirits of the people who died there. The cave on the headland at Red Rock marks one end of McDougalls' Run, the northern extent of the coastal strip between Red Rock and Arrawarra headlands where Herbie and Abraham McDougall walked as the protectors of that coastal strip. Abraham McDougall was guardian of the cave at Red Rock and he took the young men there to learn about that place.

> The Red Rock headland, that's where Michael McDougall's mother and father walked in that cave there, yeah. He wanted to take us in there but I was too frightened. It was below the tide, and he walked right the way in there, all proud he was, he was a game man though [laughs]. He offered to take me and Keithy, and Michael and Brucey too. Clarrie went down, he was down a long time. You can only climb down a little bit, up near the beginning, kick all the crabs and things out of the road. Some of them go right up to Old Farm, that's where it goes to. Michael got down there from the headland, McDougall's headland. But he can't talk lingo, you gotta talk

to that thing before you go there. Michael's father could talk
lingo, yeah, that's all they talk, nothing else. (Bing Laurie)

In telling this story, Bing describes the courage required to go into the cave, which was exposed only at very low tides. Only those who had been through initiation were fearless enough to brave its depths. As guardian of the cave, Abraham McDougall taught the young men its stories. He told them that the cave on the Red Rock headland was the place where the men escaped the massacre and walked through the labyrinth to the birthing grounds at the Old Farm. Whether the cave always had a spirit presence, even before the massacre, is unclear, but Bing portrays this spirit as an entity which continues to live there and has to be addressed in Gumbaynggirr. This is the language of the spirit world that all the Old People spoke; the younger generation had to learn through the translation of the stories into English.

Further down the coast at the other end of McDougalls' Run the rainmaking place on the headland at Arrawarra was also a place of power and taboo. As the protector of the rainmaking place Jimmy Runner taught his sons its stories when they went there for a weekend of fishing.

Jimmy Runner is the only man who knew how to make rain at Arrawarra. Arrawarra, round the headland we used to get big, big drummers and gropers. A heap of really good tucker, big ones. We used to spend the weekend up there and come home ready for school on Monday. Told me how he makes the rain and all that. He used to come back from Arrawarra and tell us there'd be a big rain comin' here soon, big rain – in about a week you'd see the clouds build up, there'd be rain. Stir her up, and she gets wild, and the biggest rain comes. (Bing Laurie)

It is likely that the significance of the big fish is part of this story because the fish traps were also located just below the Arrawarra headland. Tony said that they called Arrawarra 'Comeback' because it was a dangerous and powerful place for children. They were told not to throw pipi shells there because the high-pitched sound would disturb the spirits of the rainmaking place and they would be deluged with rain. Jimmy Runner also told Bruce and Bing not to poke around in the rock pools or throw stones because the big rains would come before they even got home. The 'rock pools' are part of the ancient fish traps where rocks were placed to trap fish by the cycles of the moon and tides. They are also likely to be part of the place's taboo.

> Yeah, Jimmy Runner told us never, ever, whatever you do, poke around the rock pools. 'Don't throw stones', he said. Or the breadfruit tree, don't break anything off the breadfruit tree or you'll get rain, you know. He said, 'Never throw stones, don't throw stones around that headland, especially at Arrawarra. Don't ever poke 'round the headland, those rock pools. You'll bring rain', he said, 'straight away, and by the time we get home we'll get wet'. Clouds'd build up, just like that. Wouldn't let – we never used to throw stones there, we made sure we never did that. He'd know if we did anything wrong, he knows. (Bruce Laurie)

The spirit powers of the weather belonged to the rainmaking place at Arrawarra. The breadfruit tree, linked to that place, is still believed to hold power over the rain and storms and children are warned that pulling leaves from any breadfruit tree will bring deluges of unwanted rain. Even recently, when a big gathering down at the Old Camp was flooded out, Margie explained it was because some children had pulled the leaves off the breadfruit tree. In the old days, in the swampy land at the back of the dunes in transient shelters made of bark or tin, people were vulnerable to cyclonic winds, rain and storms so the spirit powers of the weather were critical to their daily lives. During storms the Old People used to sing out in language to send the storms away. Later, in the absence of the Old People themselves, the Elders continued to call out to the storms in Gumbaynggirr language, waving the clothes of the Old People that were imbued with the spirit powers that had lived in their bodies.

Spirits in places

> Yeah, yeah, the Old People used to wave their dresses and sing out, wave their Old People clothes, wave them, sing out 'Waalga ngarri', push away, push that way storm, push it away then, over in that direction. It used to go around then, it used to go around that way then. Yeah, used to sing out all the time, you know the old fellows, until it goes around. Special, you know, it goes round you. Yeah, sing out, 'This old house is no good', sort of thing, you know, 'Yaam nguura yuunggu, yaam ngoora yoonggu. Jaalgarra', they sing out 'jaalgarra' you know, then the storm go that way then, goes round the other way, sing out. (Bruce Laurie)

The weather, the tides, the cycles of the moon and the seasons were an integral part of their lives in No Mans Land. The great cycles of the sea were closely associated with the powers and significance of food from the sea. The story of the Old People singing the dolphins is an iconic story for everyone who lived at Corindi Lake of the powers of spirits in places and is told in many different versions.

> Yeah, they used to sing to the fish and everything. Oh they could sort of sing, stand on the headland, call out, and then sing out, and draw all the porpoise in. The porpoise'd come round and they'd circle and they'd keep singin', keep singin' all the time, and it was just like a message, it was goin' straight to the porpoise, and the porpoise'd come in and they'd go right around. You'd see 'em in the circles. Then they'd get plenty of schools of fish, they'd drive 'em in. Drive 'em right onto the beach, right close, and then when they'd finished drivin' them in they'd give, throw fish to the porpoise there. Then they'd talk and sing to the porpoise and the porpoise'd swim off, gone. (Tony Perkins)

In late winter the dolphins migrate north at the same time as many of the fish are migrating in great schools up the coast. It is a time of fecundity and excess, a time when big groups of people gathered for ceremony because many people could be fed. The signs of these ceremonies remain in the middens at the great gathering places, and the middens themselves are inspirited with these sacred places.

> Mindi was a really big tall, man and, and he just walked the beach, he just walked the coast, just go along the beach eating the pipis. He use' to sit, and I mean a big man, and there'd be lots of shells, and that's what they'd say, 'Oh well Mindi's been here'. When we were kids, Mum, you know, you'd see a big pile of pipi shells and they'd always say, 'Oh look, you know Mindi's been here'. (Robyn Duroux)

For children, Mindi is simply a character in a story, an unusually big man who walks up and down the beaches eating so many pipis that he leaves big piles of their shells for all to see. For knowledgeable adults he is one of the creation ancestors who is part of the ongoing ceremonies and stories of spirits in places. Two big middens marked the gathering places in northern Gumbaynggirr country: at Jewfish Point and at Arrawarra (see Chapter 3). The Arrawarra midden was washing into the sea so the people asked us to collect and analyse its contents and then give them back to the sea where they belong. The Red Rock midden was carefully explored with a few selected squares excavated and analysed by the people, and these too were carefully returned to their places.

When the encroaching white settlement made these ceremonial places no longer accessible new ones were made for some parts of their ceremonies and the sacred objects were kept near to those new places. In this way some of the powers of song, dance and ceremony were brought to the Old Camp at Corindi Beach.

> And that's where he [Clarrie Skinner] kept it, kept that stone, at the bottom of that tree. But when he was livin' up here, one night there was a lot of noise outside, you know, they'd be havin' a bark. And we went out there and had a look, and there was lots of these, like, they were like bats. But they looked like a coupla foot high, about two or three foot high. And they were like small bats, and they were on the outside,

at the place there. And he came out, came out and he took 'em back down to that tree and told 'em that they weren't to come out of there. That's where he kept 'em, where that old tree is there what's died, and that's where he kept the stone and, oh, other things too, other property. (Tony Perkins)

The tree where Clarrie Skinner kept his 'property' was the dead tree that Bing pointed out when we were walking up the track from the Old Camp. The recurring stories of these bat-like creatures are some of the most mysterious of the spirit stories. They are right at the limits of my understanding, and the ability of the English language to transmit Gumbaynggirr meanings. Tony struggled to find words to tell the story. My sense was that people enacted the exchange of form and identity from animal to human and human to animal through dance, song and body paint, as in the brolga dancing story. The spirit creatures that Clarrie brought to the Old Camp somehow participated in this exchange. Tony used the idea of 'totem' to explain his grandfather's connection with these bat-like creatures and the organisation of the different clan groups of Gumbaynggirr people. Each of these clan groups, he said, had a relationship to particular country and to the special places and animals within that country.

Yeah well see that's his, that was my grandfather's. They were like things that I suppose protected him, you know. I think he was a bat, sort of thing, was his totem. Yeah, 'cause that's what he used to keep, used to keep them there. Some had a frog, and some had a owl, all things like that. Because, see, some wouldn't eat different things. Because that's the way that, if everyone ate the same thing, they'd be nothing left sort of thing, you know. So each group had a, one lot mightn't have had that, and the next lot didn't have this and there were some restrictions sort of placed and that way you didn't wipe it all out. (Tony Perkins)

In the statement 'he was a bat', Tony reveals the depth of the identity exchange involved in the process of human-becoming-animal that is part of the spirit powers of ceremony. This is related in turn to the different animals that each of the clan groups were identified with and their responsibility to protect their particular animal and its living places. Part of this protection was a prohibition on eating the totemic animal, a ceremonial taboo, but also an intensely practical and deeply held responsibility for the wellbeing of the animals and their places. This wellbeing is, in turn, connected to the spiritual wellbeing of the person and for this reason the power of healing is as much a spiritual act as a physical one. It permeates all ceremony and all stories of spirits in place and is not only about the wellbeing of human beings but it is about living well with all living things and their places.

These deeply held beliefs were what the people who lived at Corindi Lake learned, even in the absence of ceremony. 'Things were very special, you know, very special thing here, you had to really look after that. You grow up and you know you went through all your life, you grew up with it, with what was given to you to look after.' Even without the detailed and articulated understanding of the relationship between people and the spirits in places that Tony has, a sense of identification with other living creatures and their places remains.

～

The Old People were connected to the special story places. Through their embodiment of these spirit stories and places they passed them on in their changing forms to the next generation, Tony's generation. In this way the powers of the Old People, conferred through ceremony, permeated the lives of people in No Mans Land. These spirit powers belonged to the Gumbaynggirr language but were translated into English stories and transmitted orally through storytelling rather than through ceremony. Where parts of the ceremony became associated with particular places in No Mans Land, new places became inspirited. The stories continued to be part of their daily lives in that place and through the stories the knowledge of spirits in places continued in a different form. These stories integrated the human and non-human worlds as well as the material and spirit worlds. They embraced the natural forces of the sea and weather. All of the landscape, its creatures and non-living elements were imbued with a sense of power, or spirit, and the wellbeing of people and places were intimately connected. Communicating with this spirit world, translating its meanings and acting where necessary was the province of the Old People. It is now the domain of the Elders of today who have the knowledge of the spirits in places and these Elders are responsible for making decisions about how to pass on these stories.

Initiation

The Old People used to feed him
the tongue of a blue-tongue lizard
when he was a young fella.
If they thought you were a bit slow in talkin'
they used to give you
the blue-tongue lizard's tongue.
He knows a lot about all that
he was with our grandmother most of the time
he seen her when she was old
he seen it all, yeah he knows a lot.

The beach is edgy this morning. Lumpy grey clouds, thick like porridge as I face the roaring sea, wind pounding in my ears. I hear the crash of the waves' constant movement but along the water's edge, the space in-between dry and wet, the smoothed-out sand is still and glassy as each wave retreats. Above the edge of the tide the sand is dun-coloured and packed flat by rain, one dimensional after heavy rain last night. I stand in this still space suspended between the flattened sand and the sea, all movement and noise, white waves crashing. In this edge space the smooth wet surface of the sand reflects my own image and the clouds. The skirts of the ocean froth around my ankles and balls of froth blow in patterns across the smooth wetness. Pipi holes appear in the glassy surface and I remember squirming toes in wet sand between each wave to feel the hard surface of shell and – quick – grab before the next wave comes. In a disgruntled greyness the odd seagull hovers. Stones, bits of seaweed and debris litter the tide mark from last night's heavy rain. It is these edges that I love.

Initiation is an edge place. It is the time when young boys and girls make the transition to adulthood. I learned ceremony from living in the desert with old women who had only lived in contact with white people for eight years. They wanted me to drive them to their country to dance. Each time we sat in a circle in the shimmering heat, each of us rubbed in turn with kangaroo fat. We sang to the rhythm of clap sticks as ochre designs were painted on breasts and arms. I imagine it was inconceivable to these Pintupi women that anyone would not know singing and dancing in country. I was, however, profoundly a not-knower. I learned through my senses, through the sound and rhythm of music and singing, the smell of kangaroo fat, feeling of ochre and red dirt on skin, touch of feet on earth, and movement of dancing. I left there a not-knower, I had no words for this experience.

When I left the desert I began working with Aboriginal women in Armidale, on the western edge of Gumbaynggirr country. As a teacher I arranged visits to many special places as part of their learning, but no matter how benign a place seemed the women would never get out of the car. They told me how one old man had recorded a story with an anthropologist about the last big initiation ceremony near Point Lookout. After telling that story 'he was finished up', he died. There was a great deal of anxiety around initiation. I had only questions and no answers about the relationship between my prior experience in the desert and Aboriginal life in Armidale. We learned lots together, we even visited Alice Springs, but there was a great yawning gap in that space in-between. My learning about spirits in places did not begin again until I began working with Tony at Yarrawarra and heard the stories of the spirits of the Old People translated into English and contemporary forms of meaning.

Tony explained the loss of power consequent on the 'release' of the knowledge of the Old People. The power that was conferred through ritual practice in initiation ceremonies was transferred to oral stories, and the release of knowledge through oral storytelling is a transmission through the breath, of the power of naming and language. In an oral culture, sounds, and especially songs, are believed to hold the powers of spirits in places. The multiple translations of this knowledge from song and ceremony to oral storytelling, and then to recorded story and the written word, are complex. In this writing I stay close to Tony's teachings.

I wondered, when I first began to contemplate the many stories about initiation, about how and why as a woman I was told these stories. I had heard stories about initiation over many years and from several of the Elders and they told me it was all right because of my age and because I had four children. I was surprised when I traced the initiation stories in the transcripts of my conversations with Tony that almost all of them contained stories about initiation. I was also surprised to discover that Tony introduced these stories in our very first recorded conversation. Many of the same stories were told on different occasions and each time the level of information was slightly different as I was able to understand more. It is this process and these stories from Tony that I mainly draw on here.

Tony emphasised stories of initiation from the very beginning of our research as an important dimension of their lives at Corindi Lake. In a sense, to separate out stories of spirits in places is already to distort the sense of the spiritual in the everyday stories. He began by telling me how his grandfather had shown him the scars on his body. 'I remember him showin' me the initiation marks on him, on his chest' that were undeniable evidence of his knowledge and authority in country. He explained his feeling of the raised up initiation scars on the bodies of the men as the first part of his coming to understand what initiation ceremonies meant.

> When you're really young, when you're only getting nine and ten, like I didn't understand at that time, nine, ten, eleven, twelve, and thirteen, you couldn't sort of understand – they'd tell you what they were doing, what they wanted you to do, but a lot of time, 'cause you'd never give cheek or anything like that, you stood there but somehow you couldn't understand why this was goin' on. Then they explained why, you know, why it was gettin' done. Oh yeah he told me about – he said over time they'd draw on your chest and that, and mark it, rub the ashes into it. (Tony Perkins)

On the next occasion Tony told me that the marks were made by burning and then the ashes were rubbed into the burn to help produce the raised up scars. The making of the marks on bodies and landscapes that signified the knowledge transmitted in initiation ceremonies became more detailed as the learning progressed. It became clear that the body of the grandfather mediated his teaching and learning about the meaning of initiation ceremonies.

> I remember they showed us everything, they showed us
> lots of things, we were told the sort of thing that goes on.
> Showed us all the scars and that sort of thing on the chest,
> and on the arms, all the burn marks. Like, the burns, used to
> have a lot of burns on the chest, and the scars on the arms,
> top of the arm sort of thing. Rubbed, you know, with ashes.
> You know, rub the ashes in, and all that. (Tony Perkins)

For Tony the marks on the bodies of initiated men at Corindi Lake came to symbolise all of the knowledge of initiation. Over the years, Tony's grandfather introduced him to the places, the stories, the spirit powers and the practices of initiation. The places were first introduced as taboo, dangerous places where he was not allowed to go. These taboos were to protect the uninitiated from being harmed by knowledge or experiences that were too powerful for them. These taboos are often seen by non-Aboriginal people as containing the threat of the uninitiated to these place and their spirit powers. The sense that I got from Tony's story is that the concern was the other way around; that the places, objects, experiences and stories of initiation are so powerful that they would cause harm to the uninitiated person who came too close to their power.

> And we were always told that there was two places we should
> never've been seen or never ever went to, and not to be there
> after dark, and all that type of thing. There was one, one
> tree. There was a really, really big gum tree, with a really big
> fig tree growing out the top, and you know there were places
> that we were never allowed to go anywhere near that part
> of it. That's where they keep the spirit itself. They call 'em

ghosts but really it's a protective spirit of a tribe, sort of thing.
It's not a harmful thing, but it's something that should – it's a
law not to be there after dark. (Tony Perkins)

For Tony, as a young boy, learning these taboos was an important part of learning to understand and respect Aboriginal Law. The taboos were about avoiding particular places that were made powerful by the actions and meanings of Gumbaynggirr people in relation to that place. His grandfather used to say to him, 'What I've got to do with all of you young ones is get you to understand the Law'. Understanding the Law was traditionally learned through the cycles of initiation ceremonies. In the absence of traditional practices of initiation, over the years the processes and places of taboo came to stand for power of initiation itself.

Like for years and years like no-one ever told anyone where
anything was. There's been more said in the last couple of
years than anyone ever told anyone, you know. You used to
just sort of walk around and just know where everything was
and what happened, and you just didn't sort of tell anybody.
(Tony Perkins)

The stories of initiation, like all spiritual knowledge, are also the subject of powerful taboos about what can be spoken and what must remain silent. Tony believed his brother Billy had deep spiritual knowledge because of his close relationship with his grandmother, who was a healer. But of all the Elders who received parts of the knowledge that made up the jigsaw puzzle, Bill remained the most silent. When Bill was a child, Tony told me, the Old People used to feed him the tongue of the blue-tongue lizard because he was slow to talk. The association of speech and silence with spiritual knowledge, embodied in this practice, is significant.

The Old People used to feed him the tongue of a blue-
tongue lizard, when he was a young fella. If they thought that
you were a bit slow in talkin' they used to give you the blue-
tongue lizard's tongue. He knows a lot about all that. He was

with our grandmother, he was with her most of the time, and he seen her when she was old, he seen it all. Yeah he knows a lot. (Tony Perkins)

Speech and non-speech, silence and sound, naming and non-naming are significantly associated with the spirit world. I was told this story about the blue-tongue lizard's tongue twice and on the second occasion from a Gumbaynggirr artist about his own experience as a child. Like Billy, he was fed the tongue of the blue-tongue lizard because he was slow to talk. This story was linked to his vision and knowledge as an artist, to the idea that in his art he can express complex spiritual understandings and powers that cannot be expressed in words. There is a strong sense that the knowledge associated with spirits in places cannot be spoken because of taboos but also because there are no words to express it. Once this knowledge is separated from the places and ceremonies through which it was transmitted its power and meaning is threatened. Tony's brother Billy never spoke about his knowledge of spirits in places. An important lesson for me to learn was to know when silence is the most meaningful sound.

For Gumbaynggirr people, sound and silence, speech and naming, are powerful acts. The Gumbaynggirr language is associated with important cultural knowledge and, after years of resistance, the Garby Elders have now made a decision to teach the language to their own people. Place names are powerful and the decisions about how to name places are important as names call up the spirits in places. Silence about stories often means that a story has a deeper meaning that I am not yet ready to hear. I know, for example, that although I have been told about initiation practices since my very first recorded conversation with Tony, the knowledge that I am given is only the public level of knowledge that is safe for me to hear. As I learned more and deeper cultural knowledge I became aware of the depth of trust and the significance of my own silence. Making decisions about what to reveal, about what constitutes 'getting the message out' and what needs to be protected in silence, is a dangerous and risky edge place.

The decision of Gumbaynggirr people to record their knowledge and transmit it differently was difficult. In the context of initiation, the difficulty of this decision takes on a new and poignant meaning. In the past, the cultural learning of the deepest knowledge of country was symbolised in initiation rituals. Through ceremony the young men were recognised as having deep cultural knowledge and authority in country. The fact that the Old People were initiated meant that they had the power to make legitimate decisions about knowledge transmission, about when to reveal and when to conceal knowledge. This authority was recognised in the symbolic power of the marks of initiation on their bodies. The Elders of today had to make this decision without access to this legitimate authority as none of them were fully initiated in the traditional sense.

Immediately after explaining about the processes of knowledge transmission in our first interview, Tony told a story about the special place at the Old Camp just near where his grandfather lived. He moved from the symbolic marks on the individual bodies of the initiated men to the place in the Old Camp of their new practices. He began the story by locating it very precisely in relation to where we were sitting and to where Clarrie Skinner had his camp. It is the story of a particular night and a very particular memory of spirits in places that he told over and over again.

> I still remember the time we were down, just across the road here, and he had an old place just up the hill from the other camps. One night we were at his place and I still remember he went outside and when he went out, we could hear him talkin', and when we went out t' have a look he was wavin' back but there was like, they were like miniature people but they looked like they had, like when a bat opens up its wings, it sort of looked like that, but they were very real, like they were only small, and I remember seein it. There seemed to've been, when we looked outside, and he told us later, that that was his property, and that they came from where he kept his stones and things. Yeah, where he kept it for when they used to do initiations and that. He said they come from there.
> And the strangest thing is, when he died, the tree where he kept all his property, it died the same year, the same year.
> (Tony Perkins)

This story was told to me many times and with many minor variations, as if by the very repetition I would come to know and understand. The story gives a powerful sense of how ritual objects and practices came to imbue the Old Camp with meaning and how the full meaning of this knowledge belonged only to the Old People. Beyond this, the story about Clarrie Skinner's spirits, while deeply emplaced and embodied, remains mysterious and unknowable. It does, however, gather connections to other special places and stories and it is these connections that finally give the story meaning for me. At each larger level of meaning, more special places are connected to each other. Like the pieces of a jigsaw puzzle the individual pieces only have meaning in relation to each other, but also like the pieces of a jigsaw puzzle some pieces will always be lost.

The way Tony performs the story is also meaningful. He begins with a careful place-time mapping in relation to where we sit, and to the past. The time of the past is signified by the use of the word 'old', as in the Old People and the Old Camp. The image of his grandfather waving, however, brings the physical body of his grandfather directly into the story in the present performance. The creatures that he is waving to are introduced in hesitant, searching language, as if the English words cannot quite stretch to describe this manifestation that inhabits a space somewhere between the spirit and the material worlds. The bat-like spirit creatures live in the place where his grandfather keeps his 'property', another English word curiously adapted to name the secret objects imbued with the ritual meanings of initiation. 'Property' in English signifies worldly possessions, including ownership of land. For Gumbaynggirr people this sacred property is invisible yet it is something that gives them spiritual power. The epilogue to the story, that the tree died soon after Clarrie did, reinforces the sense of powerful connection to a particular place. The life energy of place, person and spirit are intricately intertwined.

In the next part of the initial interview Tony went on to talk about the places of initiation. He moved from the intense focus on a single tree near his grandfather's camp at Corindi Lake to the places of the great initiation cycles. 'He wanted to take me to Cunjaree Mountain. He said he'd take me up there for three weeks and sort of do the stages, the stages there. Then, then you had to go then on to Pillar Valley, to the big place there.' In this first conversation these special places are only reference points because we do not actually go there, even in conversation, at this point in time. The extraordinary detail of the first stage of the initiation ceremony is further revealed, however, in Tony's account of the re-creation of the smoking ceremony, the first stage of initiation, in No Mans Land.

> You know then – but where he kept his stones and things like that, he used to have a tallow wood tree, used to, not far down from there, used to be a big tallowwood tree, and he wanted, we weren't allowed to go there, and I remember him tellin' me one time, he said when I gather all the young ones up, he said what we're going to do, he said you get the leaves, he said and we'll rake up all the leaves from underneath, he said, an' we'll make a big ring round that tallowwood tree. And he said you stand on the inside, he said, and 'cause there was Pa Laurie and McDougalls, Michael's father and uncle. And they were all initiated and what he was going to do then was, the old ones was to be on the outside and he was goin' to put us in the inside for the first smoking and that was goin' to be here, right there. (Tony Perkins)

It is unlikely that even this first stage of initiation would have been carried out at Corindi Lake before the Old People found themselves alienated from their traditional initiation grounds. It was an act of necessity. The new initiation grounds of the first smoking ceremony were marked by another significant tree, the big tallowwood tree. The leaves of this tallowwood tree were to be raked up to make the ring and those same leaves would be burned to make the smoke for the ritual cleansing. The actual bodies of the old initiated men formed the outer circle. The young men of Tony's generation were to be placed inside the circle of the old men's bodies for the first smoking. The sense of loss of these stories is told in the loss of both of the trees that marked these special places. The big tree with the fig growing out of the top where Clarrie Skinner kept his ceremonial objects died when Clarrie died, and the tallowwood tree where the cleansing ceremony was performed was cleared for white settlement.

> And what they done, where that tree was, that's all gone, all been cleared from there. People who bought that property later, later in years, they pushed all that out. Anyway I can still show you the spot where that tree was growin'. Not very far, sort of across, straight across from the other tree where he kept all his things. (Tony Perkins)

In this way the ceremonial places around Corindi Lake were imbued by the power of the spirits through their ritual practices. Each time these practices changed, their transmission depended more on memory and story. Although the trees are gone Tony still remembers the place and evokes it in his storytelling. All of this story, and the changing place practices of initiation, were remarkable acts of translation.

It was only in looking back over the transcripts of these conversations many years later that I understood the significance of these stories that were told in our first interview. When I traced the thread of these stories throughout our conversations I became aware that in almost every interview we added another piece or layer of knowledge about initiation ceremonies and their special places. It is interesting to contemplate how apt the analogy of the jigsaw puzzle is to my own experience of this learning. Over the years of recording, as we revisited these stories, small pieces were added to the jigsaw puzzle. This seemed to happen precisely in conjunction with my ability to know and understand. It was in a conversation at the end of ten years of this research partnership that Tony said to me 'You have been initiated into Gumbaynggirr ways of thinking'.

This happened when I gave back to him some of my growing understanding and asked a question about connections and meanings. In Gumbaynggirr knowledge I had just turned ten. As Tony had said of himself, at ten, eleven, twelve and thirteen years old he began his learning. I could, by then, just catch a glimmer of the whole. My sense of the intensities of the special places at the Lake and their connections to the other parts of the initiation cycles grew over all this time. Although I never went there I knew from the beginning that Pillar Valley was the place where the major part of the initiation cycle took place, the main learning part 'where you started goin' through the Law there'. Much later Tony explained more about the special place at Pillar Valley in the cycles of learning through initiation ceremonies.

> Pillar Valley, there was a ring dance there. There's a ring there on the other side of Pillar Valley, when you're goin' back towards Ulmarra way, this ring was there. Pillar Valley was more like one of the main learning places. That's where they put the fear and the respect into you there. Temptation, that was over here, at Cunjaree Mountain. That's where the temptation was done there. The fear, and the respect was put forth there. Valla was where they, you know, they used to come out. They used to come out, when they was proven. To prove themself, that they could go through that respect, they could go through that fear, they could go through that temptation. Then they classed themselves as a man then, because they come out the other side. (Tony Perkins)

Each of these places played a major part in the initiation cycle marked by 'the rings' and the 'ring dance' of the ceremonial grounds. The English translation, like the English place names that are substituted for the Gumbaynggirr names of these special places, offer only the most impoverished sense of the meaning of these ceremonial performances. At the end of the thread of his initiation story that I traced through many conversations, Tony returns not to a sense of loss but to his bodily presence in his memory of the first smoking.

> And then initiation, you know, all the old fellas would sit round the outside of a – all the leaf you know, when you piled leaf all around, had to make a big circle and then you raise it all with all the leaf on the ground and young fellas'd get in the middle, inside the circle, and all the old fellas'd sit on the outside, and when you light it, smoke the circle. Then the old fellas sit on the outside and burnt, they'd sing another song there, because the child's goin' into manhood. They all sit on the ground with one leg sort of flat, and the other leg

sort of the knee up, and stamp the feet, make the rhythm that way. Yes, all singin' around the circle while the young fellas gettin' smoked in the middle. Because that was cleansin', cleansin' all the, everything from the young fellas to go into, start the manhood. (Tony Perkins)

Tony remembers this experience in his body. In the telling of this story I get a sense of the intensity of the place formed by the outside circle of the old initiated men and the inside circle of the young men. I can smell the smoke of burning eucalypt leaves, feel the thud of stamping feet and hear the rhythm of singing that marked the ritual cleansing of the beginning of the passage to manhood. Tony said he and the other young men of his generation did not go beyond this first stage of initiation. 'I never got to go to Cunjaree, never ever went, you know.' While this story is permeated with a profound sense of loss, it is a loss that opens the way to an equally profound transition. Tony left Corindi Lake at the time for a different process of initiation into the ways of the contemporary world, after which he came back and gave birth to new forms of cultural transmission.

There are many profound acts of translation in the telling of this story. The story has travelled through the bodies of the old initiated men to the young men, crossing not only generations but two different epochs of Gumbaynggirr place-time. The place of the story has moved to the Old Camp, energising and inspiring a new place. The songs are still sung in Gumbaynggirr and the story is told in English, stretching the coloniser's language to the limits of its meaning. The oral story is recorded and transcribed into writing in a decision to transmit this knowledge in a different way. All of these translations involve loss but they equally open the possibility for singing this country differently. In the embodied traces that remain in people, in places and in stories, lies the possibility of transformation.

CHAPTER 6

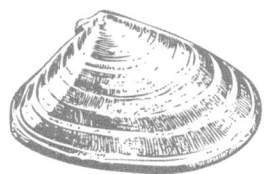

A language of landscape

The Muurrbay Tree

Yaamagay ngiyanggidam gagaaynga.
Warriwarri yandaarray. Yamagaay warriinga ngalangala
ngayinggirri jawgarr ngilina ngiyanggidam.
Biyambiyayirri. Biyambangagay.
Yaarrigay garrugundu nyaawang.
'Galang, yaam! Yarrangbarrway! Yaam ngiyanggidambu
gabaayngadu barrway biyambang; ngiyaanya gala
yaam junuy ngurraang. Galang! Gujaarri nyaaga!' …
Wurraangagay ngilina muurrbay bundeeni;
Wurraang; maaningagay.
Ngilinagay waruungga ngiyanggidam. Birrung ngilina.[33]

> Muurrbay's a white fig. The people from the west'd come down and they'd all feed from it until sometime one of 'em looked around the other side of the tree and said, 'Oh they got more figs', you know bigger figs and got a bit jealous and then they started rowing about who the figs were for. Then the creator just said, 'You're arguing too much about this so I'll just take it back'.

> Some stories they have birds taking it up and some of where they tried to cut off branches to save the tree and grow it but basically it was gone. It's also part of the story about when you die you go to that tree there and people sing out to you and if they don't hear you anymore you're there at the tree.
> (Gary Williams)

To enter the country of southern Gumbaynggirr people I drive off the Pacific Highway through the town to the lookout on the southern headland. Here the whole estuary is laid out before me, draped in its finery. Layers of dark and light aqua, delicate silk chiffon over shapes of islands and sand bars that change form and colour from moment to moment with tides, weather, seasons, and time of day. To the south, there are curves of beaches and headlands as far as the eye can see. In the west, deep purple mountains of the Great Dividing Range mark the western extent of Gumbaynggirr country, the place I have come from.

I can never look at this scene without it taking my breath away. It fills me as if I have taken in a huge breath of spiritual grace along with the salt air. I take my leave and drive down into the belly of the estuary, past all the little islands, and the story places I have come to know, until I cross the highway again at a bend in the river. Just south of Nambucca I turn west past shabby fibro houses and an out-of-the-way shopping centre to a small white wooden building with an Aboriginal flag and a sign outside that names its story, with the word Muurrbay and an image of a fig tree.[34]

It is here at Nambucca Heads that the work of connecting language back to country takes place. Corindi Lake and Nambucca Heads mark the northern and southern ends of Gumbaynggirr language territory, with 80 kilometres of beaches and headlands stretching in-between.

Muurrbay

A lot of the stories here were held
by old Tiger Buchannan,
he was the fella who knew them all.
He was the last of the storymen

that was here in Nambucca.
He believed knowledge
was to be shared,
had the foresight to look into the future
and realise that one day people
will want their language back.

'Ginnagay jinda. G'day sista', Pauline greets me at the door. Pauline invites people in, makes cups of tea, cleans up, organises, knows everyone's state of wellbeing, and has her finger on the pulse of life in Nambucca. The kitchen has a large painting of the Muurrbay story and two big tables where we have many gatherings. When we bring all the poster maps we have made from our research everyone is invited to a big feed. Pauline chooses fresh prawns, salads, bread rolls and fruit and makes special fish for the Elders, cooking it herself so it is just right. Auntie Rose sets up her jewellery stall at the back door. Gary, Ken and Amy cover the big round table on the verandah with maps, and the tables in the kitchen are laden with food. Soon the place is filled to overflowing with people of all ages. At lunch there are speeches and then the storytelling begins, using the maps we have made to tell the special storylines of Birrugan, the hero ancestor, and The Women Who Made the Sea, of Stuart Island and the Mission. We are soon in the midst of talking important political business about country. Muurrbay is buzzing with life and meaning.

The room immediately adjacent to the kitchen is a classroom with long tables and rows of chairs, a whiteboard, and another painting with life-size figures of the Birrugan story. Other beautiful brightly coloured paintings made by the students fill every spare wall space. On some days the classroom is full of Gumbaynggirr students studying language and culture. They have an art room in the backyard where they can paint, sculpt, pot and make mosaics. In the next room there is a large open-plan office with desks, computers and bays. Here is the work of the Many Rivers Language Centre which supports the maintenance of language and culture from Tweed Heads down to Sydney. Beyond the open-plan office is the inner sanctum where the Elders, who are the knowledge banks behind all this activity, have their space. There are more desks, computers, recording equipment, posters and paintings. We have our meetings outside on the back verandah where we sit overlooking the backyard with a small swimming pool and some ragged scrub over the fence. Beyond this is the river. At one time two ducks moved in to the pool and we watched as they came and went and introduced their ducklings.

Muurrbay was not always like this. When we first came it was quiet, mostly closed with drawn blinds, a caretaker and a barking dog. It became more and more vigorous during the time of our research. But even before this it had its own history. Ken Walker, the chairman of Muurrbay, said the building was originally a church, built in 1952 'for all the people here on the Mish [Mission], because they never used to like going down town to church'. Pauline shows us photos of young girls in white confirmation dresses and veils, and shiny patent leather shoes. The boys have white shirts, bow ties, dark pants and long socks. She talks about the time when the church on the Mission was full.

> This church has been full with all the blackfellas on the Mission – I mean we've got some photos. Like I've been in the church when it first opened. Ken and Gary were the altar boys, as well as Colin Jarrett, and even Michael Bryant I think. They were altar boys. But a lot of the Kooris on the Mish were all baptised and made their first kind of communion here. I mean I know I made it, I was baptised here, and my godmother is Ruthy Bryant, and I think it used to be Patsy Mundell. (Pauline Hooler)

Gary remembers that the kitchen area is where the altar once was. His current experience of the place is layered with images of the nave and altar, and the sounds of church services held in Latin. The sense of the church remains with a full-length painting of Birrugan and the hero ancestor's mother, Gawnggan[35], coloured like a stained-glass window, in a recessed area in the wall. Gary can map each part of the building as it was when it was a church. He says that when the Catholic diocese sold it to become a residential dwelling the loss of the building was 'like a running sore'.

Ken Walker tells the story of how a group of the Old People got together with Brother Steve Morelli in an old church building in Kempsey to begin the work of language revival. He became involved and they decided to buy back the old church on the Mission to 'bring the language back home'.

> When Brother Steve and Sharon and them started to develop all this program over at Kempsey, and I started to go over there I got out of all this other stuff and just concentrated on language. I enjoyed all the time I done with it. I especially enjoyed purchasing this building because this building was originally built as a church for Aboriginal people and Gary and myself were two of the altar boys that were here when they opened this church. It went through a few hands, private buyers, in-between all of them we had the opportunity to buy it and we bought it and we brought all our language back home. (Ken Walker)

Buying back the old church as a house of language recovered the place as a house of cultural work and spiritual practice. Ken explained that Sherwood near Kempsey, where they had been doing their language work, was a 'mish-mash' place because the people were all mixed up there. They had been moved from their country onto reserves and missions, displaced by government policies and practices. Language and people were separated from their places.

> They didn't belong over there, it's different country. The Old People that started it off were Gumbaynggirr people, and they were forced over there in the early days by the Welfare Board and they kicked them off Yellow Rock and took them over to Kempsey and that sort of stuff, then had 'em scattered between Yellow Rock and Kempsey, see there was like a big mission over at Clybucca, yeah. (Ken Walker)

For Gumbaynggirr people Kempsey was a 'different country'. The boundaries of country were the boundaries of language and Kempsey was traditionally Dhanggati country with different language and cultural practices. Despite being moved and separated from country, however, the Old People had 'kept the Gumbaynggirr side of 'em' so that they could pass on their language to their grandchildren. That is why the language work of Muurrbay came about.

> These are people like, some of their families were from Yellow Rock and so they married over there and grew their families up and everything like that but still kept that Gumbayngirr side of 'em. So it was only that they wanted it [the language] to be known for their grandkids, that really is how the dictionary and this place came about and then the language then went from there back to country, back to the church. (Gary Williams)

For Gumbaynggirr people, language belongs in country. After their experience of dispossession and dispersal and the sale of the church, the return of the Gumbaynggirr language to this building brought a renewed sense of home and belonging. In relocating the activities of the Gumbaynggirr language group back to Nambucca they returned the language to country in a process of repatriation. Country was symbolised by Muurrbay, the church building, which became the home place for the language. Gary, like Ken, regarded the purchase of the church building to house their language artefacts, as bringing language home.

Muurrbay is a house of many meanings and translations. When I asked Gary about what it meant to be an altar boy he laughed and reported a conversation with Gary Foley about having a funeral ceremony when they die. 'We're all suckers for ceremony, Aboriginal people', he said. He went on to add that despite his connection with the Catholic religion, 'I never think of Mary other than Brolga now you know'. Encoded in this apparently simple statement is the intersection of two worlds of meaning. On another occasion, Gary explains that the Lord has now become Birrugan and Mary is Gawnggan.

> Anyway people call Birrugan the Lord now, and of course you've got Mary's Waterhole up there which is the women's place. Gawnggan is the name. Funny enough when my aunt

said the story, she never called her by Gawnggan, she just said that she's a brolga, so she used to just say the brolga.
The brolga, yeah. (Gary Williams)

The Birrugan story is one of the major songlines and an important part of bringing the language home. These storylines were recorded by the Old People with linguist researchers and 'brought home' to Muurrbay and compiled into *Gumbaynggirr Yuludarla, Gumbaynggirr Dreamings*. In these recordings the Christian Holy Trinity and Mary, the mother of Jesus, are identified by older Gumbaynggirr speakers with their own hero ancestors. Thus Birrugan is Jesus, Yuludarla is God the Father, and Gawnggan is Mary. Cultural stories grow and change and re-emerge in country. It is, however, a two-way process in which hybrid understandings make new meanings of country possible. The Old People, in the process of translating their Gumbaynggirr stories of country into English, drew on complex symbols and stories from the Catholic religion through which to translate their meanings into English. The meanings communicated in the Gumbaynggirr dictionary reveal some of the language work that helps us to unravel some of this crossing over.

The story of Birrugan is the great epic storyline of the actions and events of the hero ancestor in creating the landscapes of Gumbaynggirr country. His mother, Gawnggan, features prominently in the story. Mary's Waterhole is a women's special place in the Birrugan story, a place where Birrugan and his mother stayed, and intersects with other women's storylines. In this account Gawnggan is also the name of the Evening Star, related to the ending of the Birrugan storyline in sky country. At the place where Birrugan was finally killed, prior to going to his resting place in the sky, Gawnggan turned into a brolga, Giilan. Hence the transposing of Gawnggan (all woman) to Brolga: 'I never think of Mary other than Brolga now'.

In these acts of translation they shifted both the meanings of the Gumbaynggirr stories to the entirely new situation in which they found themselves, and also the meanings of the Catholic church. They profoundly transformed the meanings of the Catholic religion to forge a connection to their country, to the sea, the beaches, the rivers, estuaries, creeks, and mountains of Baga-baga.

Gumbaynggirr people, their language and stories had become disconnected from their places since the first white timber-getters arrived in the Nambucca Valley in the mid-nineteenth century. Dispossession, as land was taken up by white settlers, meant that people no longer had access to the special places where ceremonies were performed and knowledge was passed on from generation to generation. Knowledge of special stories and story places could not be passed down because the young men of the next generation could not be initiated. As well as being disconnected from country by alienation from ceremonial places, some Gumbaynggirr people were moved onto missions and government reserves, further segregating people from their lands and their people. Language and kinship relationships broke down. Deliberate policies of the suppression of language and cultural practice were also put in place, exercised through schools and the activities of the Aborigines Protection Board and the Welfare. These were reinforced by the threatened removal of children – the ultimate cultural erasure. Most people we talked with recognised the great loss of language and cultural practice that had occurred since white settlement.

There was a sense that there was a great wellspring of knowledge about country stored up in language, story and its connection to place that could not be spoken. However, language speakers from all over Gumbaynggirr country – including Frank Archibald and Lenny de Silva from Armidale, Clarrie Skinner, Bruce and Bing Laurie and Keith Lardner from Corindi Lake, and Harry 'Tiger' Buchannan from Nambucca Heads – recorded Gumbaynggirr language with non-Indigenous linguists and researchers. Tiger Buchannan is one of the few people who spent many hours systematically recording Gumbaynggirr language in order to leave a legacy for future generations.

Tiger Buchannan was the last storyman in the Nambucca Valley. He was born at Cow Creek in 1898 and although he took the white property owner's name of Buchanan he did not lose his Gumbaynggirr name, nor his Gumbaynggirr identity. In *Gumbaynggirr Yuludarla* his name is given as Maruwanba[36] Maruungga. The first, Maruwanba, is his initiation name. The second, Maruungga, is his clan name. Tiger was moved from the reserve at Cow Creek to Stuart Island and then to 'the Mission', along with other Gumbaynggirr people in the Nambucca

Valley. In all of these places he continued with the tradition of initiating young people into the stories and places of the sea, river and estuary. Gary remembers Tiger stopping when he walked by their house to talk stories over the fence at the Mission.

Tiger Buchannan recorded stories with a number of linguists and anthropologists over the years including T Crowley, WG Hoddinott, Howard Creamer and Diana Eades, translating the language that he recorded with them. It is not clear why he was so passionate about recording language and cultural stories. However, the introduction to *Gumbaynggirr Yuludarla* notes that 'he had fourteen children of his own and liked to share his culture with the young'. He was also 'a great fisherman', acknowledging the profound connection between language and place for the people of the sea and river.

> A lot of the stories here were held by old Tiger Buchannan, he was the fella who sort of knew 'em all, he was the last of the storymen that was here, in Nambucca. He believed that knowledge was to be shared … He had the foresight to look into the future and realise that one day the people will want their language back and he prepared himself I think quite early, in the sixties I think. Most of the stories that we have in our story books are his, or other parts of Gumbaynggirr territory, see a lot of the stories relate to up around Grafton, Nymboida, Coffs Harbour and all them places too, and they have significance too, well it relates back to the sea story, so they have a northern version of that too. (Ken Walker)

Tiger's knowledge was held in oral stories. While language is the fundamental basis of connection between people and specific places in the landscape, it is story that holds the meaning of language. It is story that embodies the connections between people and places. The work of recording and translating language and recording and translating stories was carried out simultaneously, each one dependent on the other. Through this work, the process by which people, language and story were connected to country was made visible. Tiger's stories connected people to country over a vast area, extending beyond the Nambucca Valley to the length and breadth of Gumbaynggirr country, typical of the knowledge of initiated men. Knowledge about language and story is knowledge about country and the highest level of this knowledge was handed down during initiation. As Pauline Hooler says of her grandfather, Lambert Waddy, if he hadn't put Tiger Buchannan through the rules, the knowledge could not have been passed on.

> When we goin' to Muurrbay, talkin' about Birrugan and Gawnggan and Yuludarla and all these Dreamin' stories I said look, they wouldn't even be here 'cause it was grandfather who put Tiger Buchannan through those rules, you know, initiation ceremonies. Grandfather would have been one of them to take care of that spirituality, someone else would teach him something about the healing powers and someone else would teach him about hunting, each Elder had their role and would have passed it down to a certain male when they was at that initiation stage, they'd be given that knowledge. (Pauline Hooler)

For Gumbaynggirr people in the Nambucca Valley, as with the people at Corindi Lake, story knowledge is held collectively, shared between generations, between men and women, and resides in country. Holding knowledge is a collective responsibility. In this sense each individual has only partial knowledge, each has a piece of the jigsaw puzzle. This was especially evident during the early impact of colonisation when, as Tony explained, the Old People decided to transmit different aspects of knowledge to different people according to their interests and talents. The story knowledge that Tiger Buchannan recorded was partial because of the nature of the transmission of knowledge but also because of the constraints of recording and the limits of translation. The Dreaming stories presented in *Gumbaynggirr Yuludarla* were a compilation of a number of different versions. 'We had to intertwine both, both to make one great story, because there were bits and pieces missing from both, so we had to combine them to make it one good story, so that's how it works.'

The revival of Gumbaynggirr language and story was a collective effort of recording, collecting, consolidating, translating and publishing and by a large number of people. All of the Elders were significant in this work, some specifically involved in the formation of the Gumbaynggirr Language and Culture Group[37] at Kempsey. Ken Walker, Gary Williams and Pauline Hooler have been involved in the ongoing language and story work at Muurrbay. They have all had to (re)learn the Gumbaynggirr language. Ken recalls wondering if he would be able to learn the language again, but says 'somewhere in me brain the sound was still there' and 'it just all come back to me'. Gary remembers a similar experience of finding the language that was in his body when he had to produce a language song at a conference in New Zealand. 'They just went berserk just hearin' my singing in language and Gary Foley said, "I didn't know you can do that" and I said, "Neither did I!" ' Everyone is learning and teaching too, connecting more pieces of the jigsaw puzzle through this work.

> It's one of those things where you'll never get the jigsaw puzzle back but there's enough there and you can consolidate on things … However, one good thing is that you kind of dream, you know how they say about the Old People dreaming in language, you kind of find yourself dreaming in language a bit and I thought, oh it's a lovely feeling you know. (Gary Williams)

For Gary, one of the rewards of this work is to be able to dream in language. 'Dreaming' is the English word often used to describe the time of creation and the making of creation stories. The Dreaming is a cyclical time that is continually re-enacted in the present where new Dreaming stories can be made through a dream-like state. Dreaming in language is part of this cycle of creation and re-creation of stories and places. Thinking through language is a different lens through which to view the world. 'You look at history through language rather than through just dates and actions or reactions to things and it just kind of brings those actions alive.' For Gary, it is what makes history come alive. For Ken, too, his sense of history is transformed through language.

> Yeah well, it just goes to show you that you had a history that was a wonderful history, you had a great history. There's

not only white history that you've been taught about, they thought that was the only history that existed, but really you've got to go back and find your own traditions and your own stories that you know are irreplaceable and they go back a long time before, before anybody else's stories, because, you know, we're probably one of the oldest people on this planet. (Ken Walker)

Thinking history through language and stories of place gives a sense of continuity in deep time. Deep time links people and place with their own stories and traditions of the deep past as the oldest living culture on this planet. The deep time of the Dreaming, however, is cyclical and returns and returns in the present. It is also the time of the future. As Ken says, following the tradition set by Tiger Buchannan, language work is for future generations, 'in fifty, sixty years from now or more, what I'm tellin' you is, you never know what sort of difference is that gonna make to some kid'. The ongoing recording of language, story and place in our project is seen as a continuation of this Dreaming in deep time. Together with Ken, Gary, Pauline and Virginia Jarrett we developed new collaborative research processes of connecting people to country that we described as 'deep mapping'.[38]

In deep mapping we map the storylines of the places where Gumbaynggirr people live now and where they lived in the past, and the creation stories of the ancestors. The story we produce here follows the same processes as deep mapping, beginning with the present and moving back into the deep past. The past is always partially visible in the present, it is never completely erased.

We begin with Muurrbay today as the place where the language was brought home. The next layer of stories is about Stuart Island in the Nambucca River, a place that is special for all Gumbaynggirr people in the Nambucca Valley as a place in-between the deep past and the present time. Finally the creation storylines of the great ancestral beings are mapped as part of the deep past. However, the deep past is cyclical, it returns and is recreated in the present each time a story is told in its place. So the deep mapping storylines belong in the present in Muurrbay just as they belong in the earliest layer when the world and everything in it was created. People continue to inhabit all of these places through visits, through stories and through the imagination.

The Island

That one's Plover, Girr Girr[39],
that's Bandicoot, bandicoots have big holes
if you don't watch you'll break your ankles.
Mirubay is Egg
kids weren't allowed to go there on their own
had to go with Elders
birds're nesting there, sandpipers, oyster catchers, curlews
they didn't want them destroying nests
so it was called Egg, Mirubay.
You could walk across, mud flats and lotsa crabs.
Swimming from Wandarrga
that Blue-Tongue place
to get to the Island.
Wandarrga is the name of the blue-tongue lizard.

It is high tide and partly overcast as we stand at the Blue-Tongue Lizard place on the Nambucca River overlooking the estuary towards the sea. The channels of water and sand are marked by light and dark shades of blue-green. Before us lies the spread of the estuary with its islands of dark green mangroves. From here Gary and Ken name each of the sand islands between us and the sea. Each island is named and known for its particular habitat and inhabitants. Mirubay is the Egg island where the migratory shore birds nest; Bandicoot Island with the big holes; Girr Girr, the Plover island; and the Blue-Tongue Lizard place, Wandarrga, is where we stand to take in this view. One island, Girr Girr, stands out from all the rest. Amy Marshall said, 'I think they used to call that Girr girrjuga, that's Plover Island. That was before Stuart come there, and so they named it after him'.

In 1883 Stuart Island was declared a reserve for Aboriginal people, or, as Pauline put it, 'Queen Victoria said, "Give them fellas some land". So that's when they give 'em the Island.' People were moved from Cow Creek to Stuart Island. Then in 1952 the Lands Department declared the Island a recreational reserve and it was turned into a golf course. Gumbaynggirr people were moved again to much less desirable land without a view of the estuary and sea, to Bellwood Reserve, or 'the Mish', as it is more commonly known. Girr Girr is the place that bridges the past and present for southern Gumbaynggirr people. The deep past is represented in the storylines of Birrugan's last battle and The Women Who Made the Sea, and the present is represented by Muurrbay and the Mission where they were relocated in the early 1950s. But Gary said 'to us the Island's still the main thing'. It is the Island that holds their cultural stories.

In many ways memories of life on the Island are symbolic of life on the Nambucca estuary. Gumbaynggirr people have always inhabited this wide stretch of estuary, beach, river and creeks, fishing and living off the river and sea. Mapping the Island is mapping water country as well as land country. The maps we made show tracks all over the Nambucca estuary, across the water between the islands, up Worrell Creek, across to South Beach. Amy remembered going camping up the river every weekend with Uncle Tiger Buchannan, building shelters and collecting seafood that was cooked on the coals with damper and johnny cakes. 'An easy way of livin'', she said.

> Me Uncle Harry used to take us campin' every weekend. Used to go up the creek, like Worrell Creek, Second Bay, Third Bay, anywhere you like, you thought it was a good place for campin' along there. We'd ah, he'd make us all get wood, like, soon as we'd get there – help him build a lean-to. Like he'd have one this side and one on the opposite side and have the fire, a little fire in the middle like through the night. All the girls'd be over 'ere an' all the boys over that side. So, early in the mornin' we'd get up and go over to the beach – pipis, worms, get a few worms for fishin' – and Auntie Mabel, she used to stay back and she'd cook a coupla dampers, like johnny cakes – on the coals and by the time we got back they'd be cooked, and then Uncle Harry'd have some fish and we'd have the pipis – we'd just throw 'em on the hot coals – like it was just an easy way of livin'.
> (Amy Marshall)

In their journeys with Tiger they learned to know Worrell Creek – Second Bay and Third Bay, making shelter, collecting worms, catching fish. Inhabiting the estuary, creeks, river, bays and beaches in this way, they learned how to live in this place. The intimate knowledge of eating from that place was an important part of their relationship to the islands and the river. They also learned its stories. Every part of the landscape was resonant with stories. There was Biddy's Farm, and Wijiirjagi the cannibal woman, men's and women's special places, and all the ongoing cultural stories of living in this landscape. Martin Ballangarry remembers travelling up Worrell Creek with Tiger Buchanan and the Old People too, and some of the stories that were told about those places.

> We used to go up the creek, up the Worrell Creek there, putt putt, and then the Old People used to say, 'Now this is where we got a farm, Biddy's Farm there. All you little boys gotta duck under this tent.' So they put the tents over us and we used to look out like that, but no you gotta be very quiet when we go past this place. She was a old woman, very jokey woman, I suppose she was clever woman, and she loved little boys. So they used that 'cause she would throw her hair around us, round that boy and take you off to her farm, Biddy's Farm.
>
> See we've got a story here in our old country, our own Dreamtime story, about the Wijiirjagi Woman see, she was a sort of witch, clever woman. So even when we got off there we used to go across the beach, grab the sticks. All the little boys they can leave their footprints behind see, but us bigger boys, we had to go like that, every time we grabbed a bush, even the old fellas grabbed a bigger bush, they used to 'swish swish', rub all the footprints, yeah be walkin' and rubbin' the footprints. (Martin Ballangarry)

Martin's telling of the story of Biddy's Farm was a performance. He demonstrated the peeking out from the tents and the Old People's warning, and the swish-swishing of the branches to rub away the footprints from the sand. The telling evokes the high performance of a special place. For Martin, the story is about 'the old country', a Dreamtime story of the Wijiirjagi, the cannibal woman. Layers of past landscapes come alive in the present through the telling of this story. This story belongs in the landscape and particular places each have their part of the story. As they pass the spot where Biddy's Farm is, the young boys are covered with the tent. On the shore they have to brush their footprints away from the sand so they will be safe. Auntie Val Cohen also described the many special places along Worrell Creek where they left their story traces on the landscape.

> Up Worrell Creek here, this end up near Scotts Head, all along here is women's business. Gummang, that's where Uncle Lambert used to initiate the young fellas. But as we look at Worrell Creek [pointing on the map] somewhere on here's the men's initiation ground. As far as I know this is the women. My mother showed me lot of things that grow along that area and one certain bush that grows there has little berries on it and she said to me if a woman doesn't wanta have a baby, she eats about maybe a dozen of them. Just like sweet berries. And she showed me that bush. (Val Cohen)

Embedded within this cultural landscape of living and story places was Girr Girr, Stuart Island. Like the area around Corindi Lake, the Island became intensified with cultural meanings because of the concentration of living there. 'There are – up the bottom end of the island there's burial grounds there as well and I think there's like a ceremonial grounds there where you could go across as well over to the bigger ground.' There were three Elders who each had particular traditional knowledge: a storyman, an initiation man and a medicine man.

> See there was three Aboriginal rulers when I was growin' up on that Island. One was Uncle Harry Buchanan, he was the storyteller, and Uncle Lambert Waddy, he was the initiation man. The initiation ground is over 'ere where they used to put the men, young boys through the rules. And my father [Walter Smith] was the medicine man, he used to do all the healing. And that's how I grew up, those three Elders. (Val Cohen)

A language of landscape

The storyman, the initiation man and the medicine man continued with their cultural practices, providing guidance and leadership for the people on the Island. It was a place of gatherings where the Old People 'used to come down from Armidale, come from Kempsey, come from far north, the Bundjalung tribe. They all used to come here, sit down under that tree there, smoke their pipes, talkin' the lingo.'

The Island continues to have a very special place in the hearts of southern Gumbaynggirr people today. People were born, lived and died on the Island imbuing it with special meanings. Many people began their stories with a personal statement about the significance of the Island.

> Mum [Auntie Vilma Moylan] she was born in 1926 on this island. Auntie Eva was the midwife, that's Auntie Jess's mother. That would've been Grandfather's sister. Yeah, there was a few births then, few deaths on the island. I think nowadays they got a border thing around the burial sites where they think Mum's brothers are. That's all down there somewhere. (Pauline Hooler)

Births and deaths were recorded in memory and story, and by cultural markers, prior to the 'border' arranged by the New South Wales National Parks and Wildlife Service. Val said that 'All the people that were born on the Island, like the Waddys, the Buchannans, me – all their afterbirth is buried on that Island'. People have stories about where they were born, where they camped, and other significant markers of their lives there. They remember their shacks and their daily lives in that place.

> Well, there would've been Lambert and Valerie Waddy, which was Mum's parents. And Dad's brother, Doug Waddy and then there was Grandfather's sister, Auntie Eva Waddy, she was buried over on the Island. And there was Marshalls, Buchanans, Davises, just a few of the names I can remember Mum was yarnin' about them. They all had little hut sites, camp on either end, but they also grew corn and maize and

> they had cows on there and they were fully productive. I
> think like in winter it used to flood as well. (Pauline Hooler)

When people moved to the Mission in 1952 they maintained their relationship to the Island, through frequent visits as well as stories. 'Everybody just went to the Island 'cause that's where we swam and played, just to get off the Mish 'cause it was hot you know, that's where you went, to the Island.' Pauline remembered the track down along the riverbank through the mangroves where they walked from the Mission to the Island. The Island continued to play an important part in their sense of themselves and their identity in place.

> Yeah, to me the Island is a special place and I think it's always
> been a special place for local community who've been in
> this area, who grew up in the area. I know for a start Mum
> was born on the Island so maybe that's why it has a special
> meaning for me, apart from the fact that I know that Mum,
> Dad and family relations that's where they first camped, on
> that Island there, the Island played a big role in what sort of
> community is around here. (Pauline Hooler)

The Island is a special place for Auntie Val Cohen too. We visited the Island to record stories with Val and her cousin, Auntie Rose Boston, one hot day at the end of summer. As we drive across the causeway to the Island, Val begins a running commentary on the place moment by moment – 'tide's comin' in' – gee that bank's breakin' away' – while storying every aspect of the landscape's past.

> See that oak tree, the tallest one there? That's where the
> school used to be. Over here, see where that table is?
> That's where our house was. See, drive up to that oak tree.
> Just swing it around there in the shade. This is where our
> grandfather's hut used to be. Our house was over there. All
> this part was our house, all this part there, and the well was
> just down the end of that road there, other side of the oak
> trees where the men dug a well there. And all the people –
> Uncle Jim McGrath and Auntie Emily and the Walkers, and
> the Buchannans, Uncle Harry – had a big house over there

and Uncle Fred Buchannan. The Waddys lived underneath
the fig tree up that end of the Island. (Val Cohen)

Every aspect of the place becomes a marker for memory: the oak trees, the lantana, the coral trees, the boat ramp and the river bank. Like Gumbaynggirr people in No Mans Land, Val says the Old People planted a fig tree to mark the places where they camped because they shifted a lot due to the floods. 'Every fig tree that grows on the Island indicates where Aboriginal people camped, like their house. The Mumblers, the Bryants, the Waddys – they all come under the Waddy clan. And the Buchannans.' A stand of she-oaks marks the place where Val was born.

> I was the last born on the Island. When I came into the
> world, my mother's best mate was Phyllis Flanders from
> Bowraville, and she brought me into the world supervised
> by all the grannies. There was Granny McGrath, Granny
> Buchannan, and Granny Doyle, and I think there was a
> Granny Walter. I remember the grannies. They were the
> supervision people. My afterbirth is still buried there.
> (Val Cohen)

Rose grew up with Val on the Island because her mother died when she was very young. During our visit Rose and Val both moved in and out of joint storytelling and individual conversations, often both talking at the same time. They each brought different things to our picnic table for us to look at. Val had a big collection of photos, taken in the 1950s by visiting missionaries of life on the Island. Rose brought a collection of newspaper cuttings, artwork, stories, and the gumleaves she used to make music. Rose introduced herself to the recording quite formally.

> I say hello in the game my name is Auntie Rosina Boston,
> better known as Auntie Rose. I can blow a gumleaf. I learned
> to blow a gumleaf when I was a little girl about eight years
> old. I was born on Stuart Island Nambucca Heads, and that is
> where I used to live. About five or six Aboriginal families –
> well there was more in them times – lived there when I was a

> little girl. There was a school on the Island and our teacher's
> name was called Miss Higgins. Anyway, back in those days all
> our uncles used to pick some gumleaves and sit under the big
> trees an' tell us stories and play the music. (Rosina Boston)

Both Val and Rose construct their identity as tied to the Island. Val feels connected forever to this place through the ties of her placenta buried in the place of her birth. Rose's identity as a gumleaf player is connected to the place under the big trees on the Island where she learned to play the gumleaf with the Old People. Together they created stories of their shared life on the Island. Val's father, Walter Smith, was a professional fisherman and Val and Rose used to go with him to help carry his nets and dye them with tan bark in boilers. There are many photos of Walter Smith's fishing boats, including the last boat that Val had on the Island. She inherited the fishing from her father.

> Dad was a professional fisherman, he showed me how to
> read the moon, the stars, the way they lay tells you how the
> water is working. They, the moon controls the water, the
> sun controls the earth and the way the sun, if you're looking
> at the moon in the night and the way it lays it can tell you
> is it going to be a storm and if that moon in the night got a
> ring around, it's going to be windy, going to be very windy.
> All depends the size of that wind, the size of that ring that's
> around the moon. Tells you when the rain's comin' as well as
> it's going to be windy. The stars are the same, the way they
> lay. If you watch the way the Milky Way lays, you can say
> that's low tide, if the Milky Way's leaning, laying, a different
> [way] it's high tide or comin' high tide. I still follow it when
> I'm on the Island, yeah. (Val Cohen)

In holiday times visitors came to the Island to fish and swim and Val made a living from her bait shop. Relatives gathered to camp there for holidays too. 'We used to go over there in the holiday time and just chuck up a humpy there at the Island, because they was like all family, fishin' and oyster gatherin' and go over to South Beach get pipis, all the stuff you do around the sea, just live off shellfish and fish.' Christmas was a time for the special gatherings that they remembered by the coral trees that still stand on the riverbank.

> So right where that wharf is our table was right, like our Christmas table. So that's our old coral trees along there. They're the last coral trees we grew. We used to have a table laid out straight in the middle of the coral trees. That was our job to lay the table out and get water, plenty water. We had our own well on the place, on the Island, get plenty wood because the women were doin' the cookin' and we used to help by puttin' in little shilling in the pudding [laughs]. All us kids had to bunk it underneath the trees outside and give our beds to the visitors that came in those days.
> When all the men came together they just went off and had a big yarn up, you know, where the women were doin' all the hard work like cookin'. In those days we had a copper, couple of coppers, fill those up, put the pudding in those, yeah used to, and we had to make sure that we had plenty of wood to keep it boiling and not only carrying water from the well was hard enough and going for wood was, that was our work, our daily work, yeah. So anyway it was great fun.
> (Val Cohen)

Every bit of the Island has meaning for Val and Rose and they tell that meaning in conversation and story. They include their recent and past memories of the Island, the places where they were born and lived, the plants and trees they planted, the current state of the Island, and the other people who have come down to enjoy the water on this very hot day. Just as they include the people swimming in their storytelling, Val and Rose interact with every aspect of the place and all of its creatures, weaving stories of the past into new stories for the future. They talk to and about the butcherbirds, magpies and dolphins and the audio recorder picks up all of these conversations and stories mixed with the sounds of the birds, wind in the oak trees, other voices and conversations, from all the different places. It is a soundscape in which the whole place comes alive with meaning.

> Dolphins, dolphins, come over and see. There's one there, it's wounded. There is one swimmin' in the river. [Val: Tide goin' out.] There they are, there they are. Little fish jumpin' out the water. You weren't hallucinatin'. There they are, they got that one. Look at 'em, aren't they beautiful. Big school of 'em comes up in here. They always comin' in. There's a wounded one among them, one of the boat's blades. You know the fin that comes out of the water, their dorsal fin? It's sorta shredded. Two or three gaps in it. One of the blades of the outboard, that's terrible. But they do, they shoot the waves, thud, thud, they do shoot the waves. 'We're watchin' dolphins.' [to nearby picnickers] [Val: They're playin' a bit. They wanta get outta there before the tide go out because they gonna get caught on the sandspit.] No, they'll swim around, go out that other way. [Val: They'll have to swim right around.] Up the way they're goin', they won't get caught. (Val Cohen and Rose Boston)

Each of these memories is added in layers to the richness of what the Island can mean. Later, in a more contemplative moment, Val comments on this quality of the place, 'everywhere you look is memory' and this thought triggers more memories.

> The Island itself is just, everywhere you look is memory, where you went to school, where you used to play rounders and cricket and go, where we used to go, us young girls in those photos there, we used to do a lot of moonlight swimming in those days, so beautiful. We used to go swimming when it's dark and the tide is high and when you dive into the water it's a different world. You dive into the water at night, it's not black, it's all lit up. It's like stars are shining when you dive into the water. You see a fish or crab walkin' along the bottom of the river where you're swimming, they're all lit up, sparkling. Fish go past you sparkling, so beautiful, yeah. (Val Cohen)

For Val, her life on the Island and in the Nambucca estuary extends beyond herself and her time on earth. It is a continuity of generations, a part of a deeply collective experience, reaching into the future through her children and grandchildren. Pauline experiences this same feeling of the importance of the Island and its stories to her children and grandchildren.

> There was quite a few different families over there living on the Island and I think that created a place for us people, for our generation to go there, to feel safe and know that we belong there. I mean this is our island you know and it was our golfcourse, you know all these little things that you know when we were growin' up. To me it's important because the group that I went over with, like all me mates and my cousins and that, we still friends today, even though we were growin' up, forty years later we've all got grown up families.
>
> Even when I was livin' in Sydney that was one place where I used to go to come back, when I'd come back home, to show my kids the Island. I said this is where we grew up, this is what we did, this is where we walked, you know all this same track where we walked along, so I was showin' 'em that, and that way I talked them back to this homeland, see 'cause it's their homeland, 'cause they're Gumbaynggirr kids, so that's how I feel about the Island, it's important in that I always remember it with happy memories and, and a belonging thing. (Pauline Hooler)

The Island is a bridge for southern Gumbaynggirr people between the deep past of ceremony and creation stories and future generations of Gumbaynggirr children. All of the sand islands, creeks, channels and waterways in the estuary at Nambucca are named, known and storied. To map the memories and stories of the Island is to map this water country. Their ongoing relationship with this place gives a connection between people, place and story that is mediated by language. Through Muurrbay, the work of language is the key to revitalising this connection, and this country.

Deep mapping

Baga-baga Nyambaga
that's where he fell over when he was speared
his knee was like that and his body
well the roads go over his body
and his head on an angle like this,
so the road goes right over the middle of him.
The roads change the structure of it
but they don't change the meaning of the place
it may not exist the way it did
when it was first thought
but it's always gonna be
in the memory of the people.

As I drive from the lookout to Muurrbay the road follows the line of the river. Past the RSL and the fish and chip shop, to the causeway, to the Island. For a long time people have been telling me the river is being destroyed. They tell me the concrete causeway to the Island stopped the flow of tides, the mixing of saltwater and fresh. That part of the river is dying. The protector spirit who lived at the edge of the river on the way to the Island has gone. The Elders have been campaigning to have pipes put through the causeway to allow the river to flow again.

Today it has changed. I stop at the causeway to take in this scene. The river is deep blue hugged by mangroves. Pelicans sleep on the posts of old oyster beds. Three boys play on a pontoon and splash into the water. On the other side I can see the stand of oak trees on the Island where Val was born. At my feet the tide is coming in and the river swirls gently through the new pipes in the causeway. Close up it is a translucent green and I watch schools of fish flickering back and forth in the clear water. I walk with others along the new boardwalk and watch this slow movement of the new river and wonder if the Spirit has moved back again. Back on the road I follow the river's movement, past the place of Ngambaa's knee, and the caravan park where Birrugan made his paddles from the she-oak trees, to the bend in the river where I cross the highway to Muurrbay.

The ancestral songlines that Tiger Buchannan and the other Old People recorded are the basis of the language and cultural teaching at Muurrbay. These include the story of The Women Who Made the Sea, the Birrugan story, the Muurrbay story and the story of Wijiirrjagi, the cannibal woman. Their teaching and learning connects language, story, people and country. Groups of Gumbaynggirr learners go to the special places in these storylines where the Elders and knowledge holders tell them the story. They write, paint and produce artworks in relation to these stories. This work of connecting language and story back to country is ongoing. As Gary Williams explained, 'You'll never get the jigsaw puzzle back but there's enough there and you can consolidate on things'. At each of these places it is the always-unfinished business of connecting language, story and country that underpins the process of deep mapping.

The ongoing work of reconnecting people to country through language is clearly evident in the story of 'Birrugan's knee'. This story is about the naming of Nambucca (Baga-baga Nyambaga), and the traces of Gumbaynggirr meanings held in that name. Ken Walker explained that Birrugan's knee is where the caravan park is now, the place where Birrugan fell over when he was speared. When I asked him what it meant that the roads go over Birrugan's body, he said that the meaning of the place is still there even though the place has changed. Gary remembered Tiger's reflections on the multiple translations involved in the naming of Nambucca.

> We were doing the story of the knee down here, at Baga-baga[40], at Nyambaga. At the end Tiger said there was a whitefella and a blackfella standing there on the spot and the whitefella said, 'Where are we now?' and the blackfella said, 'You're on his knee'. I don't think the whitefella can grasp the concept of standing on somebody's knee there, like a person. So they, I think that's why they chose the crooked river, that's as close as they can get to that kind of concept. He threw that

> in and I remember that bit, it's a way of whitefella thinking, blackfella thinkin', it's not the original story but that's making the point, yeah. (Gary Williams)

In this story, Tiger Buchannan and Gary are reflecting on the differences between Indigenous and non-Indigenous understandings of story and landscape. For Gumbaynggirr people the bend in the river *is* Birrugan's knee. Each time they go past that place the shape of the landscape reminds them of this story and the interchangeability of people and place, the material embodiment of places and their connections to them. Even though the structure of the place has changed, overwritten by roads and caravan parks, they still remember the story and the connection through language, Baga-baga Ngambaa, Ngambaa's knee. It is the detailed work of language that calls up these place-story memories.

> I think it's the making of Nambucca, like it's strange now because when we're switched into language and you think now well Ngambaa's baga-baga and Nyambaga, you shorten it, of course, white people would say Nambucca because it's easier but you could see them [the Old People] sitting down there now all the way back in the middle twenties on the Island there or something like that and thinking 'We'd better get it back our way a bit in sounding to Ngambaga', I think. Everybody says the Old People say Nyambaga now for Nambucca but you can see where the white person turns the Aboriginal way around but they Aboriginalise it again in the way they want it to be said to themselves. This is one of the things now with having language back again, you can muck around in this kinda way, yeah. (Gary Williams)

Baga-baga is the place where the giant Ngambaa man fell when he was killed in the Dreaming. The story is inscribed in the place, and in the language that names that place. Bringing the language home has enabled the work of language to connect the story to the place. It has also made visible the complex back and forth translations through which Gumbaynggirr people have brought these stories into contemporary meanings. Ken and Gary call it Birrugan's knee in the sense that Birrugan is not only the creator hero but the word also means man, any man. So we move between Birrugan, as symbolic of all man, and birrugan meaning any man, in the complex conversations around this story. Birrugan's knee continues to exist in the landscape through language, story and memory, despite the overlay of the caravan park and roads. When, in the process of deep mapping, the roads and towns, caravan parks and shopping centres are removed, visual images are created of these layers of place stories. Behind these images lies a deep knowledge of story, language and country.

The first Dreaming storyline that we mapped was the story of the creation hero, Birrugan's last battle. In beginning the work of mapping this storyline, Gary began with a brief summary of the story of Birrugan's last journey in southern Gumbaynggirr country to give the overall picture.

> They were living there at Valla and he got news that they needed him down there because of the war, because he was a good warrior and how they tried to kill him out there at Valla before, had to make sure that he didn't get down there because he was a clever man as well and so he beat them off and then they killed him the first time and he healed himself, and then the second time how he was beating them and they killed him but the mother came over, brolga came over, and turned the other mob into ti-trees over there so that you can see the ti-trees there at the golf course. (Gary Williams)

This general version of the narrative, as with so many of the public versions of what non-Indigenous people know as Aboriginal myths and legends, has an opaque quality that hides the complexity and layers of meaning. When such stories are translated into English, the story is separated from the landscapes which produced it and which it, in turn, produced. The places where events happened in this telling are not apparent, except for the golf course. The golf course is visible in this story because it is a distinct place with an English name that is generally recognisable. It is also noteworthy because its presence has destroyed the most important story place. The linking trails between the elements of the story are also absent. It is in the detailed language work and the cultural knowledge of the important symbolism of red clay, ti-trees, river oaks and rock wallaby, Gawnggun and Birrugan, that the story becomes meaningful as a songline. We began again with a more local, emplaced and embodied story.

> Yeah, well, the Birrugan story starts at Deep Creek and Valla. That's where 'e lived with his mother, it's part of the creek with a deep hole and that deep 'ole relates to the story itself. When Birrugan fell during the battle over at Sou'west Rocks, the magay, that's the red clay, fell off the tent pole and then when it hit the ground it formed a deep hole and that's the waterhole out at Deep Creek where they used to live, him and his mother. And in fact, there's a magay miirlarl[41] just next to it and you can almost see him picking up the clay there and walking back twenty metres or thirty metres or something like that, yes, and just sticking it up on the tent pole. (Ken Walker)

This more detailed version of the story locates its beginning at Deep Creek near Valla. Places such as these occur over and over again in stories and conversations so they begin to resonate as places of intensity. In this story, Deep Creek is the actual place where Birrugan camped with his mother, Gawnggan. It is here that Birrugan places the red ochre on the ridgepole of the tent so that if it falls his mother will know he is in trouble. The waterhole at Deep Creek is created when the red clay falls and Ken tells us there is a magay miirlarl, a special place for red ochre, just next to the deep hole. Ken imagines Birrugan walking back from the waterhole to the camp and then backtracks to an earlier part of the narrative when the messengers came through to warn him of the impending attack. Ken brings this story to life in the drama of the telling.

> That is also where he was making boomerangs there too and when the messengers came through he told his mother about the messengers, and then he went back to the boomerang

making. Then those old fellas, clever fellas from over there, decided they'd try to kill him there before he got over. Decided they'd do him in because they heard that he was such a powerful warrior, see. And that he was a clever man too. So he had powers as well. So they had to send six – *six* – powerful men over to try and kill him. So they had two tries at him. First they changed themselves into snakes and ants and things and he just brushed them aside, that's how powerful he was. (Ken Walker)

Each action and event in this dramatic story is significant, and each is associated with particular aspects of the landscape that are imbued with the story's meanings. Each action, such as the making of the boomerang, symbolises all making of all boomerangs, so each of the elements associated with that making have ritual connotations. The trees that the boomerangs are made from have a special meaning, as does the spot where Birrugan sat on the ridge overlooking the camp while making the boomerangs.

This was all around Deep Creek. Yeah, well, the thing about that place, that Deep Creek there – you know that ridge I was showin' you, that ridge up from Deep Creek there, I was taught – sorta planted that in my mind as a place where he was sitting making boomerangs up on that ridge there. It's the only little high spot there, isn't it? And that looks down onto the camp. So I'd say that would be part of it. It's a place that he went, probably for a bit of solitude when he was sittin' down makin' his boomerangs – kept an eye on the camp and his mother down there. (Ken Walker)

Ken leads us into the places of this story as he connects his intimate knowledge of the shapes of the landscape with the events in the story: where the camp was located, the waterhole that was created when the magay fell, and the ridge where Birrugan sat watching the camp and making boomerangs. As part of the storytelling of our deep mapping Ken imagines himself into the character of Birrugan through the places that he knows where the story events happened.

> So first up then those Old Men ended up killing him, and he took the spear out and put leafs on it, on his wound, and things like that and healed himself. And told his mother that he was needed down there, and left the clay from that magay spot. And he placed it on the ridgepole of the tent. And then he took off from there, didn't he. (Ken Walker)

Each action is precisely told and each has many layers of meaning. We know from this segment that special healing plants were used, and that the red clay, associated with ceremony and initiation, played an important role in the unfolding drama. As Birrugan travels, just as in people's everyday stories of their journeys down the river, other events happen that shape the particular characteristics of each special place.

> Well first of all, he left – when 'e left from Valla, apparently he even went up to Wirriimbi.[42] That's where he was supposed to have made his canoe there. So he musta come back down when 'e made that canoe at Wirriimbi there, come back down that old trail, that Newry Creek thing, down that way. So, that trail that we showed you, and that ti-tree. See Wirriimbi's an oak tree place as well, she-oak, yeah. In fact, there's easy walks that way too. There's a route that goes up there. Long way to carry a canoe.
>
> Well, that's where he come from, Wirriimbi, down to – at that caravan park and crossed there. Yes. So then, we know that he crossed the river there where the Pelican Caravan Park is, where those trees are that they can't touch. They're a stand of oak trees there. (Ken Walker)

Wirriimbi is the place on the Nambucca River near Bowraville that takes its name from the language word for the saltwater oak, a native casuarina. Birrugan made his canoe from the timber of the saltwater oak at Wirriimbi and this name then becomes code to signify this part of the creation story: the saltwater oaks, the act of canoe making from this timber, and the rituals through which all these are remembered and passed on in the lives of young men. The name Wirriimbi then evokes connections between this place and the whole storyline of the creation ancestor. The trail that Ken refers to is the one that people have described in their walking stories from Bowraville to the Island, the linking trail of Birrugan's storyline as he travels along the river. At the place where the Pelican Caravan Park is now another stand of oak trees marks the special place where Birrugan made paddles from the oak trees and crossed the river.

> Now this place here, it's on the map, Worabooraby, an' actually there was an old mill there back in the 1890s, that even old white people call it 'Worabooraby', that area. And then Ken and I were looking through the dictionary and so you've got wurraa, it means to remove, as in bark on a tree. And budii is one of those names for paddle – a canoe. So the old people must've – what to tell 'em, you know, when the whitefellas said what's the name of the place he called it Worabooraby. And this is what we're kind of generally calling Birrugan's Crossing. (Ken Walker)

The multiple acts of translation through which we can know this story are most evident in the detail of each individual place. At this place, the story encapsulates the taking up of the name, even though imperfectly, by early white settlers. In the same way that it was a good spot for Birrugan to cross the river, it was also a good spot for the timber mill that relied on the river to transport timber. It is also the place where Gumbaynggirr people camped along the river and the closest place on the river to where they are now located at Muurrbay. It is now a place for a caravan park by the river. Muurrbay has reclaimed the language words for 'removing bark from a tree' and for 'paddle', for the stand of oak trees marked with a plaque to indicate Birrugan's Crossing. The work of reconnecting story to country involves reclaiming language, story and place within a history of white settlement.

After many more adventures along the way, Birrugan finally arrives at the place of his last battle. The point of the story is that Birrugan had to get to the battleground quickly because the Dhanggati were winning and he had to add his superior skills as a warrior to the battle.

Oh, he started into them [laughs], spearin' 'em, and boomerangin'. The other spear story, the first one, was when they speared him and killed him. And they did the same thing, except they knew where – they threw the spear up high so basically the same way as coming down from – one bloke was up in the tree to do it the first time. And they used the spear – had to come from that same direction, so they had to throw the spear up high. Couldn't heal himself the second time around. So he finally died, from a spear. As soon as he died, well that clay fell off the tent pole out at Valla and his mother knew he was dead. And she done the same journey then. She done the same journey from Deep Creek. That's when she turned all them other fellas into ti-trees. When she saw that he was dead, she just turned the rest of the other side into ti-trees. And that all happened there on the golf course.
(Ken Walker)

Birrugan's final resting place is of great significance in this story. Gawnggan followed the same trail from Deep Creek to South West Rocks, no doubt with her own female adventures along the way. She arrived to find it was too late, and turned the enemy warriors into the ti-trees that you can see there today. As part of our deep mapping Ken drove us to the place on the golf course at South West Rocks where these events took place. There he reclaimed the site for Birrugan's story in a political act of contemporary performance in place.

I'm standing at the golf course at South West Rocks, this is where Birrugan ended his journey. And as we stare down the ninth fairway we can see where Birrugan's tomb was, and had a heap of rocks on it that were moved to make way for a golf links. Which the golfing community denies, but us Gumbaynggirr people know better. We know where Birrugan was laid to rest. It's runnin' down that ridge, right down there to where that clump of trees is down there and you'll see a big rock layin' down there. Where that rock was, was where they laid Birrugan and covered him with a lota rocks but when they made way for this modern-day masterpiece, golf course, an' they moved the rocks, shifted them. (Ken Walker)

At Birrugan's grave, Ken tells us, the mother turned herself into a brolga, and every year she used to come back and dance around her son's grave. That is, until someone shot one of the brolgas, and, as Ken said, 'You hardly see 'em out there any more'.

The shooting of the brolga symbolises the momentous loss of place and story. In *Gumbaynggirr Yuludarla* it is simply noted that much of the area is cleared and populated and the brolgas rarely come back there now. The detailed language work of reconnecting story to place is made visible in the more literal language translations. When the red clay dropped from the ridgepole we are told that 'Mother Gawwnggan got up. She took the red ochre and with it painted her legs. She took the red, black and white clays and painted herself with these colours'[43] and set out on her journey to the battleground. When she arrived at Birrugan's grave 'she performed a dance and became a brolga. Mother Gawnggan circled around and then flew home.'[44] A footnote tells us that living Gumbaynggirr speakers remember the brolga's regular return to dance at her son's grave and that Auntie Maggie Morris remembers seeing that 'the grass was flattened like a racecourse around Birrugan's grave'.[45]

These storylines are the basis of Muurrbay's language and culture work in country. They take Gumbaynggirr students to the special story places and tell the stories there. In deep-mapping interviews we recorded these stories and marked the places on a road map to link the story and the place. In making visual representations from the mapping interviews we scanned the road maps into the computer and removed all the roads and towns using Adobe PhotoShop software. Story text and images were then inserted onto the map to show the events in the stories and images of the places where these events happened. This is a symbolic reversal of the processes through which the grid of roads and towns was laid over earlier memories and story places.

Deep mapping replicates Muurrbay's ongoing teaching which re-connects people, language, story and country by telling the creation stories in the landscape. It is a process of repatriation whereby Gumbaynggirr histories, memories, experiences and stories are reconnected to country. It continues the process of imagining landscapes through layers of stories that was already present in the language work that Tiger Buchanan began and that Gumbaynggirr people continue. It is the process whereby a storyline, the skeleton of a story, becomes a songline again because when language, story and country are reconnected, we again open up the possibility of singing the country.

~

The work of reconnecting language, story and country is symbolised in the naming of the old church building, Muurrbay, as the symbolic home of the Gumbaynggirr language. The Muurrbay story in *Gumbaynggirr Yuludarla* is as Gary told it at the beginning of this chapter. Like all Dreaming stories it has a simplistic surface meaning when translated into English for a public audience. It is a parable about all the different clans of Gumbaynggirr country working together to achieve a common goal or, in Tiger Buchanan's words, they would 'end up with nothing'. The story of the Muurrbay tree is 'Muurrbay Bundeeni: The Tree of Life'. The work of language that goes on in the church building is the tree of life for its people.

The muurrbay tree is a white fig tree, but in one story the original tree was a Moreton Bay fig, at one time very rare in the area. In No Mans Land at Corindi Lake, and on the Island in Nambucca Heads, the Old People would plant a fig tree to mark their camp sites, a place of home and belonging. The fig tree signifies a belonging place for Gumbaynggirr people. There are at least three special places for the Muurrbay Tree when it was supernaturally taken from one place to another. Now it is located at another special place, the building that is Muurrbay, the house of the language of landscape. In a Gumbaynggirr funeral ceremony witnessed by Ivy Smith, the clever man Ngaluunggirr called out 'Yuuway! Cooee!' to the spirit of the dead man. It was only when the person finally failed to respond to the call that the mourners knew that the spirit was now eating at the Muurrbay Tree.[46] Muurrbay is also a place of spirits where the Old People reside in the talking and stories of their language. It continues the tradition of the building as a Catholic church, but translates the

Catholic story to embody the return of language and meaning back to country in the Birrugan and Gawnggan storyline.

The work of Muurrbay as the Tree of Life is represented in our mapping of living places, both past and present. These include sea tracks and land tracks, eating and camping places, places of births and deaths and daily living places. We begin with Muurrbay, the place of the present time, and the language and culture work that happens there. This also includes a sense of the deep past in the Dreaming storylines brought to life at Muurrbay, so the deep past exists also in the present. We map the historic living places on the Island and the estuary that provide a bridge between past, present and future. Like the Nambucca River estuary with its layers of transparent silk over shapes of islands and sand bars, in this layering, each previous layer remains partially visible, the past is not erased but is always visible in the present. As Ken Walker reminds us, stories of the past are held in the imagination, always waiting to be sung again.

CHAPTER 7

Connecting the dots

We're parked at South West Rocks overlooking the mountains, I don't know what they call 'em in English, but the Gumbaynggirr people call them Marrgaan⁴⁷, the place of the rock wallaby. And Margaret's got out to take a photo as usual, thank you very much.

Gula points in Gumbaynggirr territory to all the mountain peaks. Hills all have a storyline attached to them that interconnects each and every one of 'em. Just like its people, oh just like your story, Margaret, you know, your connecting the dots story.

Gumbaynggirr people done it thousands a years before you even thought of it. Whadya think of that? Tra-la-la.
(Ken Walker)

In the final phase of our project we connected northern Gumbaynggirr with southern Gumbaynggirr knowledges. Ken Walker and Gary Williams travelled from Muurrbay to Moonee Beach to a disused motel, recently purchased by Yarrawarra. At the time I did not understand why Tony had chosen this place for southern and northern Gumbaynggirr to meet. It was noisy, as it was right on the Pacific Highway, uncomfortable because it was not yet set up, and had a feeling of abandonment and disuse. Looking back now I can feel the significance of this meeting place as an almost electric intensity. Moonee Moonee is the location of the mother place, the place of creation for northern Gumbaynggirr people.

At our meeting with Ken and Gary, Tony was right in the centre of his country, pointing in one direction then another. To the Yellow Waterholes and Mary's Waterhole, to the white pipeclay from Corindi Beach, the Old Farm, the brolga dancing place and the birthing grounds. Ken and Gary deferred to Tony's greater knowledge as visitors in his place. Each of them was intent on connecting their different stories of Gumbaynggirr country. When Tony talked about the rare plants on the headlands at the mother place, Ken said DNA testing has shown these plants to be distinct from each other, even though they look similar and only grow in these special places. We ranged over the whole of Gumbaynggirr country recording stories from the edge of living memory. Many of these stories were partial, some secret and not for public access, and all were part of the fragile process of piecing together the jigsaw puzzle.

Tony continued to provide advice and leadership throughout this part of the project, offering the big ideas through which this regional knowledge could be researched and understood. Gumbaynggirr people who had been trained to work as researchers were employed to interview key Elders in Gumbaynggirr country about these regional knowledges. This was also part of their intergenerational learning. We continued the deep-mapping work, expanding our processes as required by these new research questions. Road maps no longer proved adequate to our purposes. We needed to cover larger stretches of country, and especially country where there were no place names or towns to guide us about location. We used satellite maps that showed the forms of the landscape – mountains, ridges and valleys – to enable us to record the lines of story and connection.

From our three years of research with Yarrawarra we learned that there were categories of place knowledge that moved beyond the local and extended across Gumbaynggirr country and beyond. These categories of regional knowledge included boundaries, language, movement, kinship, exchange, storylines and ceremony. When we were finished recording the regional interviews it became clear that they could be clustered into three parts of a narrative that build up our understanding of how regional knowledge works. These are: boundaries and identity; linking trails and storylines; and special places of gathering and ceremony.

Boundaries and identity

They always told me first
up here is your mother
it's like a spirit mother
of the Gumbaynggirr people.
Up this way people would say
that's your mother, your mother's from here
it's important area to you
that's where your spirit mother
she come from there.

For Gumbaynggirr people a sense of the boundaries of one's country is constructed from the inside, from the centre of one's being. Boundaries are important because they signify identity and knowledge in country. Each of the three knowledge holders introduced himself in relation to his particular location and connections in Gumbaynggirr country. Even when Tony was interviewed about his regional knowledge by a young Gumbaynggirr researcher well known to him, he began with a statement of his own identity. He performed it as a form of address, a formal protocol of introduction:

> Tony Perkins, the name. I am a local person from the northern area of the Gumbaynggirr. All my relatives come from this area but I got associated with other Elders' groups within Gumbaynggirr through different types of marriage in the clan groups. The things that I say are things that have been passed on, like knowledge passed on to me from Old People that is now deceased. Mainly all the things that are knowledge that I will be saying has been told to me from the Elders in the Red Rock – Corindi area. (Tony Perkins)

In introducing himself, Tony summarises the intertwining of self, people and place in personal identity. He describes himself as a 'local person', identified with a particular area of Gumbaynggirr country. Through marriage across clan groups he is connected to the wider territory, to 'other Elders' groups'. His authority to speak is related to knowledge of country that was passed down orally by the Old People and by Elders who are recognised as having authority in the Red Rock – Corindi area. Throughout the rest of this interview, and in other conversations about regional knowledge, Tony expands on the relationship between self, family, clan, and territory.

> My mother was Clarice Skinner, my father was William Henry Perkins, and this is really hard to work out, my mother was a Skinner but my grandmother on my mother's side, she was a Harvey, so my great-grandmother was a Harvey and she came from the Urunga area and my father, his mother was a Jarrett and they're Nambucca-based Aboriginal people. (Tony Perkins)

Through names people trace their family connections to other parts of Gumbaynggirr country. In his personal naming Tony gives his English name, Tony Perkins, but this does not even reveal the family name of Skinner given by the white landowners. Skinner is one of the main Aboriginal family names of Corindi Lake from the initiated Clarrie Skinner. We know that the name Skinner was given by white landowners in northern Gumbaynggirr, as was the case with Uncle Harry 'Tiger' Buchanan at Cow Creek in southern Gumbaynggirr country. In his case we know his Gumbaynggirr name as Maruwanba Maruungga. The first name recognises his individual authority in country as an initiated man and the second identifies him as part of a particular clan group through his kinship or skin name. In this way Gumbaynggirr names described one's relationship to country, to other people within that country, and one's authority to speak for country. Now English family names have to serve a similar function.

> When you go back on how it all works, that's why we got that connection with Nambucca Heads, Yellow Rock

connection, and up here connection and over at Nymboida and up at Copmanhurst. When everybody tracks back if you're Gumbaynggirr, you got a link to Gumbaynggirr somewhere, you will find that you got links to each of those places. The only way you have that link and you still got it is because going way back in them times, in my circumstances one of my people, my grandmother on one side come from Nambucca, and then my grandfather on the other side up at Pillar Valley that way, but then on the other side my grandmother come from Yellow Rock at Urunga. The grandfathers and the grandmothers come from different areas 'cause they wasn't allowed to marry inside their clan and that's how they worked it, that's why we had all the links to the different clans. (Tony Perkins)

Tony traces his links to different places across Gumbaynggirr country through his grandparents. He uses this process to illustrate the connections that were made through the marriage rules in his grandparents' generation. Other Elders too, especially the women, comment on the way that marriage outside of one's clan group forged connections across country and between groups of people. Maintaining this knowledge of the relationships of people to each other, and people to country, is ongoing cultural work and part of the protocols of introduction and welcome to country.

Ken Walker introduced himself for his regional interview by taking us to his grandfather's country. He had shown me a photo of a fish trap on the wall in his office in Muurrbay and said that his grandfather was the custodian of that fish trap, so we set off for Crescent Head. Ken directed our journey and some way down the road indicated the first stopping place. He signalled to me to take a photo of him beginning his story there and he got out and turned the recorder on to introduce his great-grandfather's country.

We just come across the Smithtown bridge as you look down to your left you'll see Fatarini Island and this place is where my great-grandfather, with a couple of other families, cleared this land and were producing vegetables. After they'd been using the land for so long the white settlers got up a petition to have them removed from the island and shifted to somewhere else. The local authorities at that time controlled all black movement so they uprooted the families that were on Fatarini Island and took 'em into Clybucca township. I guess it woulda been then because that's where there was a great congregation of Aboriginal people that were intermingled into all different tribes, and intermingled together and that's where my great-grandfather reared most of his family. (Ken Walker)

Connections to country are now intertwined with the history of white settlement. Up and down the coast Gumbaynggirr people were camping in the same places they always had, often near special places so they could protect them. Even when they conformed to white expectations – such as clearing land and growing vegetables – they were moved to 'mixed-up places' where lots of different language groups were brought together. This is not the whole story however. Ken's story also makes the connection to the Clybucca middens. 'It's all [close to] the middens that run from Gumma right through to Stuarts Point, right up to Crescent Head.' These middens mark a great gathering place where different language groups came together over thousands of years, it was already a 'mixed-up place'. As Larry Kelly said, 'The midden's eight kilometres wide and sixteen kilometres long and we don't know how deep it is but it's one of the oldest sites in New South Wales and you could imagine how many people gathered there in those old days'. Ken's is a story of origins that tells us of both connection and displacement.

Gary begins the story of his regional knowledge in a similar way to Tony and Ken. He describes the Island at Nambucca as his home place, but in his introduction he names his actual birthplace in his father's country of the adjacent Bundjalung language territory.

I suppose you'd have to start off with a bit of my own story, and that is my brother and I were born in Mullumbimby in my father's country. But after that we came down to Burnt Bridge and then from Burnt Bridge we came back to Nambucca and

> in those days it was just about the last days of school on the Island so I was — they moved into the Mission here in fifty-two, so I was born at the end of forty-five so that's when I would have been seven so I did the last year over there, so I would have been six or somethin' like that, and then did the Mission school here on the reserve. (Gary Williams)

He maps the journey through which he came to be at Muurrbay through his school days on the Island and then on the Mission school just up the road from Muurrbay. His place identity is tied up with white histories and schooling, but his Aboriginal learning gives him access to other knowledge and connections. Although he identifies Nambucca as the 'centre of the universe', he is connected to other places in Gumbaynggirr country through the teaching of family relations.

> In one sense Nambucca, even though it's still the centre of the universe, I've got an overview of other areas too … when we were young men down in Sydney you know, my father was gone, actually he was dead by then, and my mother said to my Uncle, Clive Williams, 'You better take over the teaching', so in fact we'd learn all about our Bundjalung heritage. So, without setting foot up in Bundjalung country we kinda knew where to go, who to see and what languages were spoken, how you approach people and where your relations are and things like that. So he mapped it all out, in fact he'd sing songs in Bundjalung and everything like that. (Gary Williams)

When young Gumbaynggirr people moved far away to the city their parents and grandparents took responsibility for teaching them about their identity in place. Even without going into Bundjalung country Gary knew 'where to go, who to see and what languages were spoken'. It was a way of mapping country through relationships and connections. His uncle also sang songs in Bundjalung, another way of mapping connections through the songlines that connect neighbouring language groups. Gary said that this knowledge of country gave him a sense of connection but not belonging. For him a sense of belonging and familiarity in home places is instinctive. 'The people had specific knowledge, it's all the area around here, you just knew that you know the boundaries.' It is this instinctive sense of local belonging and identity that Tony explained young people learn from everyday stories and conversations with their Elders.

> Johnny Laurie wouldn't put a tent on his back now and travel up around Dorrigo and camp there because he knows he's outside his area … it's just instinct with him, he doesn't feel right. He knows he's outside this area. It's not his home. I suppose it's because listenin' to Bing and Keith and all them over the years and years about certain places. And to him he picks up over time that they're not talkin' about this place and that place, so they're identifying only certain areas they talk about all the time. (Tony Perkins)

Local boundaries are linked to story knowledge that was 'passed down … when the Old People were around'. There were so many stories of their places of belonging and identity that they become familiar with their country. This sense of the boundaries of their clan country was also related to familiarity with the places where they habitually travelled and camped. 'We can put lots of dots on a piece of paper within a certain area, but outside that area you might find only a coupla dots, but they're more ceremonial-type camping areas when you're travellin' from one area to another.'

The boundaries of local territories were learned from the inside in an experiential way and through listening to stories. Tony said the new way of putting lines on a map to represent boundaries and identity in country causes many problems. Lines on a map, he said, 'hem people in' because they are contrary to a sense of local country defined from within. These lines do not conform to country as it is understood through the delicate negotiations with others involved in boundary work. 'A lot of time we had to spend with people from Yamba and Maclean trying to work out a line running from there at Minnie Waters and them places. We're tryin' to work out a line. Where will it run? How do we get that line?'

Lines on a map are a construct of a western culture of writing. To understand a relationship to country that is not defined by print literacy is to understand country through other knowledges: through walking and camping, eating from a place, oral stories, spiritual intensities, relationships, connections and negotiations. The move to putting lines on a map as a matter of political necessity is another process of translation. In formalising the boundaries of their clan country, Tony and the Garby Elders have translated their intimate knowledge onto a map so they can define the area of Gumbaynggirr country that they have authority over.

> We come from under Moonee Creek and then we go out to the Orara River out at Nana Glen we go across, follow that river and we come out there at – we cut across that Two Mile Lane this side of South Grafton, go across there on the Two Mile Lane then we go across to Coldwater back to Wooli, well just past Wooli on the northern side then we come back down the coastline. That's our clan group, the Elders' area in this top end. (Tony Perkins)

This intimate and infinite local knowledge defines the clan territory of the Garby Elders. For Tony, a sense of home and identity is related to this clan area rather than to Gumbaynggirr country as a whole. He said that the Old People talked about the whole of Gumbaynggirr country as the mother, and the clans were like children, branching out from the mother and shaping smaller areas within country.

> We talk about the Gumbaynggirr Nation, and I always say that that's like a mother, the mother. Then from the mother becomes the children, then and those children go out and form their own territory. Then those boundaries are already set, those clans are what we call the children's boundaries – that's the clan boundary. (Tony Perkins)

The mother place is where the children left the mother to become the clans of Gumbaynggirr country. Tony, from the northern area, and Ken and Gary from the southern clan area, are brothers within the larger Gumbaynggirr territory. Together they translate their sense of the edges of the larger Gumbaynggirr country onto a satellite map. Ken and Gary talked about a 'buffer zone', a 10-kilometre-wide strip that enables people to negotiate boundaries where they have mutual interests in country. They also identified areas that are 'mixed-up places': 'a sort of mutual understanding ground where everybody comes together'. They explained that the area of the Clybucca middens is such a place where people from different clan and language groups always came together for gatherings. 'A lot of people were born there, so it seems to be a meeting place of both sides in a sense. That's where, down here, that's where the old middens – the real big middens are.' These mixed-up places are marked by 'blurry boundaries' where different language groups acknowledge shared country. Even well-defined boundaries are open, and crossing boundaries is associated with the protocols of entering country. Tony likened this to knocking on the door when entering someone's house.

> When we talk about entering a person's territory it's like when you visit anybody in his house. You knock on the door before you go inside and you ask, you give 'em permission to go inside, the same as a bloke when he goes through his boundaries, he's gotta do the same thing, he's gotta knock to get permission to go inside that next fella's boundary. That's why you find that in one Elders' territory, you'll have a number of Elders in there who can speak a couple of languages, 'cause he can go both – he can go west or he can go south 'cause he can talk that language around him, he can talk to the other fella, that's how it worked. (Tony Perkins)

Language is the key to moving across boundaries that are primarily understood through language differences. The contemporary versions of acknowledging traditional owners and welcome to country are reciprocal protocols for entering country outside of one's boundaries. When Bing welcomes visitors to country at Yarrawarra he speaks in Gumbaynggirr language. The welcome described in Chapter 4, 'Darruyagay biyambaygu yuraal', invites visitors to 'be happy and eat food' at Yarrawarra. Sharing local food is a way to share knowledge about one's country and is related to the way clan groups were associated with particular foods or totems. Knowing one's totemic identity is another way of crossing boundaries. Ray Kelly said that to cross into another territory you had to call out your 'skin' (totem) to introduce yourself. Emily Walker, whose father was Birrbay and mother Dhanggati, described how Granny Ballangarry introduced her to Gumbaynggirr country through a ritual associated with her totem.

> So I'd say that I am in Gumbaynggirr 'cause Granny Ballangarry she gave me my first piece of possum, just her and I by ourselves out in the bush. She skinned a possum and cooked it on the coals and gave me my first piece of possum and it wasn't until later on in my life that I found out that possum was my totem. (Emily Walker)

Acknowledging the spirits of the ancestors in places is another important aspect of entering country that is associated with language. Keith said that speaking in Gumbaynggirr language to the spirits of a place protects him when he goes to a different place outside of his own area. 'You're all right to go anywhere as long as you can talk for yourself. If you don't talk you probably will see something. "Yaam guumunbu ngaya yirringin ngaya yilaaming", that mean "Spirit, don't come here".' The Old People provided this protection for them when they were moving through country in the old days. They knew where it was safe to go and where it might be a special place of taboo.

All of these protocols are related to intensity of local place knowledge and identity. Tony emphasised, however, that while a strong sense of identity in particular local places is important, it is equally important to understand that identity for Gumbaynggirr people is broader than the local. He believes that Indigenous knowledge is diminished when people are seen as only having knowledge of a restricted local area. Through Law and custom Gumbaynggirr people learn about connections across country made in linking trails and songlines.

> Lots of people believe that we're only connected to a very small area. They say, 'Yeah but you fellas only based at Red Rock', and they're pretty happy 'cause it's just that little area of Red Rock, that keeps them happy. Well that's right in one sense but then you gotta go out on that long journey on knowing how the Law and how the custom, how it works

for Aboriginal people living at Red Rock, then you start
to understand why it's important to know about the links
from Yamba right through to the Nambucca area, across to
Armidale, all them places so it becomes a bigger picture. It's
far greater than just a small area, it links up, it might not be
used today, that sort of linking trails, there's reasons behind
that, but it's part of history and it's a part of our culture and
it's part of our heritage, that's what it is and that'll never
go away, whether we use it or not it's part of our lives.
(Tony Perkins)

The long journey is both a physical and a metaphysical journey. It is a process of coming to know country through the walking tracks that connect across vast areas of country, but also the long journey of coming to know through greater spiritual knowledge. Linking trails are as much a part of people's place stories as their intimate knowledge of local places. A sense of place identity and belonging begins with one's family relationships and is learned through stories from the Old People. Through these stories, home places become familiar and instinctive while others are recognised as outside of one's country.

Boundaries are defined from within local knowledge rather than through lines on a map. Connections to other places are made through marriage outside of the clan group. Movement outside of these local boundaries is made through knowledge of languages, totems and spiritual knowledge, the kinds of knowledge passed down through Aboriginal Law. This regional knowledge of the way places are connected to each other across Gumbaynggirr country is embodied in linking trails, and is an important part of Gumbaynggirr cultural heritage.

Linking trails and storylines

When they comin' across
they were linked up
like the Southern Cross
that's the way you find,
you gotta have a pointer

> when you're coming to sites.
> Lot of times it was the stars were used
> like a pointer in the sky
> then you got pointers on the ground
> rock formations with a point
> comin' to the site
> rock formations put in.

Linking trails are primarily walking trails that link local places to each other across country. To understand how they work it is important to experience them as actual tracks along which one might travel from place to place. As part of our work with Muurrbay we mapped Uncle Martin Ballangarry's memories of walking from Bowraville Mission to the Island, recording his story as we marked the places of his journey on the map. To do this is to enter this world of knowing country through walking. It begins as a journey from one place to the other and like all good travelling stories departs in the middle with a digression about cobras, revealing the intricacies of walking knowledge and intersecting trails.

> Here's the river, we walk from here down, we walk all the way down there and just up a bit from there, Wirriimbi Island, there's another place. No, that's it – that's a property there, used to come across there, all the Old People used to meet there. On that side there. We used to meet 'em there. Down here – probably because we'd meet 'em here on this little part here. On that little flat there. Here's a little creek goes up there, inside that there. And that's where all the women and kids used to wait for us as we'd walk down there spearin, and collectin' and gatherin' fruit. (Martin Ballangarry)

In this mapping interview we are walking with Martin down the Nambucca River. Martin orients himself to the map by finding the river and then the different places along the way. Place is infinitely detailed as he marks Wirriimbi Island, a 'property' they walked through, a little creek that flows into the river, and a flat where they used to meet up with the women and children. It seems from this that the boys were already learning special knowledge as they walked with the Old People, spearing, and collecting and gathering fruit. It was on these walks that they learned how to collect food. 'The uncles of me, they taught me to do the spearing – how to do things.'

As the walking proceeds, stories are told about the past and the present as the story places open up along the way. We pass an area that Martin describes as a 'no-go zone', marked by the sign of a diamond tree, 'maybe there was a massacre site there'. A diamond tree is a tree carved with the Gumbaynggirr symbol of the diamond that marks special places of initiation and burials. This particular diamond tree has a guardian and we learn something more of the history of the place through his story.

> There was an old diamond tree, cemetery and we weren't allowed to go camping. Jimmy used to stop us from going – he was the guardian of that, Jimmy Dotti. He was a deadly swimmer. They used to get 'im when any white fellas get drowned around here. They used to get Uncle Jimmy used to do all the divin' – him and his older brother – they [had to dive] to find someone in the muddy water. They'd get the old blackfella to go and do the divin' for them. Because the whitefella couldn't stand to be under water too long, so they used to do that, Uncle Jimmy and Uncle Bill Dotti, yeah. So that's a diamond tree there. But it's not, it's not standing no more because the farmer cut it up. You couldn't do much about this. (Martin Ballangarry)

Walking trails are dynamic interactions between people and place. As we walk with Martin we learn about the more recent histories of black–white relations in country. Places always had their histories and the changing events that were significant in those histories were remembered in particular places as they walked. Jimmy Dotti was the guardian of the special place with the diamond tree and his story is symbolic and iconic. We learn that his hero status is recognised by both black and white people because of the rescue story. Everything in this brief episode signals other larger stories and connections, all is code for another series of stories just like the epic Birrugan storyline. Even though the diamond tree is now gone its details are remembered in the story told along the way as passing places evoke memories of events along the trail. The story changes as the travel through country changes. Further on down the trail we begin to map the water tracks across the river.

> Lot of shallow parts and then we'd float across on a log anyway, depending on which way the tide's comin', you'd get on a log and float across if the tide's goin' out you'd get on up here and you'd float across there. That's us little fellas, us younger ones with the food, put 'em on a man-made raft, make your own little raft, just to float us across, you know, the younger ones. With the food and the spears an' the axes – oh the axe'd be down here. So you wonder how they got cobra out in the early days before the new technology of axes come along, eh? They must've hit him with the old, the big axe – big rock ones. They'd have to. See we used to go from here all the way down, walk right down.
> (Martin Ballangarry)

The places where it is possible to cross the river, the detail of the tides which determine the direction and place of crossing, and the means of crossing the water on a log, or making a raft, are all part of the walking trail story. Each item is a significant part of the events in this story. Martin's memory of carrying the axes recalls their purpose in cutting through the rotten logs to extract the cobra worm. It is here that Martin departs to walk metaphorically along another linking trail, the trail of collecting cobra. The intersecting cobra story is especially important for Martin because of his identity as a 'guguurr fella'.

> As for the Macksville mob, I don't know, you know, which way they go, they come our way or they go that way. But if they want a feed of cobra they all come up to Bowra – we were the guguurr fellas, we were the main fella for guguurr, cobra. They fella, they get very salty from here down. So the saltwater is good for cobra, but up this way they get a little

bit bigger, and they get longer up round our country up here.
Yeah. Bigger. The salty ones they sorta stay stunted and then
they just all get growth more. (Martin Ballangarry)

Cobra is a prized food and important in Martin's identity in place. Martin's knowledge of cobra comes from walking through the landscape, catching cobra at all the different places, knowing where the best and biggest cobra grow, and the precise conditions that make that growth possible. Cobra grow biggest in the tidal part of the Nambucca River at Bowraville where the particular mix of salt- and freshwater is the best for their growth. The Bowra people are therefore 'the guguurr fellas', identified with the cobra and the place where they grow best. This identification is Martin's translation of a totemic clan identity. Part of the walk from Bowraville to the Island provokes him to reflect on this intense identity with his local country. The cobra story evolves into other stories about journeys; how the saltwater moves from the sea up the river, the journeys of the cobra going out to sea to breed, and his own journeys to collect cobra.

> We eat them. I live off it. That's my culture food. That's its main staple diet today.
> The main salt stops right up here at Bowraville. So it's got to have certain amount of salinity in it for the cobra to breed. When they decide that, they go out to sea, go right up to Raleigh. Oh, this is another cobra area for me [pointing]. Sometimes we'd start from up here, too, see, come down, that's another travelling route. They'd walk down from Seven Oaks – they'd go from Seven Oaks down – oh that's just another thing, but sort of go all hunting for cobra, beautiful – all up the creek. Another story, another time.
> (Martin Ballangarry)

All walking trails intersect with the storylines of other walking trails. The places where these trails intersect are particularly powerful. Martin's finger follows the cobra as they travel out to sea to breed and then back to the local waterholes on the Nambucca River at Bowraville with its local unmapped name, Seven Oaks. During this digression Martin describes in intimate detail the way the bodies of cobra inhabit the logs with their bodies twisted around each other.

He knows which logs will be good for cobra, and where they are, and describes cutting them out with an axe so as not to damage their soft bodies. We talk about the virtues of eating them raw or preparing them for cooking, and how they are important as medicine. This intimate knowledge of the bodies of cobra and their living places is only a minute part of the knowledge of local food ecologies that belongs in particular places on the linking trails. The walking trails connect such places of intensity in ever-increasing webs of connection, extending even to the journeys of Captain Cook as Martin explains about the impact of the cobra worm on Cook's journeys in timber vessels and the need to stop to repair the boats from their damage. For him, he says, the cobra is survival; for Cook it was an inconvenience to his ever-onward journeys of exploration.

Finally, after this long digression and intersection with all of the other journeys, we map the last part of Martin's walk from Bowraville to the Island. Here we mark the places where only 'the old fellas' were allowed to collect crabs, the special Blue-Tongue Lizard place, and then the crossing to the Island for a big picnic.

> So we went all down around, you know, and we then stayed on this side of the river too, right down to Nambucca. We get along there, this is where us young fellas walk around while the old fellas go round this way 'cause he go 'round and get the crabs, see. The old fella get all the crabs from 'round in that area. Yeah, they're mud flats this is. Now you can just go 'round there, get some mud crabs, and then they'd come out on the highway and then go down, like that. So just down 'ere Blue-Tongue – but they'd go 'round and 'round the mud flats then they'd come out and then they'd go to the Blue-Tongue come down then they'd walk down the road. Then they'd move over to the Island then. Walk down the highway, spear along their fish then go over to the Island then. Big picnic, eh [laughs]. (Martin Ballangarry)

As they get nearer to the Island their food gathering intensifies and they go round and round on the mud flats collecting crabs and spearing fish. They pass Wandarrga, simply called Blue-Tongue after its Dreaming story, and then across to the Island, for 'a big picnic'. There are no details of the big picnic, the point of the story is not the arrival but the journey itself. The story of the big picnic, of the gathering place, is another story of its own. The story of walking through country, where food is collected, places learned, histories recorded, where all the places are storied and marked, is the quintessential linking trail.

There are many elements of Martin's story that parallel Birrugan's journey from Wirriimbi to Worabooraby along the Nambucca River. Birrugan leaves his home camp and many events happen along the way. His journey is also a story of intertribal politics through which histories in land are told. Birrugan left the home place where he was camped with his mother to engage in a fight with a neighbouring tribe at Scotts Head. On his journey he hunted and collected food and made a canoe and paddles from the trees growing by the river. On the way he crisscrossed many of the other story places and songlines. At the arrival place more significant events happened that are marked in that special place time and time again through gathering and ceremony.

The mapping of Martin's walking trail gives me insight into the basis of the songlines that crisscross Gumbaynggirr country. A songline is a walking trail that links the story events, the path that the creation ancestors followed as they did the same, walking through country, collecting food, and living out the events in their lives that are marked forever in the landscape. At each of the special places along the way a song is sung and the songs are connected in the songline of the linking trails. It is through these linking trails that connections are made across Gumbaynggirr country and beyond, connecting with the storylines of neighbouring language groups. Tony said they are like Central Railway Station, with travel routes connecting in all possible directions.

> You can see the connection, it's like gettin' off at Central Railway Station. It's not the end of the line, you jump off there and jump on the next train over here, it's gonna take you somewhere else and that's what it's like, like Central

Railway Station to us, but it's like Central Railway Station to these people too because they come along and met us here, we came down and met them there and what we'd find is some of our own names are, family names are down through here, is connecting from here right up to where we are, so we can see that these lines were used and there was a type of sharing, sharing in, may have been sacred or spiritual sites or trading sites, all those type of things. (Tony Perkins)

The Old People travelled outside their local clan areas on recognised walking trails. 'There's a lot of lines within your own area but then they're branchin' out over the top of other areas.' These walking trails crossed clan and tribal boundaries, connecting places from different clan and language groups in traditional patterns of movement. Through these movements and connections relationships were forged, material resources were exchanged and the highest level of spiritual knowledge of country was shared. Movement across country was never random but followed cultural trails that were based on the tracks of traditional songlines. Gary describes 'movement from the western way, big clans, tribe that way come across. There's so many storylines, different, governing different things'.

There are many traditional travel routes that cross Gumbaynggirr country. Gary pointed out that the road I drive on from the tablelands down to the sea follows the old linking trails. These east–west movements were based on 'long-term arrangements' by which people from the mountains travelled down to meet up with people from the coast. These travels from the northern tablelands to the coast are enshrined in the story of the muurrbay tree. Similarly, people travelled in the reverse direction from the sea to the inland reaches of Gumbaynggirr country to the big ceremonial places on the edge of the tablelands at Point Lookout and Serpentine. Uncle Ray Kelly described another travel route running north–south through Gumbaynggirr to Dhanggati country which finally led to the Clybucca middens, another important place of gathering and ceremony.

As we map these linking trails we begin to recognise common elements in these storylines. They follow the lines of rivers and ridges, marking features such as mountains, headlands and other lookouts, all identifiable on topographical maps that show the shapes of the landscape. The places they pass through are often remote, rugged gorge country commonly regarded as unnamed and uninhabited wilderness. The linking trails are dotted by miirlarl, special places where people gathered for ceremony and exchange. They had many different purposes and meanings. There were smaller trails within local boundaries and larger trails that crossed clan and language boundaries. There were trails for camping and food, women's trails and men's trails, and trails that the young and uninitiated learned to respect as powerful and taboo. The different meanings of these linking trails were an important part of place learning.

> Yeah, some of them places you used to go had more different types of meaning to it when you're travelling. One of the trails you're took on only for camping or food and that sort of thing but then another one you go and you're not allowed to go down them until you're with the Old People. That might be where you're going back and forth to collect the initiation stones or power stones, what we call glowing stones. Them travel routes you just can't travel them by yourself.
> Then there's other ones just 'specially for women. They're the ones like birthing routes where the women travelled to their special places and back to their birthing ground and that sort of thing, for children to be born, they had the special areas where they went. Each trail had their special significance, why they were there and that's what you had to learn as a kid, which ones you could go on and which ones you can't go on. (Tony Perkins)

The meaning of the different trails was as significant as the meaning of the special places on these trails. As a young man Tony learned the everyday trails that they were allowed to travel on by walking them. The storylines that followed the ceremonial trails were only taught in stories by the Old People 'because we never got the chance to do all the old travelling ways'. These were the stories that Tony told when I sat with him beside a map of Gumbaynggirr country. He began with the mother place at Moonee Beach where all the clans began. He then oriented himself back through his own clan territory in the north to the ceremonial places near Red Rock. We followed these trails on the map across Gumbaynggirr country, north to the Clarence River and west to the powerful place near Point Lookout. The most powerful meeting places seemed to be at the edges of country where different clan and language groups came together for ceremony.

Within a local area there are smaller linking trails, each with their special places. These are in turn linked to larger storylines and special places, as Tony explained in his metaphor of Central Railway Station. The impact of Tony's story, however, was not about the special places or the individual trails but in the diamond-shaped patterns that connected linking trails across Gumbaynggirr country. These networks of diamond-shaped trails mirror the diamond shape of the star constellation the Southern Cross. Linking trails connect sky country to earth country and to water country. At the most elementary level the stars of the Southern Cross were used to guide their journey along the walking trails to the special places in far away country. The stars are symbolically represented on the ground with rock formations that mark the way to these special places. The diamond pattern of the stars of the Southern Cross is also deeply embedded in the storylines and symbolism of the creation ancestors.

In mapping the storylines of Birrugan and The Women Who Made the Sea we were following the process of reconnecting story to country in the work that Tiger Buchannan began and Muurrbay continues. It is through this work that storylines can become songlines again, songs can be sung again in their places in a new way. In making their connections with each other, Tony, Gary and Ken were reconnecting the larger songlines throughout Gumbaynggirr country. They talked about the patterns of linking trails across Gumbaynggirr country, connecting northern and southern stories and extending beyond their own clan areas.

The first part of The Women Who Made the Sea begins in southern Gumbaynggirr country at Scotts Head in 'the time when we all began'. The two sisters, angry that they had been left behind and pursued by an unwelcome lover, decided to make the waters rise and cause their errant tribe to be stranded out at sea. They began their journey to make the coastline of what we now know as Australia, at Moonee Beach[48], the place of the mother. One went north and the other went south and they met up again at Moonee Beach at the end of their journey.

After they completed their circle of Australia, as we call it now, makin' the sea and the sand, they met again at Moonee Beach and they swam out to the ocean and they crossed their yam sticks. An' the place where they crossed them is called Split Solitary Island. If you look from a certain angle you'll see it like crossed yam sticks. And from there, the sisters went up into the sky, up into a star cluster we call Janagan. You'll know it better as the Seven Sisters or the Pleiades. And that's where the story ends. (Ken Walker)

The story of The Women Who Made the Sea, however, is part of a trilogy that is repeated up and down the coast, connecting across different language groups. Although each songline has a beginning and end in each territory they are connected to further episodes of the same story in other places, or simply repeated in similar versions of the same storyline in different places. The section of the story of The Women Who Made the Sea in southern Gumbaynggirr country at Scotts Head connects to the story of the koala brothers who made a bridge to the land with their intestines to rescue the people who got stranded when the two sisters made the sea. This story involves many other characters such as Baalijin, the native cat, and Guubuny, the mopoke owl. This part of the story ends when the koala brothers were turned to stone at Mount Yarrahappini, 'yarriabini', meaning 'koalas rolling down', in Dhanggati country. The koala brothers can be seen in the two humps at the top of Mount Yarrahappini. The storyline, however, continues on, joining to other stories further down the coast.

The Birrugan story continues on down to Seal Rocks, just north of Newcastle beyond Dhanggati in Birrbay country, 'where the story really ends after he climbs the myrtle tree and then goes into the sky and becomes the Southern Cross. And the two pointer stars are the wives.' The translation of the name Birrugan is also given as the name for the Southern Cross[49] symbolised in the diamond patterns of the linking trails and the diamond symbols on the carved trees that mark the special places in Gumbaynggirr country. The Birrugan songline makes connections in many directions, linking earth, heavens and sea, and connecting people, stories, languages and places. The layers of connection deepen as stories and contemporary places intersect.

We know from Gary that Birrugan's mother is known as Gawnggan, meaning 'all woman', and as Mary the mother of Jesus, as well as Giilan, the brolga. The dance of the mourning brolga at Birrugan's grave is connected to the mother place at Moonee Beach, to the yellow waterholes, and to Mary's Waterhole (Miimiga Gawngganba Miirlarl)[50] in northern Gumbaynggirr country. At Jewfish Point the brolgas learned their dance from Gumbaynggirr people as they danced in ceremony on the opposite shore, and nearby at the Old Farm, the site of the birthing grounds, the brolgas return to dance every year. As Ken says these songlines are 'a combination of a lot of stories that flow from one to the other. That's generally how our Gumbaynggirr stories work'.

The linking trails, then, are the actual walking tracks that people followed when they travelled back and forth through country. They are the walking trails of the ancestral beings as they moved through the landscape. The storylines that follow these trails link the many smaller stories of particular events that happened along the way as they created the forms and all the living creatures of the landscape. A storyline is the plot or narrative outline of the story and this becomes a songline once again when language, story, people and place are reconnected. This happens when the intimate detail of local places is known and cared for. Deep mapping is the process whereby the larger narratives are reconnected to country, reclaiming their original status as songlines. Ongoing language work and storytelling in country keeps the local connections strong and helps people to care for country. Through listening to the conversations connecting southern and northern Gumbaynggirr knowledges, we can understand something of this ongoing work of connecting storylines to places as a process of singing country anew.

Miirlarl – special places of gathering and ceremony

Picketts Mountain the Europeans call it
we call it Nunguu Miirlarl
a kangaroo special place

> it was an increase site
> when kangaroo was scarce
> they went up and done their dances
> on top of the mountain
> so the kangaroos would come back
> that's one part of that place.

The places where people sang and danced their country on the linking trails are places of intensity connected to each other through the narrative storyline. These places of intensity are known as miirlarl which signifies a special place of gathering and ceremony. On each of the major songlines there are many small events or stories that give rise to the forms of the landscape and the animals and plants that live there. Each of these has a miirlarl. Gary said that The Women Who Made the Sea is the main songline because all of the sea creatures came from this story. 'I think that the main one is the sea story because everything else follows about miirlarls for crab, lobster, you name it, different kinds of fish, all of them – stingray – places are lost now forever.' The creation story for each of these creatures was marked by a miirlarl, where the place and its particular creature – crab, lobster, or stingray – was sung into being in ceremony.

> In the olden days there would have been thousands of miirlarl. I try and tell people it's like those dots on the dot paintings, they're all maps with differing levels of importance, and if the whole country was mapped with them basically after a while you don't need the ones that you need to walk around country when you put on the reserves and everything, you need the ones that are important. I suppose those people would still know the songs and to tell the people that's for that and that's not for this and so people would know the main ones, like you got kangaroo, you got yam, you got cobra worm, all that type of thing. (Gary Williams)

Special places and their linking trails are maps of country. There are layers of special places, including historic places imbued with the events and histories of contact. These might be living places like camps and missions, massacre places like the site at Red Rock, or contemporary cultural places like the Muurrbay church building. These local everyday places do not need to be encoded for memory because everyone knows where they are and how to care for them. The significant places outside of the local area, however, are remembered in songs and these songs are sung for all the main foods such as the kangaroo, the yam and the cobra. At the kangaroo place, Nunguu Miirlarl, the song to make the kangaroos return was sung. The places and their creatures were given new life through the singing. The songs were also revitalised through the singing of the places.

The singers were the men and women who took part in the most secret–sacred ceremonies. 'It's one of those things where the singers have gone but the song was still there, so the only difference now, the songs are still there in the areas, you still regard it with the same kind of reverence, but the singers have gone.' By the time of Ken, Tony and Gary's generation the initiation ceremonies through which people gained the knowledge to sing could no longer be performed because of the intrusion of white settlement. For Gary, however, even though the singers have gone, the songs are still there in the places. He described this sense of their closeness to the songs in these places as living in 'the shadow of initiation'.

> Terry Widders and I coined the phrase, in the early seventies, that we were born in the shade of initiation, in the shadow, because we figure we're a generation and a half away. Not much indeed and you're just brought up with it all, and the thing about being born after initiation you just, you know all the taboos. (Gary Williams)

Their generation was born 'in the shadow of initiation' because they were only a few years away from the times of singing and dancing in the special places. They grew up with the stories but they could only learn about the places of initiation through taboo. The songs and ceremonies of the initiation cycles were a way to transmit the highest form of knowledge about country but the special places for the initiation songlines were so powerful that the uninitiated had to be protected from their power. Gary imagines the last initiation in southern Gumbaynggirr country as a big party.

> I like to think of it as the last hurrah, you know the men of high degree and they could see, before they got too old you know, they could do one last ceremony before the wide world closed in fully because I think, lots of things happened in Bellbrook before they converted it into a reserve and then the station manager and that kind of thing. So like I said, they might well have just got together, sent out invitations, said, 'Look let's do it and put some people through and just do it and get together and sing our songs for the last big time in a proper way'. I can see it, you know, you can just see it in your mind. (Gary Williams)

The last hurrah was part of the larger cycle, the final stage of initiation where the ngaluunggirr, the clever men, were made. Gary remembers the story of his father and brother travelling down to South West Rocks, to the miirlarl, the special place of Birrugan's last battle, and arriving a day late. They could therefore not go to the last stage of the cycle, held at Bellbrook in 1935. Gary and Ken grew up with the Old People telling these stories of initiation but already initiated men like Uncle Harry Buchannan had begun to record the songs and stories of the special places. Tony, too, grew up in the orbit of initiation with his grandfather in No Mans Land, just one generation away.

> I think the last – I had a letter that he left with me, and it was written to, it wasn't an Aboriginal person, it was a white person and his name was McManus. He was a doctor. And in the letter this Doctor McManus was writing back to my grandfather. It was written on old brown writing paper and it was 1950. It had a date on it and I remember it. He, Doctor McManus, was sent somewhere up north and he was sent away to search for himself to gather the stones that was wanted as part of his [initiation]. And in the letter he wrote back and said that he'd gathered, what he had to gather for

> the ceremony. I actually had that letter and that was in the fifties. I was told the last initiation took place down at Red Rock here and that was in the late fifties. It was at Red Rock, on this side of Jewfish Point, that's where there used to be big gatherings there, Jewfish Point. The secret parts they used to take around, like see, Bald Nob Hill, just down halfway to Red Rock, it was a special hill too, you know, linkin' with the tree from here. (Tony Perkins)

The last ceremony was in the late 1950s when Tony was about twelve years old. He could have been initiated at this time but he chose not to. The cycle began at the sacred tallowwood tree in No Mans Land where they smoked the young men and then continued on to the special places at Red Rock. The most important thing about this story for Tony, however, is that it was a white man who was initiated. At this time Clarrie Skinner also made the decision to record his secret and sacred knowledge with non-Aboriginal linguists.

Tony, Gary and Ken are continuing the process that the old initiated men began of transmitting their stories in a different way. In connecting the storylines back to country, by mapping them onto a satellite map and recording their stories in the process of deep mapping, they are drawing on the knowledge and the work of the Old People. Tony said the Old People always began with the mother place, the place where the Gumbaynggirr nation began.

> The father, our creator, he came by water down to – they call it Look At Me Now Headland. We landed there, and he met his wife and so he could see his wife, he put her at Mount Coramba, the reason why Mount Coramba was a safe place he built, they put Mount Coramba there so that it was the highest peak, so from one, he could be there and she could be there, that's the mother and the father of the clan. And we came like children from the mother and father, we're like all brother and sister, but we're all in different clans, different clan areas, coming from that mother and father. Yeah, but we're brother and sister belong to the mother and father. (Tony Perkins)

Connecting the dots

When I asked Tony about where the mother place was he didn't answer me directly. He told me the story of how 'one time ago, Coffs Harbour City Council wanted to put a pipe through Look At Me Now Headland and out to the sea. I told them it would be like putting a pipe through the mother's head.' Like Birrugan's knee, the physical place of the headland is the body of the mother. The mother place is where they all came from and spread out as brothers and sisters to their different clan areas. Tony from the north, Ken and Gary from the south, and me from the western edge of Gumbaynggirr country, coming together at this motel at Moonee Beach. In this meeting of different knowledges about country we work at the very edge of living memory to connect storylines and fill in some of the missing pieces. The conversations grew in depth, the silences as powerful as the stories' gathering intensity. They began talking about the golden miirlarl.

Each of the different clan groups in Gumbaynggirr country had different major storylines and associated miirlarl and where these storylines meet up are the most powerful places of all. In the liminal space of the motel, I gather together the fragments of these stories at the edge of memory and outside the realms of my understanding. Tony explained: 'The three main golden spirits that belong to Aboriginal people is that Golden Eel, that Golden Dog, and down at Nambucca way they got that Golden Kangaroo'. I remember that in my first story recording with Ken when I asked him about the special places around Nambucca, he said the most important place was 'the Golden Kangaroo'. He introduced the place through its English name, Picketts Mountain, and then through its language name, Nunguu Miirlarl, the kangaroo special place. Gary also talked about the three 'golden' places, giving the language names for each as well as calling them by the English translation.

> We've got, you know, the Golden Kangaroo and if you go up, between here and Grafton and Grafton does have the Golden Dog Hotel there and they also have the Golden Eel up at the bridge at Grafton there, so they're the three sites, the Waanyji Miirlarl in Coramba, Buurrga Miirlarl at Grafton and Nunguu Miirlarl here, special places, to my way

of thinking. I think this kangaroo place is probably *the* place.
(Gary Williams)

I follow the lines of these stories and struggle to understand. It is only through my direct interaction with the places that I begin to have some sense of them. It took me years to recognise Nunguu Miirlarl in the landscape. I had been watching a particular hill from the cabin where I stay, wondering if it might be the place people talked about as Picketts Mountain. One late afternoon it seemed to shine golden from within, it was as if it was calling me to it. I went inside to get my camera and by the time I came out it had changed. I began to photograph it each day and at different times of the day as it changed from minute to minute, depending on the season, the light and cloud, the time of day. I asked Gary about that mountain, telling him of this experience, and he said yes, it is Nunguu Miirlarl, the place of the golden kangaroo. 'I always talk to Nunguu,' he said, 'driving out to Pauline's at night, shining silver in the light of the full moon, it's very beautiful.'

After this I see the mountain from all different places and different perspectives. When I walk along the beach in the afternoon there is one particular rock platform that reaches out from the curve of a headland into the sea. From there I can see the mountain in its fullness in the late afternoon sun. Or in the early morning when the sun shines on the whiteness of the waves and the sky is tinged with faint light pink, Nunguu Miirlarl is joined to rows of beaches up the coast as far as the eye can see. Making these sorts of connections has been an important part of my learning. The knowledge of places is never all there in front of me, presented for my consumption. After I have deeply experienced this place day after day, year after year, I begin to know things differently. I can go back to transcripts of conversations years later and see that some things have always been there, I was just not ready to understand. There are many things that I can never know. I learn to be comfortable with not knowing but I also hear more in future conversations that help me to connect more of the pieces.

> That's that jigsaw puzzle that we talk about, 'cause it can go right back that jigsaw puzzle and 'cause each young fella, they were taken out by the older ones when they're young and

the older ones was very clever at how to teach you. They tell some young fellas about different things and they'll tell the other young ones other things and the idea is when the young ones grow up, when they go up in age they should be talkin' to one another then about all the different types of what they've been told to one another. So they put together like a jigsaw puzzle and understand all the information, what it's all about, and that's how they used to teach us. I suppose in one way it was a more simpler way because if Keith was told a lot about Picketts Hill where someone else might have been told oh well it is a very special place but they won't go into it too much, because I suppose in their time if they distribute that knowledge to different people then different people go around and distribute to one another and that's how they used to do it. (Tony Perkins)

Each piece adds to the whole and gathers all that has come before it. In this return to the metaphor of the jigsaw puzzle Tony talks about Picketts Hill for the first time, a sideways glance, just in passing. I think of it now as Nunguu Miirlarl with the language depth of generations. I have a sense of it in my body through my daily connection with the place. I imagine the vast time depth of the Birrugan storyline and all the places near Nunguu Miirlarl in the Birrugan storyline. The place where Birrugan camped with his mother at Deep Creek, the place where he sat on the ridge making his boomerang and watching his mother's camp, and the deep waterhole made when the red ochre fell off the ridgepole of the tent when he died. All of this is in southern Gumbaynggirr country and now I hear that Tony from northern Gumbaynggirr is connected to this place too.

> There's a lot of different pictures you got to put together 'cause you know we had a link from up this end, the northern end, with Deep Creek 'cause there's a lot of powerful sites from here to there. They had a special trail running to that which would link and then the next tribe below that they would link at that special site on that boundary and they'd have their trails running, where they used to do the same

thing. There are all special different meanings to every track that was there but it took a lot, a lot of time to understand it and realise what they were for. (Tony Perkins)

The linking trails become special for me too as the places connect and deepen their meanings. The barely articulated knowledge I have from the Yarrawarra Elders of spirits in places hovers into these places too. They gather up with all that I have learned through living in these places. Through the special linking trails Tony, Ken and Gary connect their stories and I can connect the two separate parts of my work. I can know Deep Creek as the place where Birrugan camped with Gawnggan close to Nunguu Miirlarl. I can know this as the special place for the coming out of the ngaluunggirr, the clever men, the place where the women sang the sons home to their country.

Here at Valla there was a big ring there, and that was the one where my grandfather was telling me where they all come out of the travel as fully Elders, clever people by the time they come around to here. That's where he was tellin' me about the women, women would form the line between the two rings and the clever men would come through the first ring and down through the next ring and that's the first time the women'd see the men and all that so that was like a big ceremony there and he was telling me all white, all of the feather and everything they used was all white, ochre, everything, that was a special thing, they used the white when they got to there, and that was when they came out. (Tony Perkins)

Tony learned all this through the songs. 'I used to hear him, he used to sing a lot, my grandfather used to sing a lot about initiation.' His grandfather used to sing to him the special songs that were sung when the young men came out of their place of deep learning. 'He used to sing a lot of times and he used to just sing me what they used to sing for 'em when they used to come out, special songs they used to sing for when they was finishin up, like comin' out into manhood.' These songs were sung because they were part of the public ceremony when all of the people would gather together to celebrate the coming out of the young men. The songs were an integral part of the whole performance in that place. The place, the circles, the dance and the songs all came together in that powerful moment. Tony's grandfather sang the songs over and over to the young man, teaching him through story and song about the way young men were brought into the full knowledge of that place.

At the same time as he was singing these songs to his grandson, Clarrie Skinner recorded these songs. The tapes of these recordings are held in the University of New England library and over the years I had many copies made for people who wanted them. Part of the process of bringing the language home was to gather together all of the recordings that had been made over the years by the Old People and link their language and stories back to country. It was not until now, however, that I realised that Clarrie Skinner's tape recordings and their annotations offer a remarkable gift of insight into Nunguu Miirlarl and the nature of singing country.

Clarrie Skinner described these songs as Bagurlany[51], songs that were sung in the public ceremonies to welcome the young men coming out of the initiation ceremony at Nunguu Miirlarl. There were two songs, the song of the mountain and the song of the lyrebird.

Gala guuray wuugan [=wuuban]	the bloodwood flowers rain down
Guuray wuugan [wuuban] barri	the bloodwood flowers rain down
Yaarri ganga ya Gabaagu juluumgu wuuban.gu	Later it's off up here to the mountain to the bloodwoods
Wurruunda nunguugundi	here to the wing house of the kangaroos
Ya wuuban.gu guuray wuuban barri	the bloodwoods the bloodwood flower rains down
Galnyam-gal yurruunda	In the rainforest
Ngal-ngal yurruunda	I was going up and down a long way
Jaawandu girraanday ngaanya barri	A lyrebird met me and called me home
ganggaa-lay jaygal ngal-ngal yurruun(da)	up and down a long way

Like all song, these songs offer us poetry. Clarrie Skinner's songs are a poetry of place that captures the quality and intensity of a relationship to place that is both ordinary and extraordinary, everyday and spiritual. Even more poignant is Clarrie Skinner's voice talking about his memories of the Old People and their ceremonies. 'I could take you to Clouds Creek – that's where they dance. When he took me out and showed it I had a look at it and I sat on a log and I cried. That's where Old People made up that song about putting us through the Law and finishing up brought us home and showed us that.' Listening to Clarrie's voice saying these words I realise that we all live in the shadow of initiation. It is so close and there has been so much loss. There is also so much that remains in the places, in the songs, and in the stories that were handed down from the Old People, in their memories and in their recordings. It is a time to stay in this moment of 'exquisite care and attention', to feel the voice, the songs, and the places with all of our senses, emotions and intellect, and to ask again about how can we sing our places differently.

~

When I moved from northern New South Wales to south-east Victoria, Tony, Ken and Gary were incredulous. 'You'll come back home', they said. It took twelve months in my new job before I could write about Gumbaynggirr country, before I could stop taking in here and write about there, the place of my home country for thirty years. I grieved the landscapes of home. This morning, I am in the depths of writing about Clarrie Skinner's songs, about coming out of the mountain, how the bloodwood flowers rain down and the lyrebird calls him back home. The rainforest and the mountain. I remember each of the Garby Elders in turn, and our work together. I write about how 'gaabi' means swamp wallaby and it is this sign, the sign of the swamp wallaby, that symbolises the authority of the knowledge holders of that country. The right to share this story.

After three hours or so of this writing I get up and go to Morwell National Park for my Sunday morning walk. It is my green time, breathing the air of trees. Once I caught sight of a wallaby who lives at the bottom of the valley, disappearing between trees. Another time I heard a lyrebird call. On this unusually warm morning that heralds the coming of spring I ease into the green of trees and breathe deeply. The ground is moist, hoping for more rain. Last summer was hot, dry and bush fires, dirty weather. I am not thinking much, weather, trees, it is my hazy soft vision time. Gentle thoughts come and go, down the soft dirt track to the deep green floor of the rainforest. Moss on fallen logs, soft green light.

I am absorbed in the gentle movement of these thoughts when I become aware of a swamp wallaby standing in front of me on the path. He moves, slowly, and stands just off the track beside me. I stop and stand still and quiet, close enough to touch him. It is as if he is with me. He just stands there not moving. I can sense the texture of his warm dark fur, changing shades of brown, grey and cream over his body, the ripple of light in fur as he makes the slightest movement. I feel his body balanced on strong tail and muscular hind legs, front legs and paws poised in front of his chest. I can see the delicate nose, ears and mouth twitching slightly, responding to me responding to him. After a few moments he begins to nibble the small green leaves on a bush near his face, so calm, so unafraid, as if we eat here together. I walk off slowly with great care and gentleness so as not to disturb his quiet morning.

I pass Mrs Lyndon's Grove, named after a local lady who loved its native orchids, and I walk through the grove to check the little creek that was bubbling and splashing a fortnight ago. Today all is quiet except for the birds. Down on its banks, amongst fallen logs and ferns, the creek has only puddles. I think about knowing places intimately. It is only through this intimate knowing of days and seasons, years and generations, that one can know how well a place is doing. In this Sunday morning green time I think of getting to know this place, each Sunday, the rhythm and pleasure of the same, of the return.

I walk up the hill and I hear the lyrebird singing. He is chirruping and trilling, mimicking all the bird songs around, but his song is louder, more insistent, more of a performance than these birds he imitates, so I know it is him. I stand still again to listen and realise he is only a few feet away from me in the bushes. In that moment of recognition he begins to dance. He turns his back to me so his dancing feathers face me, and slowly raises and opens his lyre-shaped tail. Fully open, he holds the lacy curtain of feathers aloft, then quivers and shimmers their pearly luminescence in the green shady light. It is only a few moments but for that moment it is all eternity. It is as if we meet each other spirit to spirit in that place. He softly closes his lyre feathers and lifts his feet high, one after the other, in a deliberate slow dance as he moves away over bush and branches. In the space he has left there is a perfect cleared circle of bare earth. I imagine white painted bodies adorned with white feathers, dancing the lyrebird quiver and shimmer in the green light, feet lifting and lowering, human-becoming-lyrebird. A little way off he stops again and scratches at the leafy ground, eating what he can find there.

I walk quietly on and hold these images in my mind. It is not until later that I think about these experiences. I have never had such a close encounter in the bush with two wild creatures. It is here in this place, my new place where I struggle to find home. It takes me back, deep into the place of my writing, and feels like an encounter with the spirits of Gumbaynggirr country here in this new place. I recall Clarrie and the lyrebird calling him back to his homelands from the mountain. I remember my friends, the Garby Elders, named for the dark-faced swamp wallaby. They were so close to me in this work. We did not always communicate much in words but there was love and acceptance, a sharing and generosity of spirit. Four of them are gone now. It is as if they visited me here in this place and gave me their blessing. Even if I am unsure of the possibility of spirits, the experience remains in the quality of attention, the intensity of being in this place, and the deep connections to other places and people that it calls up. The quality of care and attention is spiritual in itself, even without the sense of spirits, but I am left with a strong sense of being held in the connection with these spirits of place.

I want to hold onto this moment but I cannot abstract it from the flux of that place, the air of trees, the green light, the light feeling of the breeze, the season, that particular Sunday morning at the beginning of spring, that walk. I think about it now as a slow Sunday of little miracles and about how we all hunger for this. I think about how I am suspended in the liminal, in-between a tradition from elsewhere and this place. It is the work of translation, the work of the spirit and the work of story. It is a work that connects people to each other and to their places, a work that makes new songs.

Epilogue: The place of creation

And so, I return to the mother place, the place of the beginning.

It is a rainy grey day at Moonee Beach when I go back there in search of the place. The whole flat of the sandy estuary where women and children were playing two days earlier is covered with water from high tide. A strong wind buffets my ears and cold rain blows against my face. All is grey, soft light.

This time I cross the little bridge over swirls of clear green water in the mangrove-lined creek. The other side is still and quiet and along the shoreline a thick mass of shells crumbles white from the dark, overhanging bank. Long, elegant spiral shells drop from their densely packed layer and lie scattered along the narrow sandy edge of the lapping tide. 'Junka', Ken calls them, 'we used to eat them in the old days'. I crawl gently over the crumbling bank and into bushes and ferns under the dense shelter of rainforest trees, now out of the buffeting wind. Through the undergrowth a path opens out, crunchy underfoot with densely packed midden shells all the way through tall lichen-trunked casuarinas to the grassy flat of the headland. How many people feasted here at this place, I wonder, and what did they gather here for?

I had met with Tony to talk about the final text of *Singing the Coast*. He spoke about the decision to record their knowledge and make it publicly available long before we began our research. When we talk about what non-Indigenous people should know about their coastal country, Tony says 'not many white people want to go deep into our culture'. He then talks again about McManus, the white doctor initiated by his grandfather in the last initiation ceremony at Red Rock. He says his grandfather believed that 'however deeply the white man wanted to go, we were willing to share our knowledge'.

I ask him about the mother place and I am given great gifts of knowledge. It is as if, in coming with the gift of the text of our book, I am given equal gifts in return. I have been there too and looked at all the intimate details of the place so I know what questions to ask. I ask him about the green dome headland on the southern end of Moonee Beach that I walked to on the crunchy pathway of midden shells. Tony says, 'We went there with Uncle Groper, he wouldn't go over the bridge, it's that women's place'. I ask about all the different headlands trying to work out which is the one where they landed from the sea and he explains that they were all part of Moonee Beach at one time. When I ask about Look At Me Now Headland he tells me the same story. 'One time ago', he said, 'they wanted to put a pipe through Look At Me Now Headland so we told them that it would be like putting a pipe through the head of the mother'.

We get out the map and look over the expanse of country – beaches, headlands, estuaries – that make up these Gumbaynggirr coastal landscapes. We move between our intimate knowledge of these places, the infinite detail of the prints in the sand, the crunch of shells in the midden and the vast lines and shapes of connection. Tony draws the shape of a triangle with his finger. There is one triangle, he says, between the southern headland at Moonee Beach, the mother place, at Look At Me Now Headland, and the Yellow Waterholes. Then he makes another larger triangle between the southern headland, the mother place headland, and Mary's Waterhole, Miimiga Gawnggan, shaping with his body the linking trails that crisscross Gumbaynggirr country. He says that the creator landed at Look At Me Now Headland, the women were always there, they were there first. He tells me that the Yellow Waterholes is the place where the two sisters banged their digging sticks to make sand and water, then one went north and the other south, making the coastline of our island continent. I ask again about the grassy dome of the southern headland with the midden along the bank of the estuary and up the path to the headland. Tony nods. 'That is the one, because when we went there with Groper he wouldn't go over the bridge, he told the men not to cross it.'

I emerge from the shelter of the midden track out onto the headland and just then, right on the edge of the green dome, another split island comes into view. I recognise it immediately as the one where the women left their ganay, their digging sticks, when they had finished their work. From there they went up into the heavens to become part of the Pleiades. I look to the north towards the mother place headland where the creator landed and 'the women were always there'. I look to the west towards Miimiga Gawnggan, the waterhole where the women came to the water of that special place. I follow the line of my vision along a silver creek that flows into the estuary towards the sea. I know it now as Ganaygal Creek where the women made their digging sticks from the grey myrtle, the ganayga tree. I can cross my digging sticks, for my work is done.

Notes

1. M Somerville & T Perkins, 2005.
2. This research was conducted over a period of ten years from 1996 to 2006 and during that time more than half of the knowledge holders that we worked with passed away. In honour of their memories we write about them in the present tense to respect the knowledge given to the project.
3. This old canoe, approximately 200 years old, is now housed and preserved at Yarrawarra's offices.
4. See ML Pratt, 1992.
5. P Carter, 1992, pp. 179–80.
6. P Cohen & M Somerville, 1990.
7. P Carter, 1992, p. 129.
8. R Stowe, 2005.
9. F Magowan, 2001, pp. 41–43.
10. ibid, p. 41.
11. ibid, p. 47.
12. M Somerville, 1999, p. 162.
13. DB Rose 2003, p. 168.
14. K Schlunke, 2004.
15. I borrow these words from K Schlunke, 2003, p. 2, Myall Creek: Dumb Places, a presentation at Writing Events: New Writing in Cultural Studies, UTS Sydney, to use as a dramatic refrain throughout this chapter.
16. P Cohen & M Somerville, 1990.
17. M Somerville et al., 1994.
18. DB Rose, 2003, p. 178.
19. Text from memorial cairn on Red Rock headland.
20. V Brady, 1998, p. 94.
21. ibid, p. 94.
22. M Tumarkin, 2005, p. 233.
23. ibid, p. 233.
24. ibid, p. 242.
25. M McKenna, 2003, p. 136.
26. ibid, p. 132.
27. P Read, 2002, p. 34.
28. M McKenna, 2003, p. 134.
29. M Somerville et al., 2000.
30. A Smith et al., 2000.
31. C Brown et al., 2000.
32. Gumbaynggirr song text and footnote text:

    Bing and Bruce Laurie of the Garby Elders had a favourite song they called 'The Gumbaynggirr Song'. This song is sung throughout Gumbaynggirr country with a number of variations on the main theme. Here it is reproduced in the original spelling and version of the Garby Elders:

    > Nganyundi baaliga Gumbaingirr
    > *My father is Gumbaingirr*
    > Nganyundi miimiga Gumbaingirr
    > *My mother is Gumbaingirr*
    > Ngaya jamay ya Gumbaingirr

I am Gumbaingirr too
Galaandi ngiinda warrga nyayagi junuygudi yu
Gosh why won't you hardly look at me sweetheart? Hey!
Reproduced from Yarrawarra Place Stories Book 3, Brown, C, Beck, W, Murphy, D, Perkins, T, Smith, A and Somerville, M 2000, University of New England.
33. GLCG, 1992.
34. **Muurrbay(ga)** N: white fig; white fig tree. 'That's the one belongs to the Lord.' **Muurrbay Bundani**: tree featured in Dreaming Story associated with the next world.
35. **Gawnggan(ba)** 1. Gawnggan, mother of the hero ancestor Birrugan, wife of Yuludarla [Sometimes translated as 'Mary', for example in Mary's Waterhole for Gawnggan's miirral at Woolgoolga.] *Miimiga Gawngganba, Birruganba bularri ngayinggi yilaa.* Mother Gawnggan and Birrugan were staying here together. 2. The Evening Star.
36. **Maruwan(ba)** N: second highest degree or school of initiation; person with this initiation.
37. Ivy Smith, Joyce Knox, Andrew 'Pop' Pacey, Jenny Brown, Maggie Morris and Jean Drew met with Shirley Kelly and Brother Steve Morelli to share what they knew.
38. The research processes were developed with, and drew on, the past cultural heritage mapping of Meg Goulding, a Melbourne-based cultural heritage consultant who had worked with Gumbaynggirr people before. They also drew on my own oral place-story recording techniques. The processes that we finally called 'deep mapping' were a co-creation with Ken Walker, Gary Williams, and other Gumbaynggirr knowledge holders who worked with us on the Muurrbay project.
39. **girr girr** N: plover. **Girr Girr** N: from (Sm) who has Giiriigirr: Stuart Island.
40. **Baga-baga**: Nambucca (more specifically Bellwood, the part of the river where the knee of the giant Ngambaa man fell when he was killed in the Dreaming.) [Nyambaga].
41. **Miirlarl** N: sacred site; (may be cave, waterhole etc).
42. **Wirriimbi** N: 1. long hair; 2. Saltwater oak.
43. GLCG, 1992, p. 47.
44. ibid, p. 52.
45. ibid, p. 52.
46. GLCG, 1992, p. 14.
47. Wallaby: Gumbaynggirr language distinguishes five different wallabies: black **gaabi,** grey **buliin,** female greyface **jirriwarr,** male scrub **girrbaam,** and the rock wallaby **maarrgaan.**
48. **Moonee Beach, Moony-Moony** Munim-Munim. Wirriiga **Wirriiga** The two Wirriiga women who made the sea went across there to become Split Solitary Island]. **Moonee Beach** (yam-stick place on) Ganaygal
49. GLCG 1992, p. 56.
50. **miimi(ga)** N: mother. Miimiga Gawngganba Miirlarl: 'Mother Gawnggan special place'. **Gawnggan(ba)** 1. Gawnggan, mother of the hero ancestor Birrugan, wife of Yuludarla. 2. The Evening Star. **Gawnggan(ba)** angel, female, good spirit.
51. Muurrbay Aboriginal Language and Culture Co-operative, (unpublished), pp. 57–8.

References and further reading

Brady, V 1998, *South of My Days: A Biography of Judith Wright*, Angus & Robertson, Pymble, NSW.

Brown, C, Beck, W, Murphy, D, Perkins, T, Smith, A & Somerville, M 2000, *The Old Camp: Corindi Lake North*, University of New England, Armidale, NSW & Yarrawarra Aboriginal Corporation.

Carter, P 1992, *The Sound In-Between: Voice, Space, Performance*, University of New South Wales Press, Sydney.

Cohen, P & Somerville, M 1990, *Ingelba and the Five Black Matriarchs*, Allen & Unwin, Sydney.

Gumbaynggirr Language and Culture Group 1992, *Gumbaynggirr Yuludarla (Gumbaynggirr Dreamings: The Stories of Uncle Harry Buchanan)*, Gumbaynggirr Language and Culture Group, Nambucca Heads, NSW.

Magowan, F 2001, 'Crying to Remember: Reproducing Personhood and Community' in F Magowan & B Attwood (eds) 2001, *Telling Stories: Indigenous History and Memory in Australia and New Zealand*, Allen & Unwin, Sydney, pp. 41–60.

McKenna, M 2003, 'A Preference for Forgetting: Some Reflections on Publishing' in *Looking for Blackfellas' Point: An Australian History of Place, Aboriginal History*, vol. 27, pp. 131–8.

Miniac, J 2005, '[Trusting in the possibility of writing.]' *Meanjin*, vol. 64, no. 4, p. 81.

Muurrbay Aboriginal Language and Culture Co-operative 2008, *Gumbaynggirr Dictionary & Learner's Grammar, Gumbaynggirr Bijarr Jandaygam Ngaawa Gugaarigam* (2nd ed.), MALCC, Nambucca Heads, NSW.

Muurrbay Aboriginal Language and Culture Co-operative 2001, *A Gumbaynggir Language Dictionary*, Aboriginal Studies Press, Canberra.

Muurrbay Aboriginal Language and Culture Co-operative (unpublished) *Gumbaynggirr Songs*, MALCC, Nambucca Heads, NSW.

Pratt, ML 1992, *Imperial Writing and Transculturalism*, Routledge, London & New York.

Read, P 2002, 'Reconciliation, Trauma and the Native Born' in *Humanities Research*, vol. 9, no. 1, pp. 29–35.

Rose, DB 2003, 'Dance of the Ephemeral: Australian Aboriginal Religion of Place' in MN McDonald (ed.) 2003, *Experiences of Place*, Center for the Study of World Religions, Harvard University, Cambridge, Massachusetts, pp. 163–86.

Schlunke, K 2004, 'Dumb Places' in *Balayi: Culture, Law and Colonialism*, vol. 6, pp. 72–81.

Somerville, M 1999, *Body/landscape journals*, Spinifex Press, Melbourne.

Somerville, M, Dundas, M, Mead, M, Robinson, J & Sulter, M 1994, *The Sun Dancin': People and Place in Coonabarabran*, Aboriginal Studies Press, Canberra.

References and further reading

Somerville, M, Beck, W, Brown, C, Murphy, D, Perkins, T & Smith, A 2000, *Arrawarra Meeting Place*, University of New England, Armidale, NSW and Yarrawarra Aboriginal Corporation.

Somerville, M & Perkins, T 2005, (Re)membering in the contact zone: telling and listening to, a massacre story, <http://www.api-network.com/cgi-bin/altitude21c/fly>.

Smith, A, Beck, W, Brown, C, Murphy, D, Perkins, T & Somerville, M 2000, *Red Rock: Camping and Exchange*, University of New England, Armidale, NSW and Yarrawarra Aboriginal Corporation.

Somerville, M & Perkins T 2005, (Re)membering in the contact zone: telling, and listening to, a massacre story, <http://www.api-network.com/cgi-bin/altitude21c/fly>.

Stowe, R 2005, *Sea Children* [song] in *Voices in the Landscape*, performance by Stephen Leeke, Brisbane.

Tumarkin, M 2005, *Traumascapes: The Power and Fate of Places Transformed by Tragedy*, Melbourne University Press, Carlton, Vic.

Index

Photographs are indicated by page numbers in italic; photographs between pages 82 and 83 are indicated thus: *82–3*.

abalone, 99–100
Aboriginal language territories, 3–4
Aboriginal reserves, 165
Aborigines Protection Board, 6, 160
ancestors *see* creation ancestors; the Old People; spirit presences
animal hunting and foods, 108–114
Archibald, Frank, 160
Armidale, 142, 169, 199
Armi's Camp, 64, 68–69, 76, *82–83 see also* Skinner, Clara (Granny Armi)
Arrawarra, 4, 11, 19, 51
    rainmaking place, 59, 126, 135
    shell midden, 62, 97, 138
authorities, avoiding intervention of, 6–7
Awabakal territory, 3

Baali (the Lord), 102
Baga-baga, 159, 178
Baga-baga Nyambaga, 177–178
Bagurlany (songs), 219–220
Bald Nob Hill, 214
Ballangarry, Granny, 198
Ballangarry, Martin, 167–168, 200–205
bamboo house (bamboo as place marker), 68–69
bark canoes, 5, 37, 63
bark collection and preparation, 7–8, 37, 63, 71–72, 183 *see also* scarred trees
bark huts and shelters, 39, 61, 63, 67–68, 70–73
    building techniques, 7–8, 61, 70–72
beach and rockpool (eating places), 94–100
Bellbrook, 213
belonging, 83–86, 186
Bennelong, Grace, 56
Biddy's Farm, 167–168
bird calls and spirits, 125, 128, 132, 134
Birrbay country, 3, 209
Birrugan story, 156, 159, 166, 177–185, 205, 208, 209–210
    Birrugan as Southern Cross, 209

Birrugan identified with Jesus, 158–159
Birrugan's grave, 184–185, 210
Birrugan's knee, 177–179
    places in, 217–218
Birrugan's Crossing, 183
birthing grounds, 35–38, 41, 48
Black Rock, 47
Blackadder Creek, 24, 25, 53
Blakeney, Maggie, 64, 66, *82–83*
Blood Rock, 24–25, 46, 52 *see also* Red Rock
Blue-Tongue Lizard place (Wandarrga), 165, 204–205
border work, 16–17
Boston, Rose (Rosina), *82–83*, 170–174
bough shelters, 61–62, 64, *82–83*
boundaries and identity, 190–199
Bowraville, 182–183, 200, 202–204
Brady, Veronica, 43
breadfruit tree, 136–137
bridges and bridge-building, 78–79
Brisbane, 4
brolga, 53, 210
    Mary (mother of Jesus) as, 158–159, 185, 210
    shooting of, 185
brolga dance, 133–134, 185, 210
brooms, 66
Brown, Angela, 62
Bryant, Michael, 156
Bryant, Ruthy, 156
Bryant family, 171
Buchannan, Fred, 171
Buchannan, Granny, 171
Buchannan, Tiger, 154–155
Buchannan, Tiger (Harry), 160–162, 166, 168, 177–178, 191, 213
Buchannan family, 169, 170–171
building
    with bark, 7–8, 60–61, 70–72
    bridges, 78–79
    with recycled materials, 73, 75–77, 79
Bundjalung territory, 4, 193–195

Index

Bundjalung tribe, 169
burial sites, 168, 169, 201
Burnt Bridge, 193
Burrabeedee, 35
bush tucker, 55, 107–120 *see also* food and food sources
bush tucker walk, 55, *82–83*, 88, 107
button fish *see* gugumbals
Buurrga Miirlarl, 215

Cain, Mary Jane, 35
camp fires (fireplaces), 65, 72–73
camps and camping places, 54–56, 61–69, *82–83*
   Flanders Camp, 54–55, 61, 66–67, 74, 110
   the Old Camp *see* Old Camp
   see also Corindi Lake
cannibal woman (Wijiirjagi Woman), 167–168, 177
canoes, 5, 13, 37, 63, 182
Casson, Dagwood, 45
Casson, Jack, 45
Casson, Ossie, 45
Cassons Creek, 24, 25, 45, 53
Catholic religion, 158–159, 186–187 *see also* Church; churches (buildings)
caves, 33–35, 48, 52, 134–135
Central Coast, 3
ceremonial places, 133–134, 138–139, 147–152
   miirlarl (special places), 8, 207, 210–222
ceremonies, 132–134, 139–140, 148–149, 158, 186 *see also* initiation
children and spirit world, 128–129
Church
   attendance at, 156
      Catholic religion, 156, 158–159, 186–187
      intervention in Aboriginal life, 6–7
churches (buildings), 156–157, 158, 186, 212
clan groups, 139–140, 191–192, 196–198, 214–215 *see also* family connections
clan territory, 196–197, 214–215
Clarence River, 4
Clouds Creek, 220
Clybucca, 157, 193
Clybucca middens, 193, 197, 206
coastal development, 10–11

cobra, 117–119, 202–204
Coffs Harbour, 132, 161
Cohen, Patsy, 35
Cohen, Val, *82–83*, 168, 170–175
Cohen family, *82–83*
Coldwater, 196
collaborative research *see* research partnership
colonial history, 17, 30, 193
colonisation, fence as symbol of, 5–6
'Comeback' (Arrawarra) *see* Arrawarra
conks *see* gugumbals
connecting people to country *see* deep mapping
contact zone, 15–17, 49, 61
Cook, Captain James, 204
cooking, 65, 112–113
   cobra, 119
   echidna, 111–112
   kangaroo, 109–110
   mullet, 106
   prawns, 90
   shellfish, 96–100
   swamp turtles, 93–94
Copmanhurst, 192
Coramba, 214–215
Corindi Beach, 4–5, 50, 62–63, 88, 105, 125, 132, 133, 134, 138
   shell middens, 62–63, 100
   source of name, 73, 129
Corindi Beach community, 14, 35, 46, 50
Corindi Lake (the Lake), 5–12, 18, 19, 53, *82–83*
   camps and camping places, 54–56, 61, 63–69, 74, 110
   dwellings, 7–8, 70–86 *see also* Old Camp
   eating place, 88–94
   key individuals, 56–61 *see also* Old People
   shell middens, 62
   see also No Mans Land
country *see* Gumbaynggirr country; traditional knowledge
Cow Creek, 160, 165
Cowan, Elsie, 27, 56
crabs, 39, 80, 91–92, 204–205
Creamer, Howard, 161
creation ancestors, 62, 138

Index

creation place (mother place), xiii, *82–83*, 189, 196, 207, 210, 214–215, 223–225
creation rituals, 22
creation stories, 1–3, 33–36, 42, 51, 163, 185–186
   rebirth stories, 33–41, 42, 47, 51–52
   see also Dreaming
Crescent Head, 193
Crowley, T, 161
Crying to Remember (Magowan), 22
crying-songs, 28–29, 44
cultural learning, 81–84, 89, 94, 125 *see also* traditional knowledge
cultural practice, suppression of, 57, 160 *see also* language revival
cultural translation, 9, 12, 14–16, 77, 78, 152 *see also* traditional knowledge
Cunjaree Mountain, 148, 151, 152

dancing, 59, 81, 139, 142, 212
dancing grounds, 134, 189
Darkinyung territory, 3
Davis family, 169
de Silva, Lenny, 160
death bird, 28
Deep Creek, 180–181, 184, 217
deep mapping, *82–83*, 164, 176–186, 189, 210
development *see* coastal development
Dhanggati territory, 3, 157
diamond trees, 201–202, 209
diamond-shaped patterns, significance of, 208, 209
Die Dunkel Erde, The Dark Earth (Wagan Watson), 22
Dirt Rock, 47
dolphins, 13, 101–102, 137–138, 174
Dootson, Noeline, 79, 80–81, 85, 95, 96
Dorrigo, 18, 195
Dotti, Bill, 201
Dotti, Jimmy, 201
Doyle, Granny, 171
Dreaming, 159, 161, 162, 163–164, 186 *see also* creation stories; songlines
drinking, 14
ducks, 116–117
the dump, 76
Duroux, Frank, 60
Duroux, Robyn, 124–125, 138
Duroux, Shirley, 129

dwelling and moving, 63–69, 79 *see also* camps and camping places
dwellings
   absence of material evidence of shelters, 64, 68–69
   at Corindi Lake, 7–8, 70–86 *see also* Old Camp
   evolution of, 10
   Old Farm, 35–41
   see also bark huts and shelters; bough shelters; camps and camping places

Eades, Diana, 161
eating places
   beach and rockpool, 94–100
   bush, 107–114
   estuary, 88–93
   river, 114–120
   sea, 100–107
   see also food
echidna, 111–112
ecotourism enterprises, 55
Edwards, Marie, 13
   on bough shelters, 64
   on Clarrie Skinner fishing, 58–59
   cooking shellfish, 96–97, 98
   on dolphins, 101
   on fig tree markers, 67
   life at the Old Farm/Red Rock, 36–41, 49
   massacre story, 29, 48
eels, 92–93, 115, 117
Egg island (Mirubay), 165
Elders, 189, 195
   Garby Elders, *iii*, 4, 11–12, 13–14, 146, 222
   southern Gumbaynggirr people, 168–169
   see also traditional knowledge
estuary (eating place), 88–94
Evening Star, 159

family connections, 191–192
   children of mixed parentage, 57
   missing family members, 30–32
   see also clan groups
family life, 83–85
fat lamps, 74–75, 103
Fatarini Island, 192–193
fear, voicing of, 28–29
fences, 5–6, 117

Index

Fig Tree site *see* Flanders Camp
fig trees
   Muurrbay tree story, 153–154, 186–187
   as place markers, 66–67, 171, 186
fireplaces, 65, 72–73
fish traps, 104, 135–136, 192
fishing, 13, 39–40, 59, 60, 81, 84, 172
   estuary, 88–93
   gathering shellfish, 94–100
   river, 114–120
   sea, *82–83*, 100–107
   see also hunting
Flanders, Gloria, 67, 69, 71, 73–74, 109–110, 113
Flanders, Jack, 60
Flanders, Jerry, *iii*, 60–61, 92, 98, 99–100, 105–106, 108, 113
Flanders, Phyllis, 171
Flanders, Therese, 68, 70–71, 84–85, 89
Flanders, Tom, 67, 69, 71, 74, 113, 126
Flanders, Tom (Old Tom), 60–61, 67, 70–71, 74, 109–110, 121, 126
Flanders Camp, 54–55, 61, 66–67, 74, 110
floors and floor-making, 36, 37, 66, 72
Foley, Gary, 158, 163
food and food sources, 7, 10, 39, 55, 80, 87–88
   beach and rockpool, 94–100
   bush, 107–114
   estuary, 88–94
   meat, 108–114
   men's food, 111
   plant foods, 107–108, 113
   river, 114–120
   sea, 100–107
   swamp, 92–94
Forster–Tuncurry, 3
furnishings and utensils, 66, 73–76

gaabi, the swamp wallaby, 11, 113, 220, 221
Ganaygal Creek, 225
Garby Elders, *iii*, 4, 11–12, 13–14, 146, 222 *see also* traditional knowledge
gathering places *see* meeting places
Gawnggan, 156, 180, 184–185, 210
   as brolga, 185, 210
   identified with Virgin Mary, 158–159
   see also Birrugan story

genealogies *see* family connections
giilan (brolga) *see* brolga
Girr Girr (Plover island) *see* Stuart Island
girriin *see* white ochre (pipe clay)
Glenreagh, 4, 36
God the Father, identified with Yuludarla, 159
Gold Coast, 4
golden spirits, 215–216
Gouding, Meg, *82–83*
Grace, Patricia, 49
Grafton, 161, 215
Green Hill, 47
gugumbals (gugalungs), 97–99
guguurr *see* cobra
Gumbaynggirr country, 4–5, 154, 158, 161–162, 189–190
   boundaries and identity, 190–199
   linking trails and storylines, 199–210
   special places of gathering and ceremony, 8, 201, 210–222
   see also Corindi Lake; No Mans Land; place learning; Stuart Island
Gumbaynggirr language, 14–15, 57–58, 146
   revival and teaching, 14, 146, 154–164, 177, 183, 185–187 *see also* Muurrbay Aboriginal Language and Culture Co-operative
   suppression of, 57–58, 160
   translating and recording, 161–164, 177 *see also* deep mapping
Gumbaynggirr Language and Culture Group, 163
Gumbaynggirr people, 2, 11–12, 41, 158, 160
   cultural centre, 5
   disconnected from country, 157–158
   identity, 47–48
   massacre of *see* Red Rock massacre
   rebirth of, 33–41, 42, 47, 51–52
Gumbaynggirr Yuludarla, Gumbaynggirr Dreamings, 159, 161, 162, 186
Gumburr (spirit protector), 78, 127–128
Gumma, 193
Gusha Gusha *see* Lardner, Margie

Harvey, Celia, 36, 39, *82–83*, 126
Harvey family, 191
haunting, 46
Hawkesbury River, 3

Index

Haydon, 95
healing powers
  medicine man, 168
  plants, 182
  of spirits, 130–131, 140
  teaching, 168
hero ancestors *see* Birrugan story; creation ancestors
history
  Aboriginal story, 30–32 *see also* Red Rock massacre
  colonial, 17, 30, 193
  importance of knowing, 49–50, 163–164
  importance of telling, 30–31, 43–45, 49, 50
  oral, 19–20
History Wars, 45
Hoddinott, WG, 161
Hooler, Pauline, 155–156, 162, 163, 164, 169–170, 175
houses *see* dwellings
hunting, 64, 81, 108–111, 112, 113, 116–117, 162, 203–204 *see also* fishing

identity *see* boundaries and identity; traditional knowledge
Ingelba, 35
initiated men, 8–9, 18, 59, 60, 126–127, 133, 143–144, 147, 149, 162, 191, 213
initiation, 8–9, 12, 31, 47, 131, 141–152, 162, 168, 212–214
  last ceremony, 213–214
  'in the shadow of initiation', 212–213, 220
  smoking ceremony, 149, 151–152, 214
  songs, 218–220
  special place markers, 201
  special places, 8, 148–151, 212–213, 218–219
  of white man, 213–214, 223
inspirited places, 50–53
intervention of authorities, 6–7
the Island, 160, 165–175
islands in Nambucca estuary, *82–83*, 165–175

Janagan (Seven Sisters constellation), 2, 209
Jarrett, Colin, 156
Jarrett, Colleen, 34, 46
Jarrett, Virginia, 164

Jarrett Family, 191
Jesus identified with Birrugan, 158–159
jewfish, 13, 58–59, *82–83*, 90–91, 101, 105
Jewfish Point, 39, 47, 50–53, 133, 134, 210
  mangrove tree, 52–53, *82–83*, 132
  Red Rock/Jewfish Point caves, 33–35, 48, 52, 134–135
jigsaw puzzle analogy of knowledge transmission, 9, 127, 145, 148, 150, 162–163, 216–217
junka (shellfish), 223

kangaroo, 108–109
kangaroo special place, *82–83*, 212, 215–218
Kelly, Larry, 193
Kelly, Ray, 198, 206
Kempsey, 157–158, 163, 169
kerosene tins, 75
knowledge of country *see* Gumbaynggirr country; traditional knowledge
koala brothers story, 209
Kooiya *see* McDougall, Herbie

the Lake (Corindi Lake), 5–12, 18, 19, 53, *82–83*
  camps and camping places, 54–56, 61, 63–69, 74, 110
  dwellings, 7–8, 70–86 *see also* Old Camp
  eating place, 88–94
  key individuals, 55–61 *see also* Old People
  shell middens, 62
  see also Corindi Lake
lamps, 74–75, 103
landscape, 2–5, 17–19, 20
  Moonee Beach, xiii–xiv
  Northern NSW, 3–4
  place learning, 19–21, 47, 189–190, 207, 216–219
  see also boundaries and identity; Gumbaynggirr country
language revival, 14, 21, 146, 154–164, 177 *see also* Muurrbay Aboriginal Language and Culture Co-operative
language speaking, 13–14, 15
  and cultural survival, 57
  prohibited, 57–58, 160
  see also Gumbaynggirr language

Index

language territories, 3–4, 154, 197–199
   measurement of territory, 18
   see also Gumbaynggirr country; Gumbaynggirr language
Lardner, Keith, iii, 13–14, 76, 79, *82–83*, 85, 118, 160
Lardner, Margie, 82–84, 125, 136
Laurie, Bing (Cecil), iii, 13, *82–83*
   on bark huts, 72–73
   on catching/preparing food, 90, 92–93, 102, 111–112
   on fat lamps, 75
   listening to the Old People, 13–14
   living in No Mans Land, 55, 64, 65, 68, 69, 76
   at the Old Camp, 78, 80, 82
   on rainmaking, 135
   recorded language, 160
   on Red Rock cave, 34–35, 134–135
   speaking language, 14
   spiritual knowledge, 13, 127–130
   welcome to country, 5
Laurie, Bruce, iii, 13, *82–83*
   on catching food, 89–90, 102
   living in No Mans Land, 64, 68, 69
   on mullet runs, 104–106
   on night bird calls, 134
   at the Old Camp, 78, 79–80
   with the Old People, 52
   recorded language, 160
   on Red Rock dump, 76
   speaking language, 14
   on weather, 136–137
Laurie, Fred (Pa), 41, 56, 79, 109–110, 125, 126, 133, 149
Laurie, Jean, 69, 78, 102
Laurie, Johnny, 80, 195
Laurie, Sadie, 56, 69, 78, 83, 109–110
Laurie, Val, 69, 78, 80, 83, 112
Laurie family, 64, 78
Leeke, Stephen, *Voices in the Landscape*, 21–22
lingo *see* language
Link Up, 82
linking trails and storylines, 198–210, 218, 224
listening, 43–44
local boundaries *see* boundaries and identity
Long, Doug and Jack, 56
Look At Me Now Headland, 214–215, 224

lyre bird, 221–222

Mac (Uncle Mac) *see* Runner, Jimmy
Mackay, Jimmy, 78, 80
Macksville mob, 202
Maclean, 195
Magowan, Fiona, 22–23, 28
manhood, initiation into *see* initiation
Many Rivers Language Centre, 155
maps, 195–196 *see also* deep mapping
Marrgaan, 188
marriage, 191–192, 199 *see also* clan groups
Marshall, Amy, 166
Marshall family, 169
Martins Point, 34, 52
Maruungga, Maruwanba *see* Buchanan, Tiger (Harry)
Mary (mother of Jesus), 158–159
Mary's Waterhole, 158, 159, 210, 224
massacres, 27, 29, 32
   disputed, 45–46
   Red Rock massacre, 17, 24–26, 33–34, 42, 45–52, 135
   Red Rock massacre survivors, 126, 135
McCallum, Johnny, 126
McCrystal, Teddy, 52, 56, 64, 126
McDougall, Abraham, 13–14, 18–19, 79, 126, 134–135, 149
McDougall, Herbie, 18–19, 34, 35, 41, 56, 126, 134, 149
McDougall, Michael, iii, 13, 76, 110, 117, 118–119, 124, 134
McDougall relations, 31
McDougalls' Run, 18–19, 134, 135
McGrath, Granny, 171
McGrath, Jim, 170
McKenna, Mark, 49, 50
McManus, Doctor, 213–214, 223
measurement of country, 18
meat, 108–114
meeting places, 4, 11, 62–63, 133, 138, 193, 197
   miirlarl (special places), 8, 207, 210–222
men's food, 111
men's places, 29, 34, 35, 207
middens
   Arrawarra, 62, 97, 138
   Clybucca, 193, 197, 206
   Corindi Beach/Lake, 62–63, 100

Jewfish Point, 138
Red Rock, 63, 133–134, 138
Miimiga Gawngganba Miirlarl *see* Mary's Waterhole
miirlarl (special places), 8, 207, 210–222
Mindi (creation ancestor), 62, 138
Minnie Waters, 195
Mirubay (Egg island), 165
the Mission, 156, 160, 165, 170, 194
Moonee Beach, 2, 36, 96, 189, 207, 208–210, 224
Moonee Moonee Creek, 2, 196
Morelli, Steve, 157
mother place, xiii, *82–83*, 189, 196, 207, 210, 214–215, 223–225
Mount Coramba, 214–215
Mount Yarrahappini, 209
moving and dwelling, 63–69, 79 *see also* camps and camping places
Moylan, Vilma, 169
mullet, 103–106
Mullumbimby, 193
Mumbler family, 171
Mundell, Patsy, 156
music and musical instruments, 40–41, 76–77
Muurrbay Aboriginal Language and Culture Co-operative, 21, 154–164, 166, 175, 177, 183, 185–187, 200 *see also* Gumbaynggirr language
Muurrbay tree story, 153–154, 186–187, 206

Nambucca (name), 177–178
Nambucca Heads, 2, 20–21, 132, 158, 191, 192, 194
Nambucca River, 4
estuary islands, 165–175
Nambucca Valley, 161–162
names
Muurrbay, 186
Nambucca, 177–178
of people, 57, 191–192
see also family connections
naming and non-naming, 128, 142, 146
Nana Glen, 4, 36, 196
Newcastle, 3
Newry Creek, 182
Ngaalgan, 3
Ngambaa man, 178
Ngambaa's knee, 176, 177–178

Nigger's Leap (poem, Wright), 42–43
No Mans Land, 5–15, 19, 31, 50, 53–56
life in *see* Corindi Lake; Old Camp; Old Farm; Red Rock
spirit presences, 123–125, 131–132, 140
Nunguu Miirlarl (kangaroo place), *82–83*, 212, 215–218
Nyambaga (Nambucca), 178
Nymboida, 161, 192

ochres, 51, 63, 73, 128–129, 133, 180, 182, 185
'old', 148
the Old Camp, 13, 27, 45, 78–86, *82–83*
ritual objects and powers brought to, 138–139, 147–148
spirit presences, 123–124, 128, 131
the Old Farm, 13, 35–41, 53, 117
the Old People, 7–9, 13–14, 125–126
fig trees and belonging places, 186
initiation *see* initiation
key individuals, 56–61, 126
meeting places, 11
protective role, 198
recordings, 219–220
separated from country, 157–158
special places *see* special places of gathering and ceremony
spirit presences, 123–131
stories and places, 47, 50, 125, 140–141
and storms, 136–137
teachings, 10, 12
walking trails, 206 *see also* linking trails and storylines
oral history, 19
oral place stories, 19–20
oral storytelling, 15, 58, 142–143, 161–162
Orara River, 196

Pelican Caravan Park, 182–183
Perkins, Bill, 145–146
Perkins, Glenda, 29, 47–48, 51–52, 65–66, 75, 111
Perkins, Tony, *82–83*
clans and clan territories, 196–197
deep mapping, 214–215
grandmother's storytelling, 27–28
massacre and creation memorial cairn, 50

Index

regional knowledge, 190–192, 208
southern and northern Gumbaynggirr meeting, 188–189
Perkins, William Henry, 191
Phillips, Gloria, 100
Picketts Mountain, 215–218
Pillar Valley, 149, 151, 192
pipe clay (white ochre)
  as building material, 73
  ceremonial use, 133
  in Red Rock midden, 63
  warding off spirits, 128–129
Pipeclay (Corindi Beach), 53, 73
pipis, 13, 62, *82–83*, 94–97, 138, 166
place learning, 20–21, 47, 189–190, 207, 216–219 *see also* boundaries and identity
place markers, 66–69, 149–150, 171, 186, 201
places
  of ceremonies *see* ceremonial places
  of gathering *see* meeting places
  of intensity *see* miirlarl (special places)
plant foods, 107–108, 113
Pleiades (Seven Sisters constellation), 2, 209
Plover island (Girr Girr) *see* Stuart Island
the Point, 70
Point Lookout, 206, 208
porcupine (echidna), 111–112
porpoises *see* dolphins
Port Macquarie, 3
possum, 113, 198
prawns, 89–92
property (sacred property), 127, 138–139, 148
protector spirits, 78, 127–128, 176
protocols, 16–17

rain, protection from, 64, 67, 71–73, 79–80 *see also* dwellings
rainmaking place, 59, 126, 135
Read, Peter, 49, 50
rebirth stories, 33–41, 42, 47, 51–52
recycled materials, 73–77, 79, 103
Red Bank, 47
red ochre, 51, 63, 180, 182, 185
Red Rock, xiv, 3, 13, 18–19
  drownings at, 29, 48
  holidays/holidaymakers at, 39–40, 41, 51, 53

last initiation ceremony, 213–214
as market place, 63
shell midden, 63, 133–134, 138
spirits, 134–135
storytelling at, 47–48
taboo place, 29–30, 50, 52
Red Rock band, 40–41, *82–83*
Red Rock – Jewfish Point caves, 33–35, 48, 52, 134–135
Red Rock massacre, 17, 24–26, 33–34, 45–52, 135
  memorial cairn and story, 42, 50, 51
  survivors, 126, 135
Red Rock rubbish dump, 76
relationships of people, 191–192
  children of mixed parentage, 57
  missing family connections, 30–32
  see also clan groups
representation, focus on, 16–17
research as a political tool, 16
research partnership, 15–17
reserves for Aboriginal people, 165 *see also* the Mission
Richards, Estelle and Doreen, 39
Richards, Tom, 36
river (eating place), 114–120 *see also* fishing
rockpools (eating places), 94–100
Rose, Deborah Bird, 26, 35
rose bush house (rose bush as place marker), 68–69, 72
rubbish tip (the dump), 76
Runner, Jimmy (Uncle Mac), xiv, 59–60, 126
  collected wild honey, 55, 121
  family, 69, 78, 82, 85
  fisherman, 59
  kangaroo hunting story, 109–110
  at the Lake, 69
  music-making, 41, 59
  rainmaker, 59, 135–136
  at Red Rock, 41, 51

saltwater oak *see* Wirriimbi (casuarina)
sapling shelters, 61–62, 64, *82–83*
scarred trees, 37, 55, 63, 67–68, 124
scars of initiation, 9, 143–144 *see also* initiated men; initiation
Schlunke, Katrina, 27, 32
Scotts Head, 209
sea (eating place), 100–107 *see also* fishing

Index

Sea Foams band, 77
sea mullet, 103–106
sea worm *see* cobra
Seal Rocks, 209
Serpentine, 206
Seven Oaks, 203
Seven Sisters constellation, 2, 209
'shadow of initiation', 212–213, 220
sharks, 105–106
shell middens, 62–63, 97, 100, 133–134, 138
shellfish, 94–100, 223
she-oak (casuarina) *see* Wirriimbi (casuarina)
Sherwood, 157
silence, importance of, 122, 145–146
singing and songs, 21–23, 194–195, 212, 218–220
  about spirit powers, 132–133
  crying-songs, 28–29, 44
  in desert country, 142
  see also speech; storytelling; traditional knowledge
Skinner, Celia *see* Harvey, Celia
Skinner, Clara (Granny Armi), 39, 56, 64, 66, *82–83*, 126 *see also* Armi's Camp
Skinner, Clarice, 37, 191
Skinner, Clarrie, *82–83*
  at Corindi Lake, 5, 58–59
  decision to record knowledge, 58, 160, 214, 218–220, 223
  favourite food, 108
  fish/fishing, 13, 58–59, *82–83*, 101
  initiation practices and spirit creatures, 126–127, 138–139, 147–148
  and protector spirit, 127–128
  at Red Rock cave, 134
  and Red Rock holidays/holidaymakers, 39–40, 41, 51, 53
  spirit presence of, 82, 125
  teaching next generations, 7–9, 51, 127–128, 132–133
Skinner, Norma, 80
Skinner, Tunny, 96
Skinner family, *82–83*, 191
Smith, Ivy, 186
Smith, Walter, 168, 172
smoked meat, 65
smoking ceremony, 149, 151–152, 214
Smoky Cape, 21

social changes, 10, 12
songlines, 3, 22, 159, 177, 194, 198–199, 205–206, 208, 210, 211, 212–213 *see also* Birrugan story; Muurrbay tree story; singing and songs; storylines; The Women Who Made the Sea story; Wijiirjagi Woman
South Beach, 166
South West Rocks, 180, 184, 213
Southern Cross, 208, 209
speaking language, 13–14, 15
  key to cultural survival, 57
  prohibited, 57–58
special places of gathering and ceremony, 8, 201, 210–222
speech
  power of voice and sound, 27–29, 128
  speech/nonspeech and spiritual knowledge, 145–146
  voices of the Old People, 132, 134
  see also singing and songs
spirit places, 131–141
spirit presences, 123–131, 198
spirit protectors, 78, 127–128, 176
spirits, golden, 215–216
spiritual knowledge, 127–130, 145–146
Split Solitary Island, 2, *82–83*, 209
Station Creek, 81
stolen generations, 17, 82
storms, 136–137
storylines, 155, 159, 166
  deep mapping, 164, 176–186
  intersection, 203
  linking trails and storylines, 198–210
  and songlines, 210
  see also Birrugan story; creation stories
storytelling, 12, 142–143
  telling and listening, 43–45, 49
  by Tony's grandmother, 27–28
  see also Buchannan, Tiger (Harry); singing and songs; traditional knowledge
Stuart Island, 160, 165–175
Stuarts Point, 193
swamp (eating place), 92–94
swamp wallaby, 11, 220, 221

taboos, 29–30, 50, 126, 135–136, 140, 144–145, 146, 198, 207, 212
Taylor, Paul, 69, 103–104, 126
Taylor family, 69

Index

tents, 67, 71 *see also* dwellings
territories *see* Gumbaynggirr country; language territories
timber working, 60
tin huts, 78, 80, *82–83*, 85, 86 *see also* the Old Camp
totems, 113, 139–140, 197–198, 203
traditional knowledge, 8–10, 15, 175
    boundaries and identity, 190–199
    collective responsibility, 9, 127, 162–163, 216–217
    holders of, 9, 58–60, 126–127, 162, 168–169 *see also* initiated men
    linking trails and storylines, 199–210
    passing on, 8–9, 12, 58, 126–127, 131, 144–147, 160–164, 223
    place learning, 20–21, 47, 189–190
    special places of gathering and ceremony, 8, 201, 207, 219–222
    spiritual knowledge, 126–131, 145–146 *see also* songlines; storytelling
Traumascapes (Tumarkin), 46
Tree of Life *see* Muurrbay tree story
triangles, 224
Tumarkin, Maria, 46
turban shells *see* gugumbals
turtles, 80, 92–94, 115, 117
Two Mile Lane, 196
two sisters story *see* The Women Who Made the Sea story

Urunga, 191, 192
utensils *see* furnishings and utensils

Valla, 70, 151, 179–180, 182, 184, 218
Virgin Mary identified with Gawnggan, 158–159
voice and sound *see* speech
Voices in the Landscape (Leeke), 21–22

Waanyji Miirlarl, 215
Waddy, Doug, 169
Waddy, Eva, 169
Waddy, Lambert, 162, 168, 169
Waddy, Valerie, 169
Waddy family, 171
wailing, 27–29
Walker, Emily, 198
Walker, Ken, *82–83*
    Birrugan story, 177, 180–185
    clans and clan gatherings, 196–197

    deep mapping, 164, 214
    language work, 157, 161, 163–164, 208
    miirlarl (special places), 215
    and Muurrbay church, 156–158
    regional knowledge, 20–21, 192–193
    'in the shadow of initiation', 212–213
    southern and northern Gumbaynggirr meeting, 188–189
    The Women Who Made the Sea story, 1–2, 209
Walker family, 170
walking distance, 18
walking trails *see* linking trails and storylines; songlines
wallaby
    food, 108–110
    gaabi (swamp wallaby), 221
    gaabi (swamp wallaby) identified with Garby Elders, 11, 113, 220
Walter, Granny, 171
Wandarrga (Blue-Tongue Lizard place), 165, 204–205
Warorimayi land, 3
washing, 65, 92–93, 114–115
weather, 20, 63, 90, 94, 104, 107, 136–137
    protection from, 64, 67, 71–73, 79–80 *see also* dwellings
    spirit powers of weather, 136–137
the Welfare, 6, 82, 157, 160
wellbeing of animals and their places, 140
white man, initiation of, 213–214, 223
white ochre (pipe clay)
    as building material, 73
    ceremonial use, 133
    in Red Rock midden, 63
    warding off spirits, 128–129
Widders, Terry, 212
Widow Tree, 114
Wijiirjagi Woman, 167–168, 177
wildflowers, 51
Williams, Clive, 194
Williams, Gary, *82–83*
    Birrugan story, 158–159, 177–179, 210
    clans and clan gatherings, 196–197
    deep mapping, 164, 214
    language work, 158, 163, 208
    miirlarl (special places), 211, 215–216
    and Muurrbay church, 156–158
    Muurrbay tree story, 153–154

Index

naming of Nambucca (story of), 177–179
regional knowledge, 20–21, 193–195
'in the shadow of initiation', 212–213
southern and northern Gumbaynggirr meeting, 188–189
The Women Who Made the Sea story, 211
Wirriimbi (casuarina), 182–183, 205
Wirriimbi Island, 200
The Women Who Made the Sea story, 1–2, 155, 166, 177, 208–209, 211, 224
women's places, 33, 158, 159, 207, 224
Wonnarua territory, 3
Woolgoolga, 18
Wooli, 196
Worabooraby, 183, 205
worms for bait, 39–40
Worrell Creek, 166–168
Wright, Judith, 42–43

Yamba, 4, 195
Yarrahappini, 21, 209
Yarrawarra, 19
Yarrawarra Aboriginal Corporation, 11, 50, 88
Yarrawarra Aboriginal Cultural Centre, 5
yellow ochre, 51, 63
Yellow Rock, 4, 157–158, 191, 192
Yellow Waterholes, 210, 224
Yirrawarra, 4, 11
Yolngu culture, 22, 28–29
Yuggera country, 4
Yulong, 4
Yuludarla, identified with God the Father, 159
yuraal (local food knowledge), 88